A KILLER GUIDE TO MAKING WINDOWS RUN YOUR WAY

D1608440

Paul McFedries

800 East 96th Street,
Indianapolis, Indiana 46240

Tweak It and Freak It: A Killer Guide to Making Windows Run Your Way

Copyright © 2009 by Que Publishing

All rights reserved. No part of this book shall be reproduced, stored in a retrieval system, or transmitted by any means, electronic, mechanical, photocopying, recording, or otherwise, without written permission from the publisher. No patent liability is assumed with respect to the use of the information contained herein. Although every precaution has been taken in the preparation of this book, the publisher and author assume no responsibility for errors or omissions. Nor is any liability assumed for damages resulting from the use of the information contained herein.

ISBN-13: 978-0-789-73822-6
ISBN-10: 0-7897-3822-8

Library of Congress Cataloging-in-Publication Data
McFedries, Paul.
  Tweak it and freak it : a killer guide to making Windows work your way / Paul McFedries. -- 1st ed.
      p. cm.
  ISBN 978-0-7897-3822-6
  1. Microsoft Windows (Computer file) 2. Operating systems (Computers) I. Title.
  QA76.76.O63M398285 2009
  005.4'46--dc22

                          2009008951

Printed in the United States of America

First Printing: March 2009

Trademarks

Warning and Disclaimer

Bulk Sales

Que Publishing offers excellent discounts on this book when ordered in quantity for bulk purchases or special sales. For more information, please contact

> **U.S. Corporate and Government Sales**
> **1-800-382-3419**
> **corpsales@pearsontechgroup.com**

For sales outside of the U.S., please contact

> **International Sales**
> **international@pearson.com**

Associate Publisher
Greg Wiegand

Acquisitions Editor
Rick Kughen

Development Editor
Rick Kughen

Managing Editor
Patrick Kanouse

Project Editor
Seth Kerney

Copy Editor
Barbara Hacha

Indexer
Tim Wright

Proofreader
Suzanne Thomas

Technical Editor
Terri Stratton

Publishing Coordinator
Cindy Teeters

Book Designer
Anne Jones

Composition
Bronkella Publishing, LLC

Reviewers
Andy Walker
Aaron Ricadela
Gareth Branwyn

Contents at a Glance

Table of Contents

About the Author

Paul McFedries is a full-time technical author who has worked with computers in one form or another since 1975 and has used Windows since version 1. He is the author of more than 60 computer books that have sold more than 3 million copies worldwide. His recent titles include the Sams Publishing books *Microsoft Windows Vista Unleashed,* Second Edition, and *Microsoft Windows Home Server Unleashed* and the Que Publishing books *Networking with Microsoft Windows Vista,* and *Build It. Fix It. Own It. A Beginner's Guide to Building and Upgrading a PC.* Paul is also the proprietor of Word Spy (www.wordspy.com) a website devoted to tracking new words and phrases as they enter the English language. Please feel free to drop by Paul's personal website at www.mcfedries.com.

Dedication

For Karen

Acknowledgments

Is it ironic that a book about tweaking Windows would itself also require tweaking? Well, no, because even the best authors need a few extra sets of eyes to make sure that the text flows, that things make sense, and that the book's sundry i's and t's are dotted and crossed. Fortunately, this book benefited by having some of the best eyes in the business give it a once- (and twice- and thrice-) over. They include Rick Kughen, who was both the book's acquisitions editor and its development editor, which means he was kind enough to ask me to write it and savvy enough about Windows to offer tons of just-so suggestions that raised the book up several notches; Seth Kerney, who was the book's eyebrow-raisingly competent and organized project editor; Barbara Hacha, who was the book's copy editor and whose sharp eyes not only weeded out all my grammatical gaffes, but also gave the book a consistent style and tone, a tough and demanding job; and Terri Stratton, who was the book's technical editor, and whose seemingly inexhaustible supply of knowledge about all things technical never fails to amaze me.

We Want to Hear from You!

As the reader of this book, *you* are our most important critic and commentator. We value your opinion and want to know what we're doing right, what we could do better, what areas you'd like to see us publish in, and any other words of wisdom you're willing to pass our way.

As an associate publisher for Que Publishing, I welcome your comments. You can email or write me directly to let me know what you did or didn't like about this book—as well as what we can do to make our books better.

Please note that I cannot help you with technical problems related to the topic of this book. We do have a User Services group, however, where I will forward specific technical questions related to the book.

When you write, please be sure to include this book's title and author as well as your name, email address, and phone number. I will carefully review your comments and share them with the author and editors who worked on the book.

Email: feedback@quepublishing.com

Mail: Greg Wiegand
        Associate Publisher
        Que Publishing
        800 East 96th Street
        Indianapolis, IN 46240 USA

Reader Services

Visit our website and register this book at informit.com/register for convenient access to any updates, downloads, or errata that might be available for this book.

INTRODUCTION

Hundreds of millions of people use Windows every day, and it's a safe bet that some of them would not describe themselves as happy Windows campers. Regardless of skill level, most people have something they dislike about Windows, and they often have a whole laundry list of gripes. "Why can't Windows do this rather than that?" "Why does Windows do X instead of Y?" "Wouldn't it be great if Windows could do Z?" Scratch the surface of most Windows users and you'll come upon a seething cauldron of unmet needs, unrequited desires, and unending frustration at being stuck with Windows the way it is.

However, a funny thing happens when you tell people that it doesn't have to be this way, that they don't have to put up with the out-of-the-box Windows experience: An initial skepticism soon gives way and their eyes light up with an almost forgotten feeling—hope. Specifically, the hope that they really can make Windows smarter, safer, faster, more flexible, and more aligned to their needs.

The secret behind this hope? Tweaks, tweaks, and more tweaks! Most people think that Windows is set in stone, but that apparently solid surface is really just a thin veneer that Microsoft slaps onto Windows to ensure that new and fumble-fingered users don't get into trouble. Strip off that veneer and a whole world comes into view, one that's eminently tweakable, moddable, hackable, customizable, and personalizable. Within this world lie tools and technologies that anyone can use to tweak and tune almost every aspect of Windows, from startup to shutdown, from the interface to the Internet, from security to scripting.

Tweak It and Freak It!

Tweak It and Freak It: A Killer Guide to Making Windows Run Your Way is your guide to this tweakable Windows landscape. With a lighthearted and lightly irreverent tone, and with a bare minimum of jargon and technical claptrap, this book takes you through hundreds of useful, unique, and easy tweaks designed to improve Windows Vista and Windows XP. The key words here are useful, unique, and easy:

- **Useful**—Any monkey can, say, reverse the interface shadows, but what's the point of doing that? In this book, if a hack doesn't help you get your work done, solve a problem, or make Windows more secure or reliable, it didn't make the cut.

- **Unique**—There are lots of Windows tweaks available on the Internet and in other books, so you certainly don't want another conglomeration of the same old Registry hacks. Instead, this book presents a fresh collection of tweaks that include many custom hacks that I've built over the years.

- **Easy**—A tweak that takes you an hour to implement and yet saves only a few seconds a day isn't much of a tweak. This book focuses on tweaks that you can implement with a few steps, or with easy-to-understand plug-and-play scripts.

My goal with this book is to empower you to take a hands-on, do-it-yourself approach to tweaking Windows. In the end, you'll no longer have a version of Windows that Microsoft thinks you should have, but rather a tweaked and tuned version that suits the way you work and play.

Who Should Read This Book?

This book is aimed at Windows users who have a gripe, a beef, or an ax to grind and are looking for ways to overcome their Windows woes and short-comings with targeted, easy-to-implement tweaks and tune-ups. This book will also appeal to curious users who want to travel down different Windows roads, rebellious users who want to thumb their noses at standard-issue Windows techniques, and power users who want to get the most of Windows.

To that end, this book includes the following features:

- A focus on practical, useful tweaks rather than mere tricks.
- Tweaks for both Windows Vista and Windows XP.
- Icons that show you which operating systems the tweak works with and the difficulty level of each tweak.
- Unique tweaks, many of which have never been seen before.
- Explanations of key concepts for novice users.
- In-depth coverage of the inner workings of each hack for more experienced users.
- A friendly and lightly humorous tone that I trust will make you feel at home with the subject and keep boredom at bay.

Conventions Used in This Book

To make your life easier, this book includes various features and conventions that help you get the most out of this book:

Steps	Throughout the book, I've broken many building, upgrading, and repairing tasks into easy-to-follow step-by-step procedures.
Things you type	Whenever I suggest that you type something, what you type appears in a **`bold monospace`** font.
Filenames, folder names, and code	These things appear in a `monospace` font.
Commands	Commands and their syntax use the `monospace` font, too. Command placeholders (which stand for what you actually type) appear in an `italic monospace` font.

Pull-down menu commands

I use the following style for all application menu commands: *Menu, Command*, where *Menu* is the name of the menu you pull down and *Command* is the name of the command you select. Here's an example: File, Open. This means that you pull down the File menu and select the Open command.

This book also uses the following boxes to draw your attention to important (or merely interesting) information:

NOTE The Note box presents asides that give you more information about the current topic. These tidbits provide extra insights that offer a better understanding of the task.

TIP The Tip box tells you about methods that are easier, faster, or more efficient than the standard methods.

CAUTION The all-important Caution box tells you about potential accidents waiting to happen. There are always ways to mess things up when you're working with computers. These boxes help you avoid those traps and pitfalls.

Online Chapters

I had such a good time writing this book that I actually ended up writing too much! Way too much, in fact, but that's not a problem in this day and age because what wouldn't fit between the covers of the book can easily fit between the covers of my website. And that's just what I've done: Six of this book's chapters are available online at my site. Just point your favorite web browser to www.mcfedries.com/TweakItFreakIt.

These files are also freely available from Que Publishing at www.informit.com/title/0789738228. There, you'll also find information on Que's other products.

Vital Performance Tweaks

The need for computing speed is seemingly infinite. I've never met any serious or semi-serious computer user who's been satisfied with the performance of his or her PC. If you use your computer a lot, you probably spend at least a bit of time every day wishing you had a faster, more powerful, machine. This isn't some newly formed flaw in the human condition. On the contrary, it's just basic human nature. For example, certain apparently complex tasks happen almost instantly on most PCs. A good example is Word's on-the-fly spelling and grammar checking: You misspell a word, and that squiggly red line appears under the offending term right away. Make a grammatical gaffe, and the green line shows up as soon as you press the period (.) to end the sentence. If these tasks are immediate, why does it often take an unholy amount of time to search for a file, open a program, or print a document?

It's also true that even as computers have muscled up over the years, the software they have to work with has grown fatter. So, yes, your current PC is probably many times more powerful than your previous machines—and probably several hundred times more powerful than your first computer—but it doesn't *feel* much faster because bloated software programs force the machine to work harder just to keep up.

We all want more performance, and as you'll see in this chapter and elsewhere in this book, there are ways to tweak Windows to make it run a bit faster. Before getting to those tweaks, however, consider a few hardware upgrades that, budget permitting of course, are guaranteed to speed up your system:

- **Add more memory**—System RAM is always the first place to start when considering a hardware upgrade for better performance. RAM is relatively cheap and relatively easy to install, and an extra gigabyte or two in your system can make a whopping difference. Most modern Windows Vista and XP systems should have at least 2GB of RAM, and 3GB is better if you often deal with large files. (Don't bother with 4GB, because 32-bit Windows machines can use only a small portion of that fourth gigabyte. If you have 64-bit Windows, you can add up to 8GB.)

- **Get a bigger and faster hard drive**—A fast hard drive (at least 7200 RPM) can do wonders for performance because the faster the drive, the less time Windows has to spend reading and writing data. A big hard drive also gives Windows lots of room to make the paging file—the area of the hard disk that Windows uses as a kind of memory extension to improve performance—as big as it needs.

- **Upgrade to a video card with more memory**—A modern-day

NOTE The memory you choose must be compatible with your computer's motherboard. If you're not sure how to check this, see my book *Build It. Fix It. Own It. A Beginner's Guide to Building and Upgrading a PC* (Que 2008). I talk about the different memory types and show you step-by-step how to install the new memory modules. I also talk about hard drives, video cards, and networking devices.

TIP The 802.11n standard is due to be finalized in mid-2009. Does this mean it's safe to purchase Draft 2.0 (or later) devices now? Probably. Most manufacturers are saying that their current Draft 2.0 products will be upgradeable; so, if there are changes between now and the final draft, you'll be able to apply a patch to the device to make it conform to the new standard. Trusting that this will be so means taking a bit of a chance on your part, so *caveat emptor.* You can eliminate a bit of the risk associated with 802.11n Draft 2.0 products by purchasing only those that have been certified by the Wi-Fi Alliance, a consortium of Wi-Fi manufacturers. After the Draft 2.0 amendment was approved, the Wi-Fi Alliance began testing Draft 2.0 devices to ensure not only that they conform to the draft specifications but that they also work well with older 802.11a/b/g devices. See www.wi-fi.org for more information.

graphics chip works as hard or sometimes even harder than the CPU, what with our monitors getting bigger, Windows requiring ever more graphical resources, and with games and other programs pushing pixels at an alarming rate. A video card with as much memory as you can afford will help push those pixels even faster.

- **Take your network to the next level**—If your Windows PC is part of a network and you use that connection to share files and other data, you owe it to yourself to set up the fastest network that you can afford. For wired connections, it's time to step up to Gigabit Ethernet, which transfers data at a theoretical top speed of 1,000 megabits per second (Mbps). For wireless, go with devices that support 802.11n, the perpetually just-around-the-corner standard for the next generation of wireless connections. Just make sure you get devices that support "Draft 2.0" (or later) of the 802.11n standard.

No budget for such things? No worries. This chapter gives you four simple ways to give Windows a bit of boost without costing you a cent.

Silence the Graphical Bells and Whistles

Easy

Windows is a graphical operating system, so it's chock full of visual flourishes. For example, when you click an item in a menu bar, the associated menu doesn't just suddenly appear on the screen; instead, it slides into view as though you really did "pull down" the pull-down menu. What's the point of such graphical shenanigans? Mostly to offer visual clues that help novice users figure out what the heck is going on. If an inexperienced user can "see" where the menu comes from, he or she will understand the pull-down menu concept that much faster. Microsoft has novice users in mind for most of these graphic goodies, including the effects you see when you minimize and maximize a window, open drop-down lists, and move a window.

That's great for your average inexperienced user, but what about the rest of us? Do we really need drop-shadows on our desktop icons and sliding menus? Probably not. Personally, I don't give a hoot what Windows effects Windows uses, but if they slow me down—either directly by hampering the performance of my PC or indirectly by making the interface harder or slower to navigate—then they're out of there.

Before I show you how to turn off some or all of Windows' graphical knickknacks, it's important to put all this in some kind of perspective. Remember that for graphics in general, and for visual effects in particular, performance is mostly determined by the amount of memory on the video card. The more memory on the card, the faster it can process the visual effects. Most new computers have a decent amount of video card memory—at least 32MB—so turning off visual effects will have little impact on over-

> **NOTE** If you don't know how much memory your video card has, Windows can tell you. Select Start, All Programs, Accessories, System Tools, System Information (or open the Run dialog box, type **msinfo32**, and click OK). In the System Information window that appears, open the Components, Display branch, and then read the Adapter RAM value.

all performance. If your adapter has 8MB or less, turning off visual effects can improve performance.

However, even if you've got scads of video RAM, you might find Windows easier to navigate and use with some or all of the effects turned off. For example, with the minimize and maximize effects turned off, windows disappear and reappear instantly, and even though this only saves you a few tenths of a second each time, it *feels* like the process is much faster.

Tuning Graphics Performance Using Visual Effects

Let's begin with Windows biggest cache of graphics settings, the Visual Effects tab:

1. Open the Run dialog box, type **sysdm.cpl**, and click OK. (In Vista, you need to enter your User Account Control credentials to continue.) The System Properties dialog box appears.

2. Click the Advanced tab.

3. Click Settings to open the Performance Options dialog box with the Visual Effects tab displayed, as shown in Figure 1.1.

4. You've got three ways to proceed here:

    ■ **Adjust for Best Performance**—Select this option to turn off every visual effect. This will give you a real minimalist interface.

> **TIP** To head directly to the Advanced tab, open the Run dialog box, type **control sysdm.cpl,,3**, and then click OK.

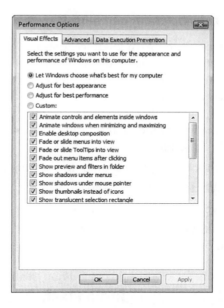

FIGURE 1.1
The Visual Effects tab is loaded with settings that control the appetite Windows has for graphical treats.

- **Let Windows Choose What's Best for My Computer**—This is the default option, and it tells Windows to activate or deactivate visual effects based on your computer's hardware.

- **Custom**—Select this option to decide which effects you want to turn off. This is usually the best way to go because it lets you leave some or more useful visual effects turned on.

5. Click OK. Windows takes a few moments to save your work and recompose the window using the new visual settings. You end up back at the System Properties dialog box.

6. Click OK.

TIP What should you leave turned on? I highly recommend leaving the Smooth Edges of Screen Fonts check box activated, because otherwise Windows text is too ugly for words. It's also a good idea to keep the Show Windows Contents While Dragging check box because makes it easier to drag windows.

Tuning Graphics Performance in Windows Vista

 If you're running Vista's Aero interface, I also recommend turning off the transparency effects. Why shun one of Vista's most famous and iconic features? Two reasons: It serves no earthly purpose that I can discern, and the text and images that bleed through the transparent sections of windows are always distracting and often confusing. In short, transparency is nothing but eye candy of the worst kind, and shutting it down is one of the first things I do on any new Vista installation. Here's how:

1. Right-click an empty section of the desktop and then click Personalize.
2. Click Window Color and Appearance.
3. Deactivate the Enable Transparency check box.
4. Click OK. Vista recomposes the screen with the transparency effects turned off.

Boost Vista Performance Using a Flash Drive

Easy

If you've purchased items from Amazon.com or iTunes, you've probably had those sites recommend books or music based on what you've purchased in the past. Vista and XP have a similar feature, although it won't help you find new books or bands. Instead, the *prefetcher*, as it's called, is a performance feature in XP that monitors how you use your system and tries to anticipate the data that you might use in the near future. The prefetcher then loads that data into memory ahead of time. If that data was indeed what your system required, performance would increase because Windows wouldn't have to fetch the data from your hard disk (because it had been already "prefetched").

Windows Vista introduced a new and improved version of the prefetcher: SuperFetch. This technology tracks the programs and data you use over time to create a kind of profile of your disk usage. Using the profile, SuperFetch can then make a much more educated guess about the data that you'll require and, like the prefetcher, can then load that data into memory ahead of time for enhanced performance.

However, SuperFetch goes even further by taking advantage of Vista's ReadyBoost technology. If you insert a USB flash drive, Vista may display the AutoPlay dialog box shown in Figure 1.2.

FIGURE 1.2

If you insert a certain kind of USB 2.0 flash drive into your system, SuperFetch can use it as its cache to improve system performance.

If you click Speed Up My System Using Windows ReadyBoost, SuperFetch uses that drive's capacity as storage for the SuperFetch cache. On many systems, this gives a performance nudge because even though data access via the flash drive is slower than with system RAM, it's still many times faster than even the fastest hard drive.

Note that ReadyBoost doesn't work with all USB flash drives. Here are the criteria:

- The drive (and the USB port you plug it into) must support USB 2.0.
- The drive must have a total capacity of at least 256MB.
- The drive must have at least 235MB of free space.
- The drive must meet certain minimum performance requirements related to read and write speeds. According to Microsoft, the minimum speeds are as follows:

  Reads—At least 2.5MB per second throughput for 4KB random reads across the drive.

  Writes—At least 1.75MB per second throughput for 512KB sequential writes across the drive.

If a flash drive doesn't meet these criteria, you don't get the option of using ReadyBoost. If you check the device properties (click Start, Computer, right-click the device, and then click Properties), the ReadyBoost tab will show you the reason. In Figure 1.3, for example, you can see that this drive isn't fast enough.

FIGURE 1.3

The ReadyBoost tab in the flash drive's property sheet tells you why it's not ReadyBoost ready.

Want more detailed info? Why not? Try this:

1. Click Start.

2. Type **event** into the Search box, click Event Viewer in the results, and then enter your User Account Control (UAC) credentials. The Event Viewer window appears.

3. Open the Applications and Services Log, Microsoft, Windows, ReadyBoost, Operational branch.

4. Click the event that was created when you inserted the flash drive.

The event tells you why the drive was rejected. In Figure 1.4, for example, you can see that the device wasn't fast across the entire drive (the "fast region"—the region that meets the minimum performance requirements—was just 120MB). In Figure 1.5, you see that when you insert a ReadyBoost-ready flash drive, Event Viewer details the drive's performance characteristics.

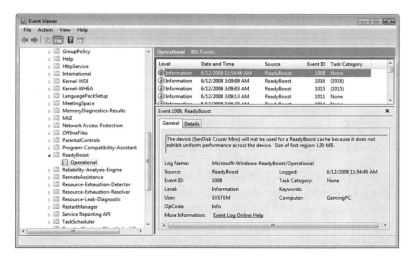

FIGURE 1.4
The Event Viewer can give you more detail about why a flash drive was rejected for ReadyBoost.

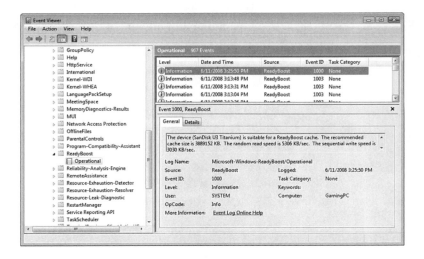

FIGURE 1.5
For a ReadyBoost-compliant drive, the Event Viewer tells you the drive's performance characteristics.

How big should the flash drive be? Ideally, it should be between one and three times the size of the physical RAM installed on your system. Here are some examples:

- **512MB RAM**—The flash drive should be no smaller than 512KB and no bigger than 1.5GB.

- **1GB RAM**—The flash drive should be no smaller than 1GB and no bigger than 3GB.

- **2GB RAM**—The flash drive should be no smaller than 2GB and no bigger than 4GB.

> **NOTE** In the 2GB RAM scenario, why is 4GB the maximum flash drive size and not 6GB? Because 32-bit versions of Windows Vista can't access memory beyond 4GB.

Note that this doesn't mean you have to get a flash drive that exactly matches the cache size you want to use. For example, suppose you have 1GB RAM and you want to use 3GB for ReadyBoost. If you have a 4GB flash drive, you can tell Vista to use only 3GB for ReadyBoost. Here's how:

1. Select Start, Computer to open the Computer window.

2. Right-click the flash drive and then click Properties to open the device's property sheet.

3. Select the ReadyBoost tab, shown in Figure 1.6.

4. Click the Use This Device option to let SuperFetch access the flash memory.

5. Use the slider to set the maximum amount of memory SuperFetch can use.

6. Click OK.

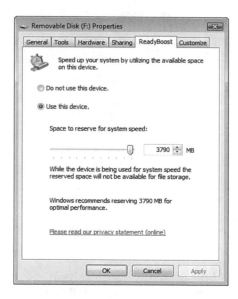

FIGURE 1.6

In the flash drive's property sheet, use the ReadyBoost tab to set the maximum amount of memory that SuperFetch can use.

Ensure Windows Is Optimized for Programs

Easy

You can set up Windows so that it's optimized to run programs. This involves adjusting the *processor scheduling*, which determines how much time the processor allocates to the computer's activities. In particular, processor scheduling differentiates between the *foreground program*—the program in which you're currently working—and *background programs*—programs that perform tasks, such as printing or backing up, while you work in another program.

TIP To head directly to the Advanced tab (although with a UAC detour in Vista), open the Run dialog box, type `control sysdm.cpl,,3`, and then click OK.

Optimizing programs means configuring Windows so that it gives more CPU time to your programs. This is the default in Vista and XP, but it's worth your time to make sure that this default configuration is still the case on your system. Here are the steps to follow:

1. Open the Run dialog box, type `sysdm.cpl`, and click OK. (In Vista, you need to enter your UAC credentials to continue.) The System Properties dialog box appears.

2. Click the Advanced tab.

3. In the Performance group, click Settings to display the Performance Options dialog box.

4. Display the Advanced tab.

5. In the Processor Scheduling group, activate the Programs option.

6. Click OK.

7. When Windows tells you the changes require a restart, click OK to return to the System Properties dialog box.

8. Click OK. Windows asks whether you want to restart your system.

9. Click Yes.

Enable Your Hard Drive's Advanced Performance Features

Easy

One of the slowest operations your computer performs is reading from and writing to the hard drive. So it makes more than a little sense that you can improve overall performance by reducing the amount of time that Windows has to spend reading from and writing to the hard drive. Fortunately, almost all hard drives come with a bit of onboard memory called the *hard drive cache*, and Windows can take advantage of that speedy cache to store frequently used chunks of data. That is, when Windows needs to read some data from the hard drive, it first checks the cache. If the data is there, great: Windows can retrieve the data many times faster than if it had to go directly to the hard disk's platters.

The cache speeds up hard drive read operations, but Windows also has to write data back to the hard drive. Does the cache help with write operations, too? Theoretically, yes. This is called *write caching*, and it means that Windows stores changed data

CAUTION Let me reiterate here that activating the Enable Advanced Performance option tells Vista to use an even more aggressive write-caching algorithm. However, an unscheduled power shutdown means you will almost certainly lose some data. Activate this option only if your system is running off a UPS or has a battery backup.

in the hard drive cache. Windows doesn't write that changed data to the disk until the system is idle, which improves performance. You can get even more of a performance boost if your system uses a SATA (Serial Advanced Technology Attachment) hard drive, because SATA drives include extra cache features.

This hard drive performance improvement is theoretical because on most systems Windows doesn't activate write caching. That's because the downside of write caching is that a power outage or system crash means that the data never gets written, so the changes are lost. For regular write caching this isn't a major concern, because changed data is flushed to the hard drive quite frequently. However, the more advanced SATA drive write caching is more aggressive, so losing data is a distinct possibility unless your system is protected by an uninterruptible power supply (UPS) or a battery backup.

To enable write caching on your system, follow these steps:

1. Select Start, right-click Computer (or My Computer in XP), and then click Manage. (In Vista you need to enter your UAC credentials at this point.) Windows displays the Computer Management window.

2. Click Device Manager.

3. Open the Disk Drives branch.

4. Double-click your hard disk to display its property sheet.

5. In the Policies tab, make sure that the Enable Write Caching on the Disk check box is activated.

6. For maximum performance with a SATA drive, activate the Enable Advanced Performance check box.

7. Click OK.

CHAPTER 2

Crucial Security Tweaks

Do you want your computer to be perfectly secure? Sure, no problem! Just follow my simple four-step plan:

- Never connect your computer to the Internet.

- Don't install any programs on your computer.

- Don't let anyone else work with or even look at your computer.

- Burglar-proof your home or office.

I kid, of course, because the truth is that if you want to use your computer (and live your life) in an even remotely normal way, you open up your machine to security risks.

That may sound like a bleak assessment, but the upside of all this is that it doesn't take a ton of effort on your part to turn your computer into a maximum security area. The security tweaks in this chapter will help you toward that goal, but first make sure you've nailed down the basics:

■ **Leave User Account Control turned on**—Yes, I know Vista's UAC is a hassle. However, UAC is the best thing that's happened to Windows security in a long time, and it's a fact of life that your computer is much more secure when UAC has your back.

■ **Be paranoid**—The belief that everyone's out to get you may be a sign of trouble in the real world, but it's just common sense in the computer world. Assume someone will sit down at your desk when you're not around; assume someone will try to log on to your computer when you leave for the night; assume all uninvited email attachments are viruses; assume unknown websites are malicious; assume any offer that sounds too good to be true probably is.

■ **Keep to yourself**—We all share lots of personal info online these days, but there's sharing and then there's asking-for-trouble sharing. Don't tell anybody any of your passwords. Don't put your email address online unless it's disguised in some way (for example, by writing it as `username at yourdomain dot com`). Don't give out sensitive personal data such as your social security number, bank account number, or even your address and phone number (unless making a purchase with a reputable vendor). Only give your credit card data to online vendors that you trust implicitly or, even better, get a secure PayPal account and use that instead.

■ **Assume the worst**—Back up your data regularly, keep your receipts, keep all email correspondence, and read the fine print.

With these basics down pat, you're now ready to take Windows security to the next level, and the following tweaks will help you do just that.

Thwart Snoops by Locking Your Computer

Easy

In Chapter 7, "Keeping the Bad Guys at Bay," you learn a few more security tweaks, including important measures such as advanced file permissions and encryption. These two features are great, but they each have one small flaw: They rely on the assumption that after you've entered a legitimate username and password to log on to your Windows user account, only you will use your computer. This means that after you log on, you become a "trusted" user and you have full access to your files, even if they're protected by permissions and encryption.

This is certainly reasonable on the surface. After all, you wouldn't want to have to enter your account credentials every time you want to open, edit, create, or delete a document. So while you're logged on and at your desk, you get full access to your stuff.

CAUTION I'm assuming that because you have files worthy of being protected by permissions or encryption, you haven't set up Windows to automatically log on.

But what happens when you leave your desk? If you remain logged on to Windows, any other person who sits down at your computer can take advantage of your trusted-user status to view and work with secure files (including copying them to a USB flash drive inserted by the snoop). This is what I mean by permissions and encryption having a flaw, and it's a potentially significant security hole in large offices where it wouldn't be hard for someone to pull up your chair while you're stuck in yet another meeting.

One way to prevent this would be to turn off your computer every time you leave your desk. That way, any would-be snoop would have to get past your login to get to your files. This, obviously, is wildly impractical and inefficient.

Is there a better solution? You bet: You can lock your system before leaving your desk. Anyone who tries to use your computer must enter your password to access the Windows desktop.

Windows gives you three ways to lock your computer before heading off:

- In Windows Vista, click Start and then click the Lock icon.

- In Vista or XP, press Windows Logo+L.

- In Vista or XP, press Ctrl+Alt+Delete and then click Lock Computer.

Whichever method you use, you end up at the Windows logon screen. Figure 2.1 shows the Vista logon screen. Note that is says Locked under your username.

TIP Windows also locks your computer when the screensaver kicks in. If this often happens while you're at your desk, constantly having to log on can get annoying in a hurry, so you might want to turn off this feature. Right-click the desktop, click Personalize (in Vista) or Properties (in XP), and then click Screen Saver. Activate the On Resume, Display Logon Screen check box (Vista) or the On Resume, Password Protect check box (XP). Click OK.

FIGURE 2.1
You see a screen similar to this when you lock your Vista computer.

Start Your Computer More Securely

Protecting your Windows user account with a password is an excellent idea, and in Chapter 13, "Crucial Password Hacks," you learn how to create a strong password that is all but unbreakable.

Easy

➤   **See** "Bulletproof Your Password," **p. 146**.

Having a sturdy password barrier is crucial for keeping snoops at bay, but unfortunately it's not foolproof. Crackers—hackers who use their skills for nefarious ends—are an endlessly resourceful bunch, and some of the smarter ones figured out a way to defeat the user account password system. The trick is that they install a virus or Trojan horse program, usually via an infected email message or malicious website, that loads itself when you start your computer. This program then displays a *fake* version of the Windows logon screen. When you type your username and password into this dialog box, the program records it and your system security is compromised.

To thwart this clever ruse, Windows enables you to configure your system so that you must press Ctrl+Alt+Delete before you can log on. This key combination ensures that the authentic logon screen appears.

To configure Windows to require that you press Ctrl+Alt+Delete before you can log on, follow these steps:

1. Display the Run dialog box.

2. Type `control userpasswords2` and then click OK. (In Vista, you need to enter your UAC credentials to continue.) The User Accounts dialog box appears.

3. Display the Advanced tab.

4. Activate the Require Users to Press Ctrl+Alt+Delete check box, as shown in Figure 2.2.

5. Click OK.

FIGURE 2.2

For a secure startup, activate the Require Users to Press Ctrl+Alt+Delete check box.

Take Steps to Thwart Crackers

Crackers, as I mentioned in the previous section, are hackers who have succumbed to the Dark Side of the Force. Their specialty is breaking into systems ("cracking" system security, hence the name), and at any given time hundreds, perhaps even thousands, of crackers roam cyberspace looking for potential targets. If you're online right now, the restless and far-seeing eyes of the crackers are bound to find you eventually.

Sounds unlikely, you say? You wish. The crackers are armed with programs that automatically search through millions of IP addresses (the addresses that uniquely identify any computer or device connected to the Internet). The crackers are specifically looking for computers that aren't secure, and if they find one they'll pounce on it and crack their way into the system.

Again, if all this sounds unlikely or that it would take them forever to find you, think again. Tests have shown that new and completely unprotected systems can get cracked within 20 minutes of connecting to the Internet!

Fortunately, keeping crackers away from your computer isn't hard, but it does require a bit of effort up front. Here are the main things you need to do:

- **Fire up the firewall**—The first and by far the most important thing you need to do to thwart crackers is to have a software firewall running on your computer. A *firewall* is a security feature that blocks unauthorized attempts to send data to your computer. The best firewalls completely hide your computer from the Internet, so those dastardly crackers don't even know you're there! The Windows Firewall is turned on by default, but you should check this, just to be safe. Open the Run dialog box, type `firewall.cpl`, and click OK. If the firewall is off, turn it on immediately.

- **Test the firewall**—A firewall's not much good if it leaves your computer vulnerable to attack, so you should test the firewall to make sure it's doing its job. I show you several ways to do this in Chapter 8, "Configuring Internet Security."

➜   **See** "Make Sure Your Firewall Is Up to Snuff," **p. 84**.

- **Take advantage of your router's firewall, too**—Why have one line of defense when in all probability you can have two! If your network has a router and that router connects to the Internet, then it, too, has an IP address that crackers can scan for vulnerabilities, particularly holes that expose your network. To prevent this, most routers come with built-in hardware firewalls

NOTE To access the router setup pages, open a web browser, type the router address, and then press Enter. See your device documentation for the correct URL, but for most routers the address is either http://192.168.1.1 or http://192.168.0.1. In most cases, you have to log in with a username and password so, again, see your documentation.

that provide robust security. Access your router's setup pages, locate the firewall settings (see Figure 2.3 for an example), and then make sure the firewall is turned on.

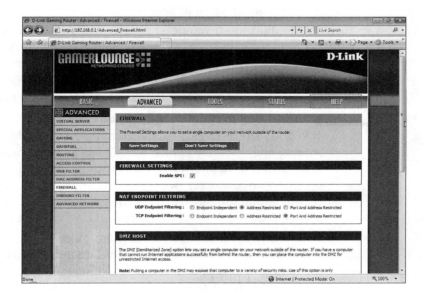

FIGURE 2.3
If your network has a router, make sure its firewall is turned on.

■ **Set up real-time spyware protection**—A firewall does you no good whatsoever if a spyware or other malware program sneaks through the front door when you install a program or access a malicious website. This can happen to anyone, so your next line of defense is a top-of-the-line antispyware program, such as Windows Defender, which comes with Vista. Whichever program you use, make sure its real-time protection feature is activated, which prevents any spyware that sneaks through from being installed. For Windows Defender, select Start, All Programs, Windows Defender, click Tools, click Options, and then make sure the Use Real-Time Protection check box is activated.

> **TIP** Many security experts recommend installing multiple antispyware programs on the premise that one program may miss one or two examples of spyware, but two or three programs are highly unlikely to miss any. So, in addition to Windows Defender, you might also consider installing antispyware programs such as Lavasoft Ad-Aware (www.lavasoft.com) and PC Tools Spyware Doctor (www.pctools.com).

■ **Update, update, update**—Many crackers take advantage of known Windows vulnerabilities to compromise a system. To avoid this, keep your PC updated with the latest patches, fixes, and service packs, many of which are designed to plug security leaks.

■ **Turn off file sharing**—If you never need to access your computer's resources from the network, you can bump up your anticracker security measures a notch by turning off file sharing on your computer. This way, even if a cracker somehow gained access to your network, you won't be exposing any resources. Here's how to turn off file sharing:

Windows Vista—Click the Network icon in the notification area and then click Network and Sharing Center. In the Sharing and Discovery Center, turn off File Sharing, Public Folder Sharing, Password Protected Sharing, and, while you're at it, Network Discovery (see Figure 2.4). In each case, click the current setting (usually On), click the option that turns off the setting, click Apply, and then enter your UAC credentials.

Windows XP—Select Start, All Programs, Accessories, Communications, Network Connections. In the Network Connections window, double-click the connection (usually named either Local Area Connection or Wireless Network Connection) to open its property sheet, display the General tab, and then deactivate the File and Printer Sharing for Microsoft Networks check box.

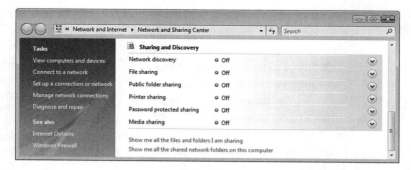

FIGURE 2.4

If you don't need to share resources with your network, turn off all Vista networking sharing features.

Take Steps to Thwart Viruses

Easy

It's an unfortunate fact that more ways exist than ever for your PC to contract a virus: malicious websites, infected program downloads, and, most often these days, infected email file attachments. In the last case, the virus shows up as a message attachment, usually from someone you know, and when you open the attachment, the virus infects your computer. In most cases, the virus then does what viruses do: It propagates by making copies of itself using your email program and your address book to ship out messages with more copies of the virus attached. The nastier viruses also mess with your computer by deleting data or corrupting files, or they install a Trojan Horse program, which enables a remote cracker to control your computer (turning it into a *zombie* PC).

Viruses are a plague upon the Earth, for sure, but if you practice safe computing, chances are that your machine will never get infected. What do I mean by *safe computing*? That you follow a few common sense procedures and configure Windows to ensure that viruses can't get a foothold in your system:

- Never, I repeat, *never* open an attachment that comes from someone you don't know. There may be an excellent reason that a perfect stranger is sending you a file, but that's none of your concern. Delete the message with extreme prejudice. (To be safe, permanently delete the message by pressing Shift+Delete.)

- Even if you know the sender, if the attachment isn't something you're expecting, assume that the sender's system is infected. Write back and ask the sender to confirm that he or she emailed the message.

- Some viruses come packaged as scripts hidden within messages that use the Rich Text (HTML) format. This means that the virus can run just by viewing the message in the preview pane! If a message looks suspicious, don't open it; just delete it. Note that you'll need to turn off your email program's preview pane before deleting the message. Otherwise, when you highlight the message, it appears in the preview pane and sets off the virus.

- What if you *think* the message is okay, but you're not completely sure? In that case, you need to

> **CAUTION** It's particularly important to turn off the preview pane before displaying your email program's Junk E-mail folder. Because many junk messages also carry a virus payload, your chances of initiating an infection are highest when working with messages in this folder.

switch your email program to read messages in plain text, which ensures that any malicious scripts won't run. Here's how:

Windows Mail and Outlook Express—Select Tools, Options, click the Read tab, and then activate the Read All Messages in Plain Text check box.

Outlook 2007—Select Tools, Trust Center, click E-mail Security, and then activate the Read All Standard Messages in Plain Text check box.

Outlook 2003—Select Tools, Options, click the Preferences tab, click E-mail Options, and then activate the Read All Standard Messages in Plain Text check box.

■ Install a top-of-the-line antivirus program, particularly one that checks incoming email. In addition, be sure to keep your antivirus program's virus list up to date. As you read this, there are probably dozens, maybe even hundreds, of morally challenged scumnerds designing even nastier viruses. Regular updates will help you keep up. Here are some security suites to check out:

Norton Internet Security (www.symantec.com/index.jsp)

McAfee Internet Security Suite (http://mcafee.com/us)

Avast! Antivirus (www.avast.com)

AVG Internet Security (http://free.grisoft.com/)

■ Make sure that the built-in virus protection features found in Windows Mail and Outlook Express are turned on. Select Tools, Options, and then click the Security tab. There are three virus protection settings:

Select the Internet Explorer Security Zone to Use—Internet Explorer implements different *security zones*, which are customized security settings for things like Internet sites and sites on your local network. From an email perspective, you use the security zones to determine whether to allow active content (such as scripts and ActiveX controls) inside an HTML-format message to run. In particular, the

> **NOTE** The email program will block any file that uses one of the following extensions: .ad, .ade, .adp, .bas, .bat, .chm, .cmd, .com, .cpl, .crt, .exe, .hlp, .hta, .inf, .ins, .isp, .js, .jse, .lnk, .mdb, .mde, .msc, .msi, .msp, .mst, .pcd, .pif, .reg, .scr, .sct, .shb, .shs, .url, .vb, .vbe, .vbs, .vsd, .vss, .vst, .vsw, .wsc, .wsf, .wsh.

Restricted Sites Zone disables all active content, so make sure this option is activated.

Warn Me When Other Applications Try to Send Mail as Me—As I mentioned earlier, it's possible for programs and scripts to send email messages without your knowledge. With this check box activated, Windows displays a warning dialog box when a program or script attempts to send a message behind the scenes.

> **TIP** What do you do if you want to send a file that's on the unsafe file list and you want to make sure that the recipient will be able to open it? The easiest workaround is to compress the file into a `.zip` file—a file type not blocked by Windows Mail, Outlook Express, Outlook, or any other mail client that blocks file types. Another method is to change the extension to something not on the list, and then tell your recipient to change the extension back when he or she saves the attachment.

Do Not Allow Attachments to Be Saved or Opened That Could Potentially Be a Virus—With this check box activated, the email program monitors attachments to look for file types that could contain viruses or destructive code. If it detects such a file, it disables your ability to open and save that file, and it displays a note at the top of the message to let you know about the unsafe attachment, as shown in Figure 2.5.

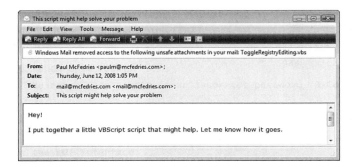

FIGURE 2.5

If Windows Mail or Outlook Express detects an unsafe file attachment, it displays a notice at the top of the message to let you know that you can't open the file.

Indispensable Interface Tweaks

I don't think I'm going out on much of a limb by claiming that *everybody* customizes the Windows interface in some way. Whether it's changing the desktop wallpaper, configuring a screensaver, or changing the Windows theme, we all like to put our personal stamp on the Windows look and feel.

I'm a dedicated customizer myself, particularly with any machine that's earmarked for personal use. I also usually have anywhere from four to six "bench" machines that I use for testing, experimenting, and creating the screenshots that you see in my books. Those machines I prefer to leave "as is" so that I can write about Windows with a "pure" setup. However, on all those machines, as well as on my personal PCs, there's a series of customizations that I simply *must* run to make the computers more efficient and more usable. I perform these customizations as soon as I get to the desktop for the first time after Windows Setup completes its labors. These are my indispensable interface tweaks, and they're the subject of this chapter.

Add the Handy Run Command to Vista's Start Menu

Easy

The Run command opens the Run dialog box, which you can use to open all kinds of file types by typing the file's address. The versatile Run command lets you launch programs, folders, documents, websites, email messages, Command Prompt commands, and more.

One of the most annoying interface changes in Windows Vista is the burying of the Run command deep in the bowels of the Start menu. To access the run command in an out-of-the-box Vista setup, you must select Start, All Programs, Accessories, Run. *Way* too much work for such a handy and useful feature!

Fortunately, Vista does give us Run addicts a couple of easier methods to get our fix:

■ Press Windows Logo+R. This is a great shortcut to know and I use it all the time, but it does have a couple of drawbacks: you can't use it on machines that don't have a Windows Logo key (such as my ThinkPad), and it's a slight hassle to switch to the keyboard if you're in the middle of a heavy mousing session.

➜   If your PC doesn't have a Windows Logo key, it's possible to reprogram some other key to mimic it; **see** "Reprogram a Key On Your Keyboard," available online in the "Dealing with Devices" web chapter.

■ Click Start, type **run** into the Search box, and then click Run when it shows up in the results. This is better than the full Start menu rigma-role, for sure, but it sometimes takes a few seconds for Run to show up in the results, and it still feels like just a bit too much work.

In previous versions of Windows, the Run command was situated right on the main Start menu, which meant that you could launch it quickly with just a couple of mouse clicks. This strikes me as the ideal mouse complement to the Windows Logo+R keyboard technique, so it fries my bananas that the Vista team moved Run to the nether regions of the Start menu landscape.

If, like me, you're a frequent Run user, you owe it to yourself to restore Run to its rightful place on the main Start menu. This is, in fact, the very first thing I always do with any new Vista installation. Here's what you do:

1. Right-click the Start button and then click Properties. The Taskbar and Start Menu Properties dialog box shows up with the Start Menu tab displayed.

2. Click Customize. The Customize Start Menu dialog box appears.

3. Scroll down the list of customizations and then activate the Run Command check box.

4. Click OK to return to the Taskbar and Start Menu Properties dialog box.

5. Click OK to put the new setting into effect.

Figure 3.1 shows the Vista Start menu with the Run command where it should be, on the bottom right of the menu.

FIGURE 3.1

That's better: the Start menu with the Run command restored to its rightful place.

Make Files Make Sense by Showing Extensions

The seemingly humble file extension—the part of the filename that comes after the dot; for example, the doc part of memo.doc—is one of the most crucial Windows concepts. Why? Because file extensions *solely and completely* determine the file type of a document. In other words, if Windows sees that a file has a .txt extension, it concludes that the file uses the Text Document file type. Similarly, a file with the extension .bmp uses the Bitmap Image file type.

The file type, in turn, determines the application that's associated with the extension. If a file has a `.txt` extension, Windows associates that extension with Notepad, so the file will always open in Notepad. Nothing else inherent in the file determines the file type; so, at least from the point of view of the user, the entire

NOTE To be fair, I should also note that Microsoft turns off file extensions *because* they're so important. That is, a novice user could render a file useless by imprudently renaming its extension.

Windows file system rests on the shoulders of the humble file extension.

Microsoft figures that, crucial or not, the file extension concept is just too hard for new users to grasp. Therefore, right out of the box, Windows Explorer doesn't display file extensions.

This may not sound like a big whoop, but not being able to see the extension for each file can be downright confusing. To see why, suppose you have a folder with multiple documents that use the same primary name. This is a not uncommon scenario, but it's a fiendish one because it's often difficult to tell which file is which.

For example, Figure 3.2 shows a folder with 18 different files, all apparently named `Project`. Windows unrealistically expects users to tell files apart just by examining their icons. To make matters worse, if the file is an image, Vista shows a thumbnail of the image instead of an icon (this happens in thumbnail views such as Tiles, Medium Icons, and Large icons). The result is that in Figure 3.2 it's impossible to tell at a glance which image is a GIF, which is a JPEG, and so on.

The need to become an expert in Windows iconography is bad enough, but it gets worse. Not being able to see file extensions also leads to two other problems:

- **You can't rename extensions**—For example, suppose you have a text file named `index.txt` and you want to rename it to `index.html` to make it a web page file. Nope, sorry, you can't do it with file extensions hidden. If you try—that is, if you click the file, press F2 to choose the Rename command, and then type **index.html**—you just end up with a text file named `index.html.txt`.

FIGURE 3.2

With file extensions turned off, it's tough to tell one file from another.

- **You can't save a document under an extension of your choice—** Similarly, with file extensions turned off, Windows Vista forces you to save a file using the default extension associated with an application. For example, if you're working in Notepad, every file you save must have a .txt extension. If you create your own web pages, for example, you can't rename these text files with typical web page extensions such as .htm, .html, .asp, and so on.

> **TIP** There is a way to get around the inability to save a document under an extension of your choice. In the Save As dialog box, use the Save as Type list to select the All Files option, if it exists. You can then use the File Name text box to type the filename with the extension you prefer to use.

You can overcome all these problems by turning on file extensions, as described in the following steps:

1. In any Windows Explorer window, select Organize, Folder and Search Options to open the Folder Options dialog box.

2. Click the View tab.

3. Deactivate the Hide File Extensions for Known File Types check box.

4. Click OK.

Figure 3.3 shows the Project files with extensions in full display.

FIGURE 3.3

With file extensions turned on, it's much easier to tell the files apart.

Give Your Eyes a Rest by Turning on ClearType

  If you read a lot of onscreen text, particularly if you use a notebook or an LCD screen, you should activate the Windows ClearType feature, which drastically reduces the jagged edges of screen fonts and makes text super sharp and far easier to read than regular screen text.

Activating ClearType in Vista

Fortunately, ClearType is activated by default in Windows Vista. To be sure, follow these steps:

1. Right-click the desktop and then click Personalize. The Personalization window appears.

2. Click Window Color and Appearance. If you're not running the Aero interface, skip to step 4.

3. If you're using the Aero interface, click Open Classic Appearance Properties for More Color Options. The Appearance Settings dialog box appears.

4. Click Effects to open the Effects dialog box.

5. Make sure that the Use the Following Method to Smooth Edges of Screen Fonts check box is activated.

6. Use the drop-down list to select ClearType.

7. Click OK in each open dialog box to put the new setting into effect.

Activating ClearType in XP

ClearType isn't turned on by default in Windows XP, so follow these steps to activate it:

1. Right-click the desktop and then click Properties. The Display Properties dialog box appears.

2. Click the Appearance tab.

3. Click Effects to open the Effects dialog box.

4. Activate the Use the Following Method to Smooth Edges of Screen Fonts check box.

> **TIP** If you're running XP, you can customize some ClearType settings using the ClearType Tuner PowerToy, available from Microsoft's PowerToys for Windows XP site: http://www.microsoft.com/windowsxp/downloads/powertoys/xppowertoys.mspx.

5. Use the drop-down list to select ClearType.

6. Click OK in each open dialog box to put the new setting into effect.

Automatically Move the Mouse to the Default Button

Easy

The power behind this tweak comes from two observations:

- Being a graphical user interface (GUI), Windows is built with the mouse in mind, which means that *everyone* does a lot of mousing in a typical day.

- One of the secrets of productivity is to reduce the time it takes you to perform a task that you repeat dozens or even hundreds of times a day. A few seconds saved each time can translate into many precious minutes at the end of the day.

This means that if you can cut some time from your mouse moves, you can save lots of time overall because you probably perform those moves so often. The mouse move that I'm talking about in particular is the clicking of the default button. In most dialog boxes, the *default button* is the command button that dismisses the dialog box and puts the dialog box settings into effect. The most common default dialog box button is the OK button. How do you know which one is the default? Windows gives you visual clues:

- **Windows Vista**—Vista makes it easy for you to find the default button by making the button glow while the dialog box is open. That is, the button's blue color gradually fades in and out.

- **Windows XP**—In XP the default button is the one that has a blue border around it when you first open the dialog box and when the focus is on any other control except a different command button. (That is, if you press Tab or Shift+Tab to move the focus through the dialog box controls and you land on another command button, that button gets the blue border.)

Many dialog boxes do nothing more than provide you with information or a warning. In most of these cases, the only thing you need to do with the dialog box is click the default button. You can get past such dialog boxes much more quickly if you customize Windows to automatically move the mouse pointer over the default button—this is called the Snap To feature—because then all you have to do is click to dismiss the dialog box. If the dialog box requires more complex input from you, you still save time because the mouse pointer is already inside the dialog box.

Here are the steps to follow to configure Windows to automatically move the mouse pointer to the default button:

1. Open the Run dialog box, type **control mouse**, and click OK. The Mouse Properties dialog box appears.

2. Click the Pointer Options tab.

3. In the Snap To section, activate the Automatically Move Pointer to the Default Button in a Dialog Box check box.

4. Click OK to put the new setting into effect.

CAUTION When you turn on the Snap To feature, it's easy to get into the habit of quickly clicking whenever a notification dialog box appears. However, if you click too quickly, you may miss the message in the dialog box, which could be important. Remember to read all dialog box messages before clicking the default button.

Terrific Web Tweaks

Most of us now spend great gobs of time surfing the Web. Whether it's doing research, buying things, getting the latest news, or keeping up appearances at your social networking sites, the Web takes up an ever-increasing amount of our apparently ever-diminishing time. To gain back some of that time, the tweaks in this chapter show you four ways to make your surfing excursions a bit more efficient. For example, you learn how to load more than one page when you start Internet Explorer 7; you learn a few handy Internet Explorer Address bar tricks; you learn how to configure Internet Explorer 7 to switch to new tabs as soon as you create them; and you learn how to disable animated GIFs (which is really more of a sanity saver than an efficiency enhancer).

Load Multiple Home Pages at Startup

Easy

As you know, a website's home page is the main page of the site, and it's the page where you often begin your exploration of that site. (Although these days, with so many people accessing sites via search engines, blogs, and RSS feeds, you're just as likely to start your site surfing on an inside page rather than the home page. For example, it's been several years since I've seen Microsoft's home page.)

A bit confusingly, Internet Explorer also defines a home page: it's the page that Internet Explorer displays automatically when you first start the program. The default Internet Explorer home page is MSN.com, but most people change that to a page that they use regularly.

With Internet Explorer 7 (which comes with Vista but can be installed on XP), the home page idea gets a boost because of its new tabbed browsing feature, which lets you open multiple pages in the same window. It makes sense, then, that if you can work with multiple tabs during a browser session, you might also want to work with multiple tabs right off the bat when you start Internet Explorer. And that's exactly what Internet Explorer 7 enables you do to. You can define two or more home pages, and Internet Explorer dutifully loads those pages into separate tabs when you launch the program.

This feature isn't a big deal if you open just a couple of sites at startup, but it pays big dividends if you regularly open several sites right off. For example, you may open a portal page such as MSN or Yahoo, a search page such as Google, your company's external or internal website, a news page, one or more blogger pages, and so on. Even if you have all those sites set up as favorites, it would still take a bit of time to create a new tab, load the site, and then repeat for every page you want to open. With multiple home pages defined, Internet Explorer handles opening all your home pages, so you just sit back and let everything happen automatically.

CAUTION When it comes to opening pages at startup, I'm afraid there's no such thing as a free browser lunch. The more home pages you define, the longer it takes Internet Explorer to start. Note, too, that if you have a home page that requires a login and you've set up that site to remember your login data, that login might fail if the page loads at startup.

TIP If you're planning to add several pages to your home page tabs, there's an easy way to go about it. First, for each page you want to add, open a new tab and use that tab to surf to the page. If you have any tabs open with pages that you don't want to include, close those tabs. Click the drop-down arrow beside the Home button, click Add or Change Home Page, activate the Use the Current Tab Set as Your Home Page, and then click Yes.

TIP If you're not connected to the Internet, you can still add a site as a home page. Click Tools and then click Internet Options to display the Internet Options dialog box. In the General tab, click the last item in the Home page list, press End, and then press Enter to start a new line. Type the address of the new home page and then click OK.

Follow these steps to set up multiple home pages in Internet Explorer 7:

1. In Internet Explorer 7, surf to a page you want to load at startup.

2. Click the drop-down arrow beside the Home button and then click Add or Change Home Page. The Add or Change Home Page dialog box appears.

3. Click the Add This Webpage to Your Home Page Tabs option, as shown in Figure 4.1.

FIGURE 4.1

Click the option shown here to add the current page to your home page tabs.

4. Click Yes.

5. Repeat steps 1 to 4 to add other pages to your home page tabs.

6. If there are any home page tabs you want to get rid of, click the drop-down arrow beside the Home button, click Remove, click the page, and then click Yes to confirm.

Become an Address Bar Guru

Medium

Internet Explorer's Address bar (and the Address bars that appear in all folder windows) appears to be nothing more than a simple type-and-click mechanism. However, it's useful for many things, and it comes with its own bag of tricks for making it even easier to use.

For example, Internet Explorer maintains a list of the last 25 URLs you typed into the Address bar. To access this list, either click the drop-down arrow on the right side of the Address bar, or press F4. You can then use the Up Arrow and Down Arrow keys to select an item from the list.

In conjunction with the Address bar list, Internet Explorer deploys the AutoComplete feature, which monitors the address as you type. If any previously entered addresses match your typing, they appear in a list, as shown in

Figure 4.2. To choose one of those addresses, use the Down Arrow key to select it and then press the Enter key.

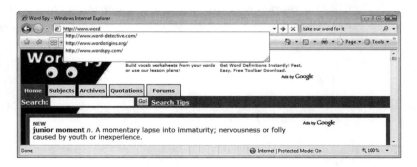

FIGURE 4.2

Internet Explorer's AutoComplete feature displays the addresses that match what you've typed into the Address bar.

AutoComplete kicks into action when you've typed at least `http://www.` or just `www.`, plus one other character. An often easier way to use AutoComplete is to begin typing the site's domain name, instead. For example, if you want to bring up http://www.microsoft.com/, start typing the *microsoft* part. Whatever you type, AutoComplete shows a list of all the typed URLs with domain names that begin with your typing. For example, you can see in Figure 4.3 that I've typed word into the Address bar, and AutoComplete shows a half dozen sites with domain names that begin with *word*. Notice how with this method I get a wider choice of sites than when I typed `http://www.word` in Figure 4.2. That's because many sites no longer use the `www.` prefix.

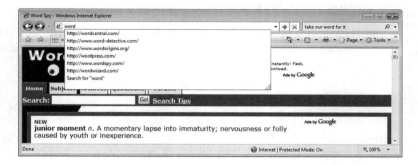

FIGURE 4.3

If you type something other than `http://www.` or `www.` into the Address bar, AutoComplete displays the URLs where the domain name begins with what you've typed.

Internet Explorer assumes that most web addresses are in the form http://www.*something*.com/, so it gives you a super-fast method for entering such addresses: type the *something* part and then press Ctrl+Enter. Internet Explorer automatically adds the http://www. prefix and the .com/ suffix. For example, you can get to my home page (http://www.mcfedries.com) by typing **mcfedries** and pressing Ctrl+Enter.

Note, too, that Internet Explorer assumes that any address you enter is for a website. Therefore, you don't need to type the http:// prefix because Internet Explorer adds it for you automatically.

> **TIP** To edit the Address bar text, first press Alt+D to select it.

> **TIP** Some websites use frames to divide a web page into multiple sections. Some of these sites offer links to other websites but, annoyingly, those pages appear within the first site's frame structure. To break out of frames, drag a link to the site and drop in the Address bar.

To search from the Address bar (a feature called AutoSearch), first type your search text. As you type, Internet Explorer adds Search for "*text*" below the Address bar, where *text* is your search text. When you've finished your search text, press Tab to select the Search for item and then press Enter. Alternatively, precede your search text with the word go, find, or search, or with a question mark (?), as in these examples:

```
go vbscript
find autosearch
search neologisms
? registry
```

Switch to New Tabs Right Away

Easy

When Internet Explorer finally dragged itself into the twenty-first century and added tabbed browsing like Firefox, Safari, Opera, and just about every other browser in existence, a huge swath of the population breathed a sigh of relief. After all, the majority of surfers still use Internet Explorer, and almost all Internet Explorer users routinely have half a dozen or more sites open at the same time. Having those sites open in separate browser windows was a hassle, but now with tabbed browsing we could open just one window and load each of our sites into its own tab.

Even better, Internet Explorer supplies each tab with its own execution thread, which means that you can start a page loading in one tab while reading downloaded page text in another tab. (A *thread*, just so you know, is a single processor task executed by a program.) You can also specify multiple home pages that load in their own tabs when you start Internet Explorer (as described earlier in this chapter; see "Load Multiple Home Pages at Startup").

The multithreaded nature of Internet Explorer's tabs means that when you open a link in a new tab, most of the time Internet Explorer leaves the current tab in the foreground, creates a new tab in the background, and loads the page into that new tab. This procedure happens when you use any of the following techniques to load a link into a new tab:

- Right-click a web page link and then click Open in New Tab.
- Hold down Ctrl and click a link in a web page.
- Use the middle mouse button (if you have one) to click a link in a web page.

On the other hand, Internet Explorer opens a link in a new foreground tab when you use any of the following techniques:

- Type the page URL into the Address bar and then press Alt+Enter.
- Click the New Tab button (or press Ctrl+T) to display a blank tab, type the page URL into the Address bar, and then press Enter.
- Click a link in another program.

Opening a page in the background in a new tab is useful if you want to keep reading the current page. However, I find that most of the time I want to read the new page right away. If you have a fast connection, the page loads quickly enough that the delay between clicking and reading is usually minimal. In such cases, you can tell Internet Explorer to switch to the new tab automatically by holding down both Ctrl and Shift and then clicking the link.

If, like me, you find this technique too awkward for full-time use, you can configure Internet Explorer to always load new tabs in the foreground. Here's how:

1. Select Tools, Internet Options to open the Internet Options dialog box.
2. Click the General tab.
3. In the Tabs group, click Settings to open the Tabbed Browsing Settings dialog box.
4. Activate the Always Switch to New Tabs When They Are Created check box.
5. Click OK in the open dialog boxes to put the new setting into effect.

Disable Annoying Animated GIFs

Easy

In the early days of the modern Web—long before embedded YouTube videos and slick Flash animations—the easiest way to give site visitors moving eye candy was to use an animated GIF image. The GIF file format supports combining multiple images in a single file, and opening that file displays its imbedded images sequentially. If those images were set up properly, the result was the illusion of motion: an animated GIF.

This was actually quite cool in the hands of an animation professional, and perhaps everything would have been okay if animated GIFs had remained a pro-only pursuit. Unfortunately, it turned out to be fairly easy to make an animated GIF, because several programs existed that would transform multiple GIF images into a single animated GIF with just a few mouse clicks. The Web was doomed.

Why? Because in the hands of amateurs, animated GIFs are almost always pure dreck: trashy, low-quality, gaudy, pointless, and really, really annoying.

The good news is that you don't see as many animated GIFs as you used to. The bad news is that there are still tons of them out there infesting the Web. Fortunately, you don't have to put up with this, because you can configure Internet Explorer to disable animated GIFs. Here's what you do:

1. Select Tools, Internet Options to open the Internet Options dialog box.

2. Click the Advanced tab.

3. Deactivate the Play Animations in Web Pages check box.

4. Click OK.

5. Shut down and then restart Internet Explorer to put the new setting into effect.

Easy Email Tweaks

These days there are more ways to converse with other people than ever. You can send a text message from your phone. You can exchange instant messages using a software program, hang out in online chat rooms, and set up an RSS feed. You can add forums to your website. You can read and respond to blog comments, send messages to microblogging services such as Twitter, and connect with friends on social networking sites such as Facebook and MySpace.

The only problem with these varied methods is that only some of the people you know use each one, so you might be able to chat with Karen on Google Chat, but if you want to connect with Tom, it needs to be on Facebook. In other words, none of these methods is even close to being universal.

Ah, but there's one way to communicate digitally that is all but universal: email. If you're online, you have an email address. Yes, I've heard that some young hipsters are shunning email, but they're such a vanishingly small portion of the online population that they barely register. Email is *the* communications medium of our times, and that goes a long way toward explaining why it takes up an ever-increasing chunk of our days (and nights). To help you get back a bit of that time, this chapter presents four easy and essential email tweaks.

Stop Windows from Adding Recipients to Your Contacts List

Easy

The email programs that come with Windows Vista and Windows XP—Windows Mail and Outlook Express, respectively—are actually decent email clients for operating system freebies. They perform all the basic chores without any fuss, have decent security features, enable you to juggle multiple accounts, set up message rules, manage folders, and more. Not bad for nothing!

However, both programs have a default setting that's positively annoying, perhaps even infuriating. If you reply to a message, no matter who it's from, both Windows Mail and Outlook Express automatically adds the sender of the original message to your Contacts list (in Vista) or your Address Book (in XP). Dumb! Most of us (I'm sure) get all kinds of messages from people and businesses that we'll never hear from again and that we'll never want to contact again, so it makes absolutely no sense to save these addresses.

If this setting was harmless, we could ignore it and get on with our busy lives. However, when you have a few dozen strangers clogging your Contacts list (or adding up in your Address Book), navigating that list becomes much harder and slower. And then when you decide enough's enough and you want to fix the mess, you have to spend a big chunk of your precious time locating and deleting the addresses that you never wanted in the first place.

So on any new Windows installation, after I set up my first account the very next thing I do is disable this brain-dead feature. Here's how:

1. In Windows Mail or Outlook Express, select Tools, Options to open the Options dialog box.

2. Click the Send tab.

3. Deactivate the Automatically Put People I Reply to In My Contacts List check box. (In Outlook Express, deactivate the Automatically Put People I Reply to In My Address Book check box, instead.)

4. Click OK.

> **TIP** If you rely on the Contacts list or Address Book to store information about the people you know, you should take steps to protect that data. Backing up your computer is an important first step, because most backups also include your email data. To be safe, you can also export your contacts to a text file. Select File, Export, and then click either Windows Contacts (in Mail) or Address Book (in Outlook Express). Click Comma Separated Values, click Export, and then follow the instructions that appear. Ideally, copy the file to a flash disk or other removable media and then store the disk in a offsite location.

Check Account Messages from Multiple Devices

Easy

It's a modern-day dilemma: How do you keep tabs on your work email when you're not at your desk or in the office? If you have a notebook computer or PDA with you, or if you have a computer at home, one solution is to set up any of these machines to also check for messages on your work account. Unfortunately, after you download a message to the other machine, your email program deletes it from the server. This means that the message is gone when you go to check your email on your work computer, which is almost certainly not what you want.

You can solve this problem by configuring Windows Mail (in Windows Vista) or Outlook Express (in Windows XP) to leave a copy of your incoming messages on the server after you download them. That way, no matter which machine you use to check your email, a copy of the message is still available when you check messages using another machine. Note that this does *not* mean that your mail client will keep downloading the same messages over and over each time you check your mail. After you download a message once to any computer, the mail program won't download the same message again to that computer.

Here are the steps to follow to configure your account to leave a copy of incoming messages on the server:

1. In Windows Mail or Outlook Express, select Tools, Accounts to open the Internet Accounts dialog box.

2. Locate the account you want to configure and double-click it to open its property sheet.

3. Click the Advanced tab.

4. Click to activate the Leave a Copy of Messages on Server check box.

5. If you want the program to delete the messages from the server after a while, click to activate the Remove from Server After *X* Days check box, and then specify the number of days after which you want the program to automatically delete the messages from the server, as shown in Figure 5.1.

6. If you click to activate the Remove from Server When Deleted from 'Deleted Items' check box, the program deletes the messages from the server when you permanently delete the messages.

7. Click OK to put the settings into effect and return to the Internet Accounts dialog box.

8. Click OK.

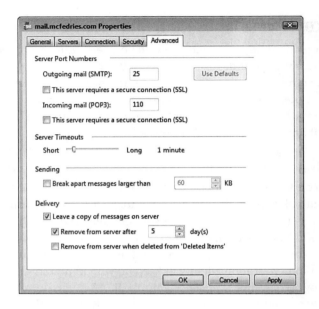

FIGURE 5.1
Use the Advanced tab's Delivery options to leave messages on the server.

Note that you probably want to configure your main computer and your secondary computers or devices a little differently:

- **Your main computer**—Activate the Leave a Copy of Messages on Server check box *and* the Remove from Server After *X* Days check box. For the number of days, choose a value that gives you enough time to download the messages using your other devices. Even if you don't download the messages on your other machines, at least they won't pile up on the server (which is important because most email servers have a maximum amount of mail that they enable you to store).

- **Your other devices**—Activate only the Leave a Copy of Messages on Server check box.

Send Messages Through a Custom SMTP Port

Easy

On the Internet, Simple Mail Transport Protocol (SMTP) is the protocol that describes the format of Internet email messages and how messages get delivered. To facilitate this, your Internet service provider (ISP) runs an SMTP server (perhaps more than one) that handles the outgoing mail for all its accounts. When you set up an account in Windows Mail or Outlook Express, the program always asks you for the name of this server, which it calls the Outgoing Mail (SMTP) server. This name usually takes the form mail.*isp*.com, where *isp*.com is your ISP's domain name. When you send a message, the program contacts the SMTP server and passes along your message. The server then routes the message toward its recipient or recipients.

This admirably straightforward sequence of events is complicated somewhat by the fact that many (now, perhaps most) ISPs insist that all their customers' outgoing mail go through the ISP's SMTP server. This makes sense for your email accounts from that ISP, but it also means that third-party accounts—for example, accounts provided by your website or blog-hosting company—have to go through the ISP's SMTP server as well. This can create problems:

- Your ISP might refuse to send messages that use the third-party account. The usual cause of this is that the ISP believes you're a spammer surreptitiously trying to relay the message through the ISP's SMTP server.

- Your ISP might at some point refuse to send messages from *any* of your accounts because you've bumped up against the ISP's monthly limits on SMTP bandwidth or total messages sent.

- Many ISP SMTP servers are busy, so it might take a while for your message to go through the server, particularly if the ISP gives higher priority to its own accounts.

For all these problems, you're better off if you can send messages from your third-party account directly to the third party's own SMTP server. The third-party server should not think you're a spammer, you're less likely to hit bandwidth or message limits if you split your messages between servers (and many third-parties have no such limits), and your message is likely to be routed faster.

Unfortunately, you usually can't just plug in the third party's SMTP server address in the Outgoing Mail (SMTP) field of your account in Windows Mail or Outlook Express. The problem here is that by default, outgoing mail is sent through port 25, and when you use this port, the outgoing messages go through the ISP's SMTP server.

Fortunately, many third-party hosts help you work around this problem by enabling you to access their SMTP server via a nonstandard port—such as 1025 or 2500. Here are the steps to follow to configure an email account to use a nonstandard SMTP port:

1. In Windows Mail or Outlook Express, select Tools, Accounts to open the Internet Accounts dialog box.

2. Locate the account you want to configure and double-click it to open its property sheet.

3. Click the Advanced tab.

4. In the Outgoing Mail (SMTP) text box, type the port number specified by the third-party host, as shown in Figure 5.2.

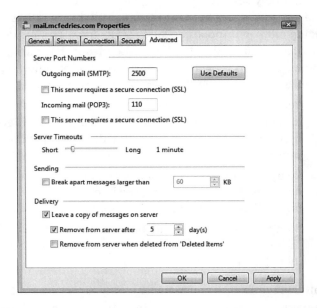

FIGURE 5.2

Change the Outgoing Mail (SMTP) value to the port number used by your third-party host.

5. Click OK to put the settings into effect and return to the Internet Accounts dialog box.

6. Click OK.

SMTP AUTHENTICATION

Your ISP (or, indeed, any of your email hosts) probably implements yet another email security feature called SMTP Authentication, which authenticates the sender of each message. If you find that your messages aren't delivered or generate an error, you may need to tell Windows Mail or Outlook Express that your account requires SMTP

Authentication. Follow steps 1 and 2 in this section to display the account property sheet. Click the Servers tab and activate the My Server Requires Authentication check box. Most SMTP authentication uses your account username and password, and this is the default in Windows Mail and Outlook Express. To make sure, click Settings and check that the Use Same Settings as My Incoming Mail Server option is activated. If your host uses a separate outgoing logon, activate Log On Using, instead, and fill in your Account Name and Password.

Configure Replies to Go to a Different Address

Easy

If you have multiple accounts, when you compose a new message or reply to or forward an incoming message, you can use the From list to choose from which account the message is sent. Normally, any replies to your message are sent to that account.

However, that might not be convenient for you. For example, you might send the message from an account that's scheduled to be deleted soon and you want replies to go to your new account. Or, you might prefer that replies go to your assistant or someone else in your department. Similarly, you might send a business message from home and prefer that replies go to your business address.

For these situations, you can configure an account with an alternative address where replies get sent. Here are the steps to follow:

1. In Windows Mail or Outlook Express, select Tools, Accounts to open the Internet Accounts dialog box.

2. Locate the account you want to configure and double-click it to open its property sheet.

3. Click the General tab.

4. In the Reply Address text box, type the email address where you want all replies to be sent (see Figure 5.3).

5. Click OK to put the settings into effect and return to the Internet Accounts dialog box.

6. Click OK.

FIGURE 5.3

Use the Reply Address text box to specify the address where you want replies sent for this account.

Fundamental File Tweaks

Psst! Want to know a productivity secret? Who doesn't these days? It's simple: Spend less time on routine, day-to-day tasks so that you can spend more time on tasks that are interesting and enjoyable. How do you do that in Windows? You figure out how to minimize the amount of time you spend performing file maintenance chores, such as selecting files, deleting files, searching for files, and so on. No one enjoys that kind of routine-but-necessary stuff, so reducing the time you spend on it lets you increase the time you spend on more engaging pursuits. This chapter shows you a few file tweaks that will help you do just that.

Easily Select Files and Folders Using Check Boxes

Easy

The buzz about Windows Vista before it launched centered around new features such as the Aero interface, desktop search, metadata, grouping and stacking, Flip 3D, and live icons. This strikes me as odd, now, because if I was ever forced to return to using Windows XP, I wouldn't miss any of those features. What would I miss? The first feature that comes to mind is Vista's new capability to let you select files and folders using check boxes.

That may seem a bit strange, so let me explain. As you know, selecting a single file or folder is easy as pie: Just click it. Selecting several files or folders in a row is a bit harder, but it's still not a big whoop: You either click and drag the mouse to "lasso" the items, or you click the first item, hold down Shift, and then click the last item.

Things start to get trickier when you need to select multiple files or folders that aren't together (that are *noncontiguous*, as the geeks say). The technique itself isn't hard: The easiest method is to hold down the Ctrl key and click each item you want to select. However, when you use this technique to select more than a few files, sometimes things can go wrong:

- You might accidentally select one or more files that you don't want. To fix the problem, you need to keep Ctrl held down and click the unwanted item to deselect it. Sure, it's not a big deal to deselect these extra files, but it's one of those small drains on productivity that bugs me (and many other users).

- You might accidentally double-click a file. For example, if you click the wrong file and then immediately click it again to deselect it, Windows might interpret this as a double-click. That's bad news, because it means that Windows will not only open the file you just "double-clicked," but it will also open *every* other file that's currently selected! Now your productivity is pretty much toast for a while because you not only have to wait while all those files (and their associated applications) open, but you must then waste even more precious time shutting everything back down again.

Vista's new check box-based file-selection technique promises to eliminate accidental selections and double-clicks, and to me that's a big deal because sometimes it's the small, incremental changes that make your life with an operating system easier and more efficient.

Follow these steps to configure Windows Vista for check box file and folder selecting:

1. In any folder window, select Organize, Folder and Search Options to open the Folder and Search Options dialog box. (You can also open this dialog box by selecting Start, Control Panel, Appearance and Personalization, Folder Options.)

2. Click the View tab.

3. Activate the Use Check Boxes to Select Items check box.

4. Click OK.

As you can see in Figure 6.1, when you turn on this feature, Windows Explorer creates a column to the left of the folder contents. If you're in Details view, when you point at a file or folder, a check box appears in this column, and you select an item by activating its check box. (In List view, the check boxes also appear beside each file or folder.) You don't need to hold down Ctrl or use the keyboard at all. Just activate the check boxes for the files and folders you want to select. Bonus technique: You can also select all the items in the folder quickly by clicking the check box that appears in the Name column.

Selected files

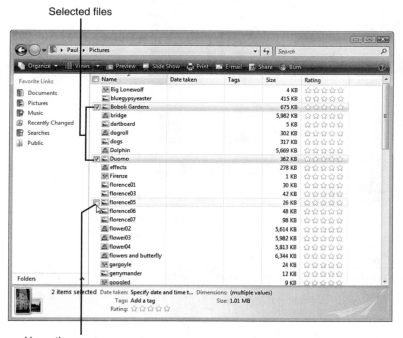

Hover the mouse over a
file to see its check box

FIGURE 6.1

In Windows Vista, you can select files and folders using check boxes.

In the various icon views—Extra Large Icons, Large Icons, Medium Icons, Small Icons, and Tiles—the check boxes appear in the upper-left corner of the imaginary box that surrounds each item, as shown in Figure 6.2.

CAUTION Selection by check boxes is a great technique, but it's not without its pitfalls. Most notably, if you miss a check box, Windows Vista in most cases will deselect everything. This happens a lot when you first use this technique because the check box is a relatively small target. However, with practice you'll find that you hit the check box every time.

Selected files

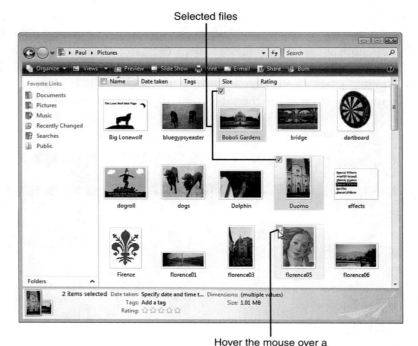

Hover the mouse over a
file to see its check box

FIGURE 6.2

In the icon views, the check boxes appear in the upper-left corner of each file's box.

Save Time by Stopping Delete Confirmations

Medium

My biggest Windows pet peeves center around tasks that require you to jump through extra hoops that are totally unnecessary. In Windows XP, for example, clicking the Shut Down command on the Start menu doesn't shut down your computer, at least not right away. Instead, a dialog box shows up and you need to click Shut Down yet again. Dumb! Windows Vista improves upon this sorry state by putting an honest-to-gosh Shut Down button on the Start menu. (Other options such as Restart and Log Off are another couple of clicks away, but you're not pestered by any dialog boxes.)

Another unnecessary dialog box is the "Are you sure you want to move this file to the Recycle Bin?" prompt that pops up when you press Delete. Now you either need to move your hand to the mouse to click Yes, or you can keep your hands on the keyboard by pressing Alt+Y. Either way, it's an extra step that just slows you down.

One way to avoid this confirmation dialog box is to click and drag the file you want to delete and then drop it on the desktop's Recycle Bin icon. That's nice to know, but most of us rarely see our desktops these days, so this method is not very practical.

A much better solution is to configure Recycle Bin to not display the confirmation dialog box at all. Here's how it's done:

1. Right-click the desktop's Recycle Bin icon and then click Properties. Windows Vista displays the Recycle Bin's property sheet.
2. Click to deactivate the Display Delete Confirmation Dialog check box.
3. Click OK to put the new setting into effect.

Now let's consider this tweak from the opposite point of view. The reason Windows displays the delete confirmation dialog box by default is to prevent you from accidentally deleting a file. You and I are savvy, knowledgeable users, so we know when we want to delete something, but not everyone falls into this boat. If you have young kids or old parents who use Windows, you know that the delete confirmation dialog box is an excellent safeguard for these and other inexperienced users.

In that case, you might be wondering if there's a Windows tweak that ensures a novice user *can't* turn off the delete confirmation dialog box. Yes, in fact, there is, although it's a bit harder to implement because it involves changing a policy setting on the user's computer. A *policy setting* is a kind of rule that an administrator applies to a Windows system, and that rule can't be overridden except by another administrator. To apply a policy setting you use the Group Policy Editor, which I discuss in detail in Chapter 35, "Controlling Windows with the Group Policy Editor."

➔ **See** "Controlling Windows with the Group Policy Editor," **p. 419**.

You can use two ways to prevent a user from turning off delete confirmations:

■ Disable the Display Delete Confirmation Dialog check box that appears in the Recycle Bin's property sheet.

NOTE The Group Policy Editor is available only with Vista Business, Vista Enterprise, Vista Ultimate, and XP Professional. If you're not running one of these versions, I'll show you how to perform the same tweak using the Registry.

- Disable the Recycle Bin's Properties command so the user can't display the Recycle Bin's property sheet.

Follow these steps to implement one of these policies:

1. On the other user's computer, open the Run dialog box, type **gpedit.msc**, and then click OK. (In Windows Vista, you need to enter your administrator's credentials to continue.) The Group Policy Editor appears.

2. Open the User Configuration branch.

3. Open the Administrative Templates branch.

4. Display the property sheet of the policy you want to use, as follows:

   - If you want to disable the Display Delete Confirmation Dialog check box, open the Windows Components branch and then click Windows Explorer. Double-click the policy named Display Confirmation Dialog When Deleting Files. If you don't have access to the Group Policy Editor, open the Registry Editor and create a DWORD setting named `ConfirmFileDelete` with the value 1 in the following key:

     `HKCU\Software\Microsoft\Windows\CurrentVersion\Policies\Explorer`

   - If you want to disable the Recycle Bin's Properties command, click Desktop and then double-click the policy named Remove Properties from the Recycle Bin Context Menu. If you don't have access to the Group Policy Editor, open the Registry Editor and create a DWORD setting named `NoPropertiesRecycleBin` with the value 1 in the following key:

     `HKCU\Software\Microsoft\Windows\CurrentVersion\Policies\Explorer`

5. Click the Enabled option.

6. Click OK to put the policy into effect.

> **NOTE** The Remove Properties from the Recycle Bin Context Menu policy has a misleading name because, when enabled, the policy disables *all* instances of the Recycle Bin's Properties command, not just on the context menu. So, for example, if the user displays the desktop in a folder window and clicks Recycle Bin, the Properties command doesn't appear on XP's File menu. It still appears on Vista's Organize menu, but choosing the command only displays an error message (as it does when the user selects Properties in the context menu).

Figure 6.3 shows the Recycle Bin property sheet with the Display Confirmation Dialog When Deleting Files policy in effect. As you can see, the Display Delete Confirmation Dialog check box is activated and disabled, so the setting can't be changed.

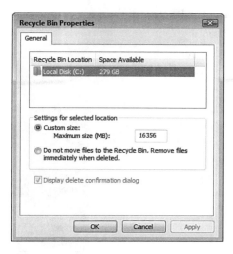

FIGURE 6.3

With the Display Confirmation Dialog When Deleting Files policy in effect, the Display Delete Confirmation Dialog check box is activated and disabled.

Search Smarter with Customized Start Menu Searching

Easy

Vista's desktop search capabilities are underwhelming right out of the box, although later in this book I show you a few tweaks that can elevate searching to a higher plane.

➤   **See** Chapter 25, "Super Searching," **p. 285**.

However, the one search feature that I've grown quite fond of is the on-the-fly searches you can perform using the Start menu's Search box. As shown in Figure 6.4, as you type characters into the Search box, the Start menu replaces the list of pinned and recently used programs with a new list that displays the following search links:

■ A list of programs with names that include the typed characters

■ A list of files (documents) with content or metadata that include the typed characters

- Other data—contacts, email messages, and sites from Internet Explorer's Favorites and History lists—with content or metadata that includes the typed characters
- A Search Everywhere link
- A Search the Internet link

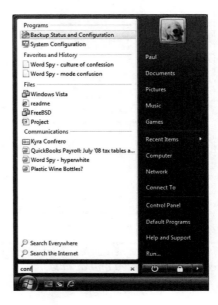

FIGURE 6.4

As-you-type searching using the Start menu's Search box.

If you see the program or file you want, click it to open it. Otherwise, you can click Search Everywhere to see the complete list of matches from the files in your user profile. If you prefer to search the Web for your text, click the Search the Internet link instead.

All in all, the Start menu's as-you-type searching is a pretty decent feature. However, many people find that these on-the-fly searches aren't all that useful because there's only so much room on the Start menu to display results, so they often don't get the match they're looking for. The problem in most of these cases is that the Start menu search feature looks for matches in a large number of file types—a half dozen in all (programs, favorites, history, documents, contacts, and email). That's convenient most of the time, but if you're getting back tons of results, you might be thinking that it would be nice if Windows Vista could dial things back a bit and not search so many file types.

Fortunately, you can tweak the Start menu to do just that. Each of the four main Start menu search categories—Programs, Favorites and History, Files, and Communications—can be toggled on or off, so you can customize searches to suit the way you work. Here are the steps to follow to customize Start menu searching in Vista:

> **TIP** You can get the Start menu to show more results by displaying a larger Start menu. Right-click Start, click Properties, and then click Customize. Use the Number of Recent Programs to Display spin box to increase the size of the Recent Programs section of the Start menu. Click OK in the open dialog boxes.

1. Right-click the Start button and then click Properties. The Taskbar and Start Menu Properties dialog box appears with the Start Menu tab displayed.

2. Click the Customize button beside the Start Menu option. The Customize Start Menu dialog box appears.

3. In the list of Start menu features, scroll down until you see the following controls:

   - **Search Communications**—Click to deactivate this check box to prevent contacts and email messages from appearing in the Start menu search results.

   - **Search Favorites and History**—Click to deactivate this check box to prevent Internet Explorer favorites and history items from appearing in the Start menu search results.

   - **Search Files**—Click to activate the Don't Search for Files option to prevent documents from appearing in the Start menu search results.

   - **Search Programs**—Click to deactivate this check box to prevent programs from appearing in the Start menu search results.

4. Click OK in the open dialog box to put the new search settings into effect.

After you remove a file type from the Start menu search results, you may find that you need to search for that particular type. Rather than add it back, in most cases Vista offers search alternatives. Here's a rundown for each file type:

- **Documents**—Click Start and then click your username to open your user profile folder. Use the Search box in the folder window to search your documents.

- **Favorites**—Click Start, click your username to open your user profile folder, and then double-click Favorites. Use the Search box in the folder window to search your documents.

- **History**—In Internet Explorer, press Alt+C (or click the Favorites Center icon) to open the Favorites Center. Pull down the History and then click Search History.

- **Contacts**—Click Start, click your username to open your user profile folder, and then double-click Contacts. Use the Search box in the folder window to search your documents.

- **Email**—Click Start, E-mail to open Windows Mail. Use the Search box to search your messages.

- **Programs**—Unfortunately, Vista doesn't offer an alternative method for searching for programs. Even if you use the Start menu's program-searching feature only once in a while (it's my favorite and most-used aspect of Start menu searches), I suggest leaving the Search Program check box activated.

Open a Document Using a Different Application

Easy

In Chapter 3, "Indispensable Interface Tweaks," you learned how Windows relies on file extensions to determine not only the file type (Text Document, Bitmap Image, and so on), but also the application associated with that file type (that is, the program that runs when you double-click a file of that type).

➜   **See** "Make Files Make Sense by Showing Extensions," **p. 31**.

Having an application associated with a file type is convenient because it means you don't have to think about what program to use. Just double-click the file you want to open and Windows takes care of the behind-the-scenes details. However, on occasion you might not want to open a particular file in the associated application. For example, you might prefer to open a text file in WordPad instead of Notepad. Similarly, you might want to open an HTML file in Notepad or some other text editor rather than Internet Explorer.

One easy way to go about this is to launch the unassociated application and open the document from there. To do so, you run the application's File, Open command (or whatever) and, in the Open dialog box, select All Files in the

Files of Type list. That will work, but it defeats the convenience of being able to launch a file directly from Windows Explorer.

Another possibility is to right-click the file you want to work with and then examine the various "verbs" that appear at the top of the shortcut menu. These verbs—Open, Edit, Print, and Preview, for example—represent the default actions associated with the file type, and the verbs you see depend on the type. For instance, a document might show actions such as Open and Print, whereas an image might show actions such as Preview and Edit.

The verb in bold type is the default action, which most often means it opens the file using its associated application. However, in some cases you can use the other verbs to open a file using a different application. For example, the default action for a Bitmap Image (.bmp file) is Preview, which opens the image using Windows Photo Gallery (in Vista) or Windows Picture and Fax Viewer (in XP). However, if you click the Edit action, Windows opens the file in Paint.

What happens if none of a file type's default actions open the file using the application you want? Your next best bet is to see if Windows has set up multiple associations for that file type. With a Text Document type, for example, Windows sets up Notepad as the default application, but Windows also sets up WordPad as a kind of secondary application. To see if a file has one or more secondary applications, right-click the file you want to open (you can also pull down the File menu; in Vista, press Alt to see the menu bar), and then examine the Open With command:

- If you see Open With..., it means that the file type has no secondary applications associated with it.

- If, instead, you see an arrow beside Open With, then it means that the file type does have one or more secondary applications associated with it. Click Open With to see the applications. In Figure 6.5, you can see that the text document's Open With command displays two applications: Notepad and WordPad. If you see the application you want to use, click it to open the file using that program.

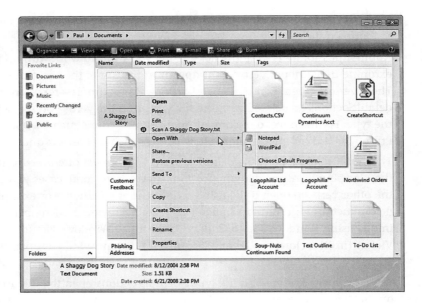

FIGURE 6.5

Click the Open With command to see the applications associated with the file type.

Still don't see the program you want to use to open the file? Okay, in that case, you need to take matters into your own hands. You have two choices:

■ **One-time only change**—This means that you open the file using a different application this time only, so you preserve the association with the default application.

■ **Permanent change**—This means that you configure Windows to always open the file type using the different application. To do this, you need to associate the file extension with the application you want to use instead of Windows' default association.

For both of these methods, you use the Open With dialog box to select the application you want to use and, optionally, to change the associated application. Windows gives you various ways to display this dialog box:

■ **Open With command**—With this method, right-click the file you want to open and then click Open With. If the file type already has multiple programs associated with it, you'll see a menu of those programs. In this case, click Choose Default Program (in Vista) or Choose Program (in XP) from the menu that appears.

- **Task pane** (Windows Vista)—When you click a file, Windows Explorer's Task pane displays a button that represents the default action for the file type. For example, if you click an image, a Preview button appears in the Task pane; if you click an audio file, you see a Play button in the Task pane. In most cases, this default action button also doubles as a drop-down list. Display the list and click Choose Default Program.

- **Set Associations** (Windows Vista)—Select Start, Default Programs, and then click Associate a File Type or Protocol With a Program. This displays the Set Associations window, shown in Figure 6.6, which displays a list of file extensions. Click the file type you want to work with and then click Change Program.

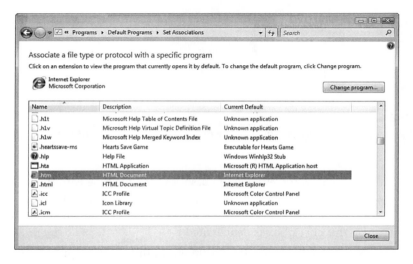

FIGURE 6.6

Use the Set Associations dialog box to change the application associated with any of the displayed file extensions.

In the Open With dialog box that appears, the icons in the Recommended Programs section are the applications associated with the file type, and the icons in the Other Programs section are applications suggested by Windows. (If you don't see anything in the Other Programs section, double-click the Other Programs heading.)

Follow these steps to select the application you want to use to open your file:

1. Choose the application:

   - **Other Programs**—If you see an icon for the application in the Other Programs area, click that icon, as shown in Figure 6.7.

■ **Browse**—If you don't see an icon for the application, click Browse, use the dialog box to select the application's executable file, and then click Open.

FIGURE 6.7

Use the Open With dialog box to choose which application you want to use to open the document.

2. If you want Windows to associate the file type with this new application, click to activate the Always Use the Selected Program to Open this Kind of File check box. (If this is a one-time only association, be sure this check box is deactivated.)

3. Click OK to open the document in the selected application.

Note that Windows remembers the unassociated applications that you choose in the Open With dialog box. When you next select the Open With command for the file type, Windows displays a menu that includes both the associated program and the unassociated program you chose earlier.

➤   To learn how to tweak the Open With list, **see** "Customize the Open With List," **p. 317**.

Keeping the Bad Guys at Bay

Some folks claim that you can never be too thin nor too rich. Other folks might give you an argument about one or both assertions, but I doubt anyone would take you to task if you added a third item to the list: Your Windows PC can never be too secure. There are just too many threats out there, and too many ways that the defenses in Windows can be breached.

With that in mind, this book gives you lots of ways to tweak Windows security. You learned about a few security tips in Chapter 2, "Crucial Security Tweaks," and you'll learn a few more in Chapter 8, "Configuring Internet Security," and Chapter 9, "Maintaining Your Privacy on the Web."

In this chapter, I focus on protecting your PC from direct attacks: that is, when an unauthorized cracker sits down at your keyboard and tries to gain access to your system. Sure, it may be unlikely that a malicious user would gain physical access to the computer in your home or office, but it's not impossible. My hope is that the techniques you learn here will help to keep these bad guys at bay.

Sneakily Hide Usernames in the Logon Screen

Medium

When you start most Windows PCs, you end up at the logon screen so that you can choose your username and log on by entering your password. The screen you see depends on the version of Windows you're using:

- **Windows Vista**—In all versions of Vista, the logon screen always displays icons for each user account, and each icon shows the name of the account. Figure 7.1 shows a typical Windows Vista logon screen.

FIGURE 7.1

The Windows Vista logon screen shows the names of the computer's user accounts.

- **Windows XP Home**—In XP Home, the logon screen also shows account icons and usernames, as shown in Figure 7.2.
- **Windows XP Professional**—In XP Pro, you see the Log On to Windows dialog box, and the User Name text box always shows the name of the last user who logged on, as shown in Figure 7.3.

FIGURE 7.2

The Windows XP Home logon screen also shows the names of the computer's user accounts.

FIGURE 7.3

The Windows XP Pro logon dialog box shows the name of the last user who logged on.

This may not seem all that important, but that logon screen is actually helping any would-be cracker a great deal. Why? The nefarious nogoodnik now has an important advantage because he knows the names of all your user accounts (or, in the case of XP Pro, one of your accounts). Yes, the evildoer must still guess an account's password, but you can make things a heckuva lot harder by forcing the snoop to also guess a username on your system. How do you do that? By tweaking Windows so that it doesn't display usernames in the logon screen. Sneaky!

NOTE These steps require the Group Policy Editor, which is available only with Vista Business, Vista Enterprise, Vista Ultimate, and XP Professional. If you're not running one of these versions, I'll show you how to perform the same tweak using the Registry.

You do that by following these steps:

1. Open the Run dialog box, type `gpedit.msc`, and then click OK. (In Windows Vista, you need to enter your administrator's credentials to continue.) The Group Policy Editor appears.

2. Open the Computer Configuration branch.

3. Open the Windows Settings branch.

4. Open the Security Settings branch.

5. Open the Local Policies branch.

6. Open the Security Options branch.

7. Double-click the Interactive Logon: Do Not Display Last User Name policy.

8. Click the Enabled option.

9. Click OK to put the new setting into effect.

If you don't have access to the Group Policy Editor, open the Registry Editor and create (if it's not there already) a DWORD setting named `DontDisplayLastUserName` with the value 1 in the following key:

`HKLM\Software\Microsoft\Windows\CurrentVersion\Policies\System`

The next time you start your computer, no usernames appear in the logon screen. Figure 7.4 shows the tweaked Vista logon screen.

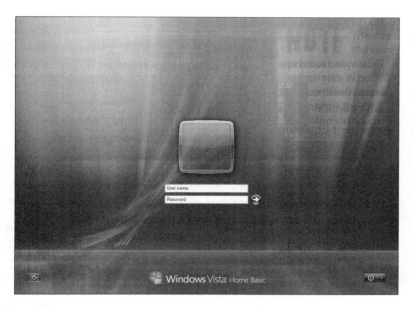

FIGURE 7.4

With the Do Not Display Last User Name policy enabled, the logon screen no longer shows the names of the computer's user accounts.

Rename Built-In Accounts for Better Security

Windows Vista and Windows XP come with a built-in Administrator account. This account is all-powerful on Windows, so the last thing you want is for some malicious user to gain control of the system with Administrator access. This is why Vista systems come with the Administrator account disabled by default. (Alas, this isn't the case in Windows XP.) However, later in this book I show you how to activate the Administrator account in Vista.

➔   **See** "Activate the Administrator Account," **p. 136**.

Both Vista and XP also come with a built-in account called Guest, which you can enable to give people temporary access to your computer. (The Guest account is disabled by default in both Vista and XP.)

➔   **See** "Use the Guest Account to Give Folks Temporary Access," **p. 130**.

If the Administrator and Guest accounts are disabled, you have no worries about these accounts. However, if the accounts are enabled, black-hat hackers have one foot in your digital door already because they know the names of two accounts: Administrator and Guest. Now all they have to do is guess the password associated with one of these accounts. If you've protected the Administrator and Guest accounts with strong passwords, you almost certainly have nothing to fret about here.

> **TIP** You can open the Local Users and Groups snap-in directly by opening the Run dialog box, typing `lusrmgr.msc`, and then clicking OK.

> **NOTE** If you're running XP and would prefer to disable the Administrator account, right-click Administrator, click Properties, display the General tab, and then click to activate the Account Is Disabled check box.

However, you can close the door completely on malicious intruders by taking away the one piece of information they know: the name of each account. By changing the account names from Administrator and Guest to new names that are completely unobvious, you add an extra layer of security to your Windows system.

Here are the steps to follow to change the names of these accounts:

1. Select Start, right-click Computer (or My Computer, in XP), and then click Manage. (In Vista, you need to enter your UAC credentials at this point.) The Computer Management snap-in appears.

2. Open the System Tools, Local Users and Groups, Users branch.

3. Right-click the Administrator account, and then click Rename.

4. Type the new account name, and then press Enter.

5. Right-click the Guest account, and then click Rename.

6. Type the new account name, and then press Enter.

Sniff Out Logon Failures

Medium

A big part of keeping any computer secure involves keeping an eye on what users do with the computer. For Windows, this means tracking events such as logon failures, because repeated failures might indicate a malicious user trying different passwords. This type of tracking is called *auditing*.

Unfortunately, Windows implements only a small subset of its auditing features, and even those that it does implement aren't all that useful. For example, Windows audits logon successes, but not logon failures. In this tweak, I show you how to enable security auditing for logon failures, and then I explain how to track auditing events.

To enable the policy for auditing logon failures, follow these steps:

1. Open the Run dialog box, type **gpedit.msc**, and then click OK. (In Windows Vista, you need to enter your administrator's credentials to continue.) The Group Policy Editor appears.

2. Open the Computer Configuration branch.

3. Open the Windows Settings branch.

4. Open the Security Settings branch.

5. Open the Local Policies branch.

6. Open the Audit Policy branch.

7. Double-click the Audit Account Logon Events policy to open its property sheet.

8. Activate the Failure check box, as shown in Figure 7.5.

9. Click OK.

> **NOTE** These steps require the Group Policy Editor, which is available only with Vista Business, Vista Enterprise, Vista Ultimate, and XP Professional. Unfortunately, security policies aren't stored in the Registry (they're stored in a separate database), so there's no Registry equivalent for this tweak.

The Audit Account Logon Events policy enables you to track when users log on to their account on a Windows PC. If you track failures for this policy, the resulting Failure Audit event returns an Error Code value, as shown in Figure 7.6. Table 7.1 tells you what the various error codes mean.

Table 7.1   Error Codes Returned for Account Logon Failure Events

Error Code	Description
0xC0000064	The user tried to log on with a misspelled or invalid username.
0xC000006A	The user tried to log on with a misspelled or invalid password.
0xC000006F	The user tried to log on outside of the account's authorized hours.
0xC0000070	The user tried to log on from an unauthorized computer.
0xC0000071	The user tried to log on with an expired password.
0xC0000072	The user's account is disabled.
0xC0000193	The user's account is expired.
0xC0000224	The user was supposed to change his password at the next logon, but he didn't.
0xC0000234	The user's account is locked.

FIGURE 7.5

In the Audit Account Logon Events policy property sheet, activate the Failure check box.

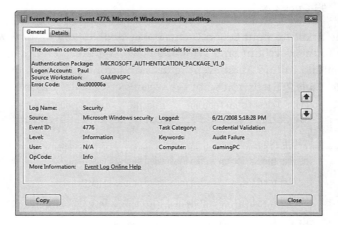

FIGURE 7.6

An example of a failed Account Logon event.

> After you've enabled this security auditing policy, you can start tracking them to look for suspicious behavior. You do this using Windows' Event Viewer, which you open by displaying the Run dialog box, typing **eventvwr.msc**, and

clicking OK. In the Event Viewer window, open the Windows Logs branch and click Security. This displays the events in the Security log, which is where the auditing events appear.

> **NOTE** The file containing the script in Listing 7.1—QuerySecurityEventLog.vbs—is available from my website at http://mcfedries.com/cs/content/TweakItFreakIt.aspx.

Unfortunately, the Security event log likely has tens of thousands of items. How do you look for suspicious behavior in such a large database? The trick is to filter the log to show just the events you want. Here how:

- **Windows Vista**—Display the Action pane and then click Filter Current Log. In the Keywords list, select Audit Failure. In the Logged list, select a timeframe (such as Last 24 Hours). Click OK.

- **Windows XP**—Select View, Filter to open the Security Properties dialog box with the Filter tab displayed. In the Event Types group, deactivate all the check boxes except Failure Audit. Use the controls in the From and To section to set the time frame, and then click OK.

An even easier way to look for logon failures is to use the script shown in Listing 7.1:

Listing 7.1   Extracting Logon Failures from the Security Log

```
Option Explicit
Dim compName, objWMI, colSecLog, objEvent, i
'
' This script uses WMI to extract events from the Security log where:
'   - The type is "Audit Failure" (5)
'   - The date is today
'   - The error code points to an incorrect password (0xC000006A)
'
compName = "localhost"
'
' Get the WMI interface
'
Set objWMI = GetObject("winmgmts:{(Security)}!\\" & _
                    compName & "\root\cimv2")
'
' Return all the events that meet our criteria
'
```

continues

Listing 7.1   Continued

```
Set colSecLog = objWMI.ExecQuery("SELECT * FROM Win32_NTLogEvent Where " & _
                              "LogFile = 'Security' And " & _
                              "EventType = 5 And " & _
                              "TimeWritten > '" & TodaysDate & "' And " & _
                              "Message Like '%0xC000006A%'")
'
' Run through the returned events
'
i = 0
For Each objEvent in colSecLog
    '
    ' Display the event data
    '
    WScript.Echo "Category: " & objEvent.CategoryString & VBCrLf & _
                 "Computer: " & objEvent.ComputerName & VBCrLf & _
                 "User: " & objEvent.User & VBCrLf & _
                 "Event Type: " & objEvent.Type & VBCrLf & _
                 "Event Code: " & objEvent.EventCode & VBCrLf & _
                 "Source Name: " & objEvent.SourceName & VBCrLf & _
                 "Time Written: " & ReturnLogDate(objEvent.TimeWritten) & _
                 VBCrLf & VBCrLf & _
                 "Message: " & VBCrLf & VBCrLf & objEvent.Message
    i = i + 1
Next
'
' Check for no events
'
If i = 0 Then
    WScript.Echo "No events found!"
End If
'
' Release objects
'
Set objWMI = Nothing
Set colSecLog = Nothing
'
```

```
' TodaysDate()
' This function creates a datatime string based on today's date
'
Function TodaysDate()
     Dim strDay, strMOnth, strYear
    strYear = Year(Now)
    If Month(Now) < 10 Then
        strMonth = "0" & Month(Now)
    Else
        strMonth = Month(Now)
    End If
    If Day(Now) < 10 Then
        strDay = "0" & Day(Now)
    Else
        strDay = Day(Now)
    End If
    TodaysDate = strYear & strMonth & strDay & "000000.000000-000"
End Function
'
' ReturnLogDate()
' This function takes the event datetime value and converts
' it to a friendlier date and time format
'
Function ReturnLogDate(logTime)
    Dim eventDay, eventMonth, eventYear
    Dim eventSecond, eventMinute, eventHour
    eventYear = Left(logTime, 4)
    eventMonth = Mid(logTime, 5, 2)
    eventDay = Mid(logTime, 7, 2)
    eventHour = Mid(logTime, 9, 2)
    eventMinute = Mid(logTime, 11, 2)
    eventSecond = Mid(logTime, 13, 2)
    ReturnLogDate = DateSerial(eventYear, eventMonth, eventDay) & " " & _
                    TimeSerial(eventHour, eventMinute, eventSecond)
End Function
```

To use this script, download the file from my website and store it on your hard drive. If you're running XP, double-click the VBS file to run the script. If you're running Vista, you need to open an Administrator-level Command Prompt session (as described in Chapter 36, "Running the Command Prompt") and run the VBA file from there. Here's how:

➤ **See** "Running Command Prompt as the Administrator," **p. 427**.

1. Use Windows Explorer to open the folder where you stored the script.

2. Right-click an empty section of the Address bar and then click Copy Address.

3. In your elevated Command Prompt session, type **cd** followed by a space.

4. Click the system menu icon in the upper-left corner (or press Alt+space-bar), and then select Edit, Paste. Command Prompt pastes the folder address.

5. Press Enter to switch the command prompt to that folder.

6. Type the name of the VBS file (including the .vbs extension) and press Enter to run the script.

➤ For an easier way to switch the command prompt to a folder, **see** "Open a Folder at the Command Prompt," **p. 262**.

➤ For a more direct way to run a script with elevated permissions, **see** "Run a Script as the Administrator," **p. 141**.

Figure 7.7 shows an example of a failed logon alert generated by this script.

FIGURE 7.7

A failed logon alert generated by the script in Listing 7.1.

Max Out Security by Encrypting Important Data

Easy

If a snoop can't log on to your Windows PC, does that mean your data is safe? No, unfortunately, it most certainly does not. If a cracker has physical access to your PC—either by sneaking into your office or by stealing your computer—the cracker can use advanced utilities to view the contents of your hard drive. This means that if your PC contains extremely sensitive or confidential information—personal financial files, medical histories, corporate salary data, trade secrets, business plans, journals or diaries—it wouldn't be hard for the interloper to read and even copy that data.

If you are worried about anyone viewing these or other for-your-eyes-only files, Windows enables you to *encrypt* the file information. Encryption encodes the file to make it completely unreadable by anyone unless the person logs on to your Windows Vista account. After you encrypt your files, you work with them exactly as you did before, with no noticeable loss of performance.

Follow these steps to encrypt important data:

1. Use Windows Explorer to display the icon of the folder containing the data that you want to encrypt.

2. Right-click the folder icon and click Properties to open the folder's property sheet.

3. Click the General tab.

4. Click Advanced. The Advanced Attributes dialog box appears.

5. Click to activate the Encrypt Contents to Secure Data check box.

> **NOTE** To use file encryption, your hard drive must use NTFS (New Technology File System). To check the current file system, click Start and then click Computer. In the Computer window, click the hard drive and then examine the file system information in the Details pane. If you need to convert a drive to NTFS, click Start, All Programs, Accessories, right-click Command Prompt, and click Run as Administrator. (In XP, just click Command Prompt.) Type `convert d: /fs:ntfs`, where *d* is the letter of the hard drive you want to convert, and press Enter. If Windows asks to "dismount the volume," press **Y** and then Enter.

> **TIP** Although it's possible to encrypt individual files, encrypting an entire folder is easier because Windows Vista then automatically encrypts new files that you add to the folder.

> **TIP** By default, Windows displays the names of encrypted files and folders in a green font, which helps you to differentiate these items from unencrypted files and folders. If you'd rather see encrypted file and folder names in the regular font, open any folder window, select Organize, Folder and Search Options (or Tools, Folder Options in XP). Click the View tab, click to deactivate the Show Encrypted or Compressed NTFS Files in Color check box, and then click OK.

6. Click OK in each open dialog box. The Confirm Attribute Changes dialog box appears.

7. Click the Apply Changes to This Folder, Subfolders and Files option.

8. Click OK. Windows encrypts the folder's contents.

Configuring Internet Security

In Chapter 7, "Keeping the Bad Guys at Bay," you learned about some tweaks designed to thwart a would-be interloper with direct access to your Windows PC. Although it's true that hands-on hackers aren't rare, they're not exactly commonplace, either. You're many, many more times likely to fall prey to an intruder who has, at best, only indirect access to your computer. I speak, of course, of the Internet and the all-but-innumerable miscreants who haunt its dark alleys and dank passageways.

Land on the wrong website, and a malicious script might do something nasty to your PC; install the wrong program, and you might end up with spyware or a virus installed right along with it; type your email address in the wrong place and you might end up with even more spam than you've got already.

How's a body to bypass these threats and still enjoy the online world? Fortunately, it's not that hard. This chapter presents a few tweaks that can help. Besides those tips, you can also do a few more general things:

- **Keep your PC patched**—Your worst enemy when it comes to online safety is actually your operating system! The sheer number of Windows vulnerabilities is staggering, and the only chance you've got to prevent some cracker from taking advantage of just one of those holes to wreck your PC is to apply any and all security-related updates that Microsoft releases.

- **Load up your machine with antimalware**—Your Windows PC can never have enough protection. So although XP comes with a firewall, and Vista also comes with an antispyware program, don't stop there. On your XP PC you need one or more antispyware programs running; on your Vista PC, adding a second antispyware program wouldn't hurt; and on both XP and Vista you really need a top-of-the line antivirus program.

- **Pay attention and use common sense**—Lots of people run into trouble online, not because cyberspace is an inherently dangerous place, but because the vast majority of those people simply weren't paying attention to what they were doing. If an offer sounds too good to be true, it almost certainly is. If a file attachment shows up unexpectedly, it probably contains something unexpected (and unwelcome). If Vista's User Account Control dialog box shows up without you doing anything, it means that something *else* is doing something, and it's a lead-pipe cinch that it's up to no good.

Windows can't do much to ensure your store of common sense is topped up, but it can help you with your PC's update and anti-malware status. The Windows Security Center offers a quick peek at your security settings and shows you right away if anything's amiss. To launch the Windows Security Center, use either of the following techniques:

- **Windows Vista**—Select Start, type `wscui.cpl` into the Search box, and then press Enter (or click wscui.cpl in the search results).

- **Windows XP**—Select Start, Run, type `wscui.cpl` into the Run dialog box, and then click OK.

Figure 8.1 shows the ideal Security Center state for Windows Vista, and Figure 8.2 shows the XP equivalent.

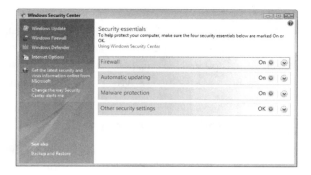

FIGURE 8.1
The Windows Security Center in Vista when it's running on all security cylinders.

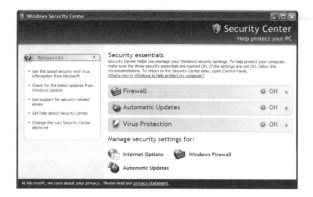

FIGURE 8.2
XP's version of the ideal Windows Security Center state.

TURNING OFF AUTOMATIC INSTALLS

The Security Center states shown in Figure 8.1 and 8.2 are ideals from Microsoft's point of view, but there's one major problem for the likes of you and me. The Automatic Updates setting that gets you the green On status in the Security Center is the one that downloads *and* installs each new update as it becomes available. Unfortunately, many updates require a reboot, so Windows will force your PC to restart. This is a real bummer if you have unsaved data or just an ideal window configuration that you wanted to use for a while. A much better setup is to have Windows download any new updates, and then notify you so that you can install them without wreaking havoc on your system. In Vista, click Start, type **wuapp**, press Enter, and then click Change Settings; in XP, select Start Run, type **wuaucpl.cpl**, and click OK. Activate the Download Updates, But Let Me Choose Whether to Install Them option.

Make Sure Your Firewall Is Up to Snuff

Easy

If you access the Internet using a broadband—cable modem or DSL—service, chances are that you have an always-on connection, which means there's a much greater chance that a malicious hacker could find your computer and have his way with it. You might think that with millions of people connected to the Internet at any given moment, there would be little chance of a "script kiddy" finding you in the herd. Unfortunately, one of the most common weapons in a black-hat hacker's arsenal is a program that runs through millions of IP addresses automatically, looking for live connections. The fact that many cable systems and some DSL systems use IP addresses in a narrow range compounds the problem by making it easier to find always-on connections.

When a cracker finds your address, he has many avenues from which to access your computer. Specifically, your connection uses many different ports for sending and receiving data. For example, the File Transfer Protocol (FTP) uses ports 20 and 21, web data and commands typically use port 80, email uses ports 25 and 110, the domain name system (DNS) uses port 53, and so on. In all, there are dozens of these ports, and each one is an opening through which a clever cracker can gain access to your computer.

As if that weren't enough, attackers can check your system for the installation of some kind of Trojan horse or virus. (Malicious email attachments sometimes install these programs on your machine.) If the hacker finds one, he can effectively take control of your machine (turning it into a *zombie computer*) and either wreck its contents or use your computer to attack other systems.

Again, if you think your computer is too obscure or worthless for someone else to bother with, think again. For a typical computer connected to the Internet all day long, hackers probe for vulnerable ports or installed Trojan horses at least a few times every day. If you want to see just how vulnerable your computer is, several good sites on the Web will test your security:

- **Gibson Research (Shields Up)**—grc.com/default.htm
- **DSL Reports**—www.dslreports.com/secureme_go
- **HackerWhacker**—www.hackerwhacker.com

The good news is that Windows includes the Windows Firewall tool, which is a personal firewall that can lock down your ports and prevent unauthorized access to your machine. In effect, your computer becomes invisible to the Internet (although you can still surf the Web and work with email normally). Other firewall programs exist out there, but Windows Firewall does a good job. For example, Figure 8.3 shows the output of the Shields Up tool from Gibson Research after probing a typical Vista computer. As you can see Windows Firewall held its own.

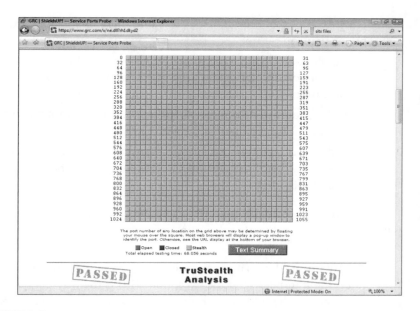

FIGURE 8.3

This standard Windows Vista PC stood up to everything the Shields Up tool threw at it.

Create a Windows Firewall Exception

Medium

I just spent the past couple of pages telling you how important a firewall is for a secure computer, so it may seem more than a little strange that I'm now going to show you how to poke holes in that firewall. Actually, this kind of thing is fairly routine, at least behind the scenes, where programs such as Microsoft Office Outlook and iTunes often configure Windows Firewall to allow them to access the Internet. That's fine, but why would you want to do something like this? There are many reasons, but they mostly boil down to needing some sort of data to get though the firewall. For example, if you want to perform administrative duties on a computer on your network, that computer's firewall needs to be configured to allow the Remote Assistance service through, something I talk more about in Chapter 30, "Making Remote Connections." Similarly, if you activate Vista's built-in web server, you need to configure that PC to allow data through port 80. (I use this as an example later in this section.)

➤   **See** "Configure a Network Computer for Remote Administration," **p. 358**.

These are examples of firewall *exceptions*, and there are actually three types of exceptions you can set up:

- **Enable an existing exception**—Windows maintains a list of programs and services that are often used as exceptions, and you can toggle these on and off.

- **Add a program as a new exception**—If the program you want to use isn't in the list, you can add it yourself.

- **Add a port as a new exception**—You can also configure a port as an exception, and the firewall will allow data to pass back and forth through the port.

In each case, you can also limit the computers that can access your computer via the exception, which is called the *scope* of the exception. Again, you have three choices:

- **Any Computer**—This scope allows any computer on your network and on the Internet to use the exception. This is the way to go if you want people on the Internet to access your computer (your web server, for example), or if you want to access your computer from the Internet, as described in Chapter 30.

➤   **See** "Connect to Your Desktop via the Internet," **p. 354**.

- **My Network (Subnet) Only**—This scope allows only the computers on your network to use the exception. Technically, it allows only those computers that are on the part of the network where they can see your computer. This means they're on the same *subnet* as you. For most small networks, the subnet and the entire network are the same thing. This is a good choice if you want everyone on your network to use the data, but still keep your PC safe from Internet intruders.

- **Custom List**—This scope is a list of computer IP addresses, and it means that only those computers on the list can use the exception. Go this route if you want complete control over who uses the exception.

The next three sections show you how to create the three types of firewall exceptions. First, use one of these techniques to open up the Windows Firewall settings:

- **Windows Vista**—Select Start, type `firewallsettings` into the Search box, and then press Enter (or click Firewall Settings in the search results). When the User Account Control dialog box appears, enter your UAC credentials.

- **Windows XP**—Select Start, Run, type **firewall.cfg** into the Run dialog box, and then click OK.

Activating an Existing Exception

The Windows Firewall Settings dialog box maintains a list of programs, services, and sometimes ports that are currently enabled as exceptions, or that are commonly enabled but currently are not. This is the easiest way to set up an exception because, as the following steps show, all you have to do is activate a check box:

1. Launch the Windows Firewall Setting dialog box.

2. Click the Exceptions tab. Figure 8.4 shows the Exceptions tab in Vista's Windows Firewall Settings dialog box.

FIGURE 8.4

The Exceptions tab lets you keep track of the Windows Firewall exceptions.

3. Activate the check box beside the exception you want to enable.

4. To change the scope, click the exception, click Properties (or Edit, in XP), click Change Scope, choose the scope option you want, and then click OK until you return to the Exceptions tab.

4. Click OK to put the exception into effect.

Adding a Program as a New Exception

If you don't see the program you want to work with, you can add it by hand. Here's how:

1. Launch the Windows Firewall Setting dialog box.

2. Click the Exceptions tab.

3. Click Add Program. The Add a Program dialog box appears, as shown in Figure 8.5.

FIGURE 8.5
Use the Add a Program dialog box to configure an application as a firewall exception.

4. If you see your program in the list, click it; otherwise, click Browse, use the Browse dialog box to select the program's executable file, and then click Open.

5. Click Change Scope to open the Change Scope dialog box.

6. Choose the scope option you want. If you choose the Custom List option, use the text box to type the IP addresses of the computers you want to allow for the exception, separated by commas. Click OK.

7. Click OK. Windows Firewall adds the program to the Exceptions tab and activates its check box.

8. Click OK to put the exception into effect.

Adding a Port as a New Exception

If you need to open a port on your computer, follow these steps:

1. Launch the Windows Firewall Setting dialog box.

2. Click the Exceptions tab.

3. Click Add Port. The Add a Port dialog box appears, as shown in Figure 8.6.

> **TIP** You can prevent computers on your network from adding program exceptions if you're worried about security. On the other computer, log on as an administrator, open the Group Policy Editor (see Chapter 35, "Controlling Windows with the Group Policy Editor"), and open the following branch: Computer Configuration, Administrative Templates, Network, Network Connections, Windows Firewall, Standard Profile. Double-click the Windows Firewall: Allow Local Program Exceptions policy, and then click Enable.

FIGURE 8.6
Use the Add a Port dialog box to configure a port as a firewall exception.

4. Use the Name text box to make up a name for this exception. This is the name that appears in the Exceptions tab, so make it reasonably descriptive. For example: Port 80 for Web Server.

5. Use the Port Number text box to type the port you want to set up as an exception.

6. Click the data protocol you want the exception to use: TCP or UDP. (If you're not sure, choose TCP.)

7. Click Change Scope to open the Change Scope dialog box.

8. Choose the scope option you want. If you choose the Custom List option, use the text box to type the IP addresses of the computers you want to allow for the exception, separated by commas. Click OK.

9. Click OK. Windows Firewall adds the program to the Exceptions tab and activates its check box.

10. Click OK to put the exception into effect.

> **TIP** If you're worried about someone on your network adding a port as an exception and possibly opening up a security hole (for example, by forgetting to change the scope to something local), you can disable new port exceptions on that computer. Log on as an administrator, open the Group Policy Editor (see Chapter 35), and open the following branch: Computer Configuration, Administrative Templates, Network, Network Connections, Windows Firewall, Standard Profile. Double-click the Windows Firewall: Allow Local Port Exceptions policy, and then click Enable.

Example: Accessing Your Web Server Over the Network

You can configure your Windows Vista or Windows XP computer as a web server by using the Internet Information Services (IIS) server. I won't go into the details about using this powerful server (the Vista version—IIS 7—is particularly nice), but I will show you how to ensure that other folks on your network can access the server after it's running.

IIS 7 is a feature in the Home Premium, Business, Enterprise, and Ultimate versions of Vista, but it's not installed by default on any of them. To install it, you need to work through the following steps:

1. Select Start, Control Panel to open the Control Panel window.

2. Click Programs to open the Program window.

3. Under Programs and Features, click the Turn Windows Features On or Off link. The User Account Control dialog box appears.

4. Enter your UAC credentials. Vista displays the Windows Features dialog box, which takes a few moments to populate.

5. Click to activate the check box beside Internet Information Services. Vista selects the most commonly used IIS features. If you want to install these default features, skip to step 7.

6. Open the Internet Information Services branch, and then activate the check boxes beside each component you want to work with. Here are some suggestions:

   ■ **Web Management Tools, IIS Management Service**—Install this component to configure your web server from any other computer on your network.

- **World Wide Web Services, Application Development Features**—The components in this branch represent the IIS programming features. If you're running IIS to build and test web applications, be sure to activate the check box for each development technology you require.

- **World Wide Web Services, Security, Basic Authentication**—Install this component if you want to restrict website access to users who have a valid Windows username and password.

NOTE To install IIS 7 in XP Pro (it's not available in the Home version), select Start, Control Panel, Add or Remove Programs, and then click Add/Remove Windows Components. Activate the check box beside Internet Information Services. If you want to configure the subcomponents, click Details, make your selections, and click OK. Click Next to proceed with the installation.

7. Click OK. Vista installs IIS 7.

Although there's not much to see, the default website is ready for action as soon as you install IIS. To access the website from the computer running IIS, you can enter any of the following addresses into your web browser:

```
http://127.0.0.1/
http://localhost/
http://IPAddress/ (replace IPAddress with the IP address of the computer)
http://ComputerName/ (replace ComputerName with name of the computer)
```

Figure 8.7 shows the home page of the default IIS website that appears.

FIGURE 8.7

The default IIS 7 website home page.

As things stand now, your new website will work properly only when you access it using a web browser on the Windows PC that's running IIS. If you try to access the site on any other computer, you get the message shown in Figure 8.8.

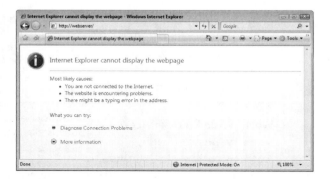

FIGURE 8.8

Other computers on the network can't access the web server yet.

The problem is that the web server's firewall hasn't been configured to allow data traffic through the World Wide Web Services used by IIS. For your website to work from any remote location on your network, you need to set up an exception for the World Wide Web Services in Windows Firewall. Here are the steps to follow:

1. Launch the Windows Firewall Setting dialog box.

2. Click the Exceptions tab.

3. Click to activate the check box beside the World Wide Web Services (HTTP) item.

4. Click OK to put the exception into effect.

With the Windows Firewall exception for the World Wide Web Services in place, you can now access the website from any remote computer on your network. You do this by launching your web browser and entering one of the following addresses:

> **NOTE** HTTP is short for Hypertext Transfer Protocol, the protocol used to exchange information on the World Wide Web.

```
http://IPAddress/ (replace IPAddress with the IP address of the IIS
computer)
http://ComputerName/ (replace ComputerName with name of the IIS computer)
```

As you can see in Figure 8.9, the network computer can now access the web server.

FIGURE 8.9

With the exception in effect, other computers on the network can now access the web server.

Boost Email Security by Reading Messages in Plain Text

Easy

It used to be that all email messages were simple text affairs. Even when email clients started including features for formatting messages, few people used them because it was unlikely that the recipient would see your formatting efforts (and might not see your message at all, depending on how ornery their email program was toward formatted messages). Nowadays, however, formatted messages—often called *rich text* messages, but they're really *HTML* messages—are pretty much the norm.

That's fine, as long as the sender is judicious with the use of fonts, colors, backgrounds, and other formatting bric-a-brac. However, the use of HTML in messages has led to a couple of security risks:

- **Malicious scripts**—Because messages can include the equivalent of web page code, they can also include the equivalent of web page scripts. Those scripts run as soon as you open or even preview a message.

- **Web bugs**—A *web bug* is an image that resides on a remote server and is included in an HTML-formatted email message by referencing a URL on the remote server. When you open the message, the email program uses the URL to download the

> **NOTE** HTML is short for Hypertext Markup Language, which is a set of codes that web developers use to lay out and format web pages.

image for display within the message. That sounds harmless enough, but if the message is junk email, it's likely that the URL will also contain either your email address or a code that points to your email address. When the remote server gets a request for this URL, it knows not only that you've opened the message, but also that your email address is legitimate.

Here are some solutions to consider:

- **Use Restricted Sites security**—If you crank up the security level in your email program, scripts won't be allowed to run. Restricted Sites is the default security level in Windows Mail, Outlook Express, and Outlook 2003, but to be safe, select Tools, Options, click the Security tab, and then click the Restricted Sites Zone option. (Note that Restricted Sites security is baked in for Outlook 2007 and can't be changed.)

- **Don't open or even preview suspect messages**—To delete a suspect message without having it display in the preview pane, right-click the message and then click Delete.

- **Block images from displaying**—This is a great way to thwart your average web bug:

    Windows Mail and Outlook Express—Select Tools, Options, click the Security tab, and then activate the Block Images and Other External Content in HTML E-mail check box.

    Outlook 2007—Select Tools, Trust Center, click Automatic Download, and then activate the Don't Download Pictures Automatically in HTML E-mail Messages or RSS Items check box.

    Outlook 2003—Select Tools, Options, click the Security tab, click Change Automatic Download Settings, and then activate the Don't Download Pictures or Other Content Automatically in HTML E-mail check box.

These are all useful solutions, to be sure, but an even easier way to keep yourself safe from malicious scripts and web bugs is to read all your messages in plain text. It's safe, you don't have to worry about deciphering someone's ugly script font, and it's easy to switch a message to the HTML view of you need to.

Use one of the following techniques to read all your email messages in plain text:

- **Windows Mail and Outlook Express**—Select Tools, Options, click the Read tab, and then activate the Read All Messages in Plain Text check box.

- **Outlook 2007**—Select Tools, Trust Center, click E-mail Security, and then activate the Read All Standard Messages in Plain Text check box.

- **Outlook 2003**—Select Tools, Options, click the Preferences tab, click E-mail Options, and then activate the Read All Standard Messages in Plain Text check box.

I use a macro to toggle Outlook between plain text and HTML. Here's the one I use for Outlook 2007:

```
Sub ToggleReadMailInPlainText()
    SendKeys "%tse%a{ENTER}"
End Sub
```

Here's one for Outlook 2003:

```
Sub ToggleReadMailInPlainText()
    SendKeys "%to%m%e{ENTER}{ESC}"
End Sub
```

In both programs, press Alt+F11 to open the Visual Basic Editor. In the project pane, open Project1, Microsoft Office Outlook, and then double-click ThisOutlookSession to open the module window. Type the macro into the module and then choose File, Save. You can create a toolbar button for the macro by returning to Outlook and selecting View, Toolbars, Customize.

> **TIP** If you get a legitimate HTML message, you can tell Windows Mail or Outlook Express to display the formatting by selecting the message and then selecting View, Message in HTML (or press Alt+Shift+H). In Outlook 2007 and 2003, click the message bar that reads This message was converted to plain text, and then click Display as HTML.

> **NOTE** You need to certify your own macros to ensure they run. Open the Run dialog box, type `%ProgramFiles%\Microsoft Office\Office12\SELFCERT.EXE` (change `Office12` to `Office11` if you're running Outlook 2003), click OK, and follow the instructions. In the Visual Basic Editor, select Tools, Digital Signature, click Choose, and then click your signature.

Reduce Spam by Blocking Messages from Certain Countries or Languages

Easy

Unless you've done an unusually good job at keeping your email address secret, you probably receive at least a few spam emails every day, and it's more likely that you receive a few dozen. Most experts agree that the problem is only going to get worse, so you need to do whatever you can to keep spam from inundating your inbox.

The best way to avoid spam is to avoid getting on a spammer's list of addresses in the first place. That's hard to do these days, but here are some steps you can take:

- Never use your actual email address in a newsgroup account. The most common method that spammers use to gather addresses is to harvest them from newsgroup posts. One common tactic you can use is to alter your email address by adding text that invalidates the address but is still obvious for other people to figure out:

```
user@myisp.remove_this_to_email_me.com
```

- When you sign up for something online, use a fake address, if possible. If you need or want to receive email from the company and so must use your real address, make sure that you deactivate any options that ask if you want to receive promotional offers. Alternatively, enter the address from an easily disposable free web-based account (such as a Hotmail account) so that any spam you receive will go there instead of to your main address. If your free email account overflows with junk mail, remove it and create a new one. (You can also do this through your ISP if it allows you to create multiple email accounts.)

- Never open suspected spam messages. Doing so can sometimes notify the spammer that you've opened the message, thus confirming that your address is legit. For the same reason, you should never display a spam message in the preview pane.

- Never respond to spam, even to an address within the spam that claims to be a "removal" address. By responding to the spam, all you're doing is proving that your address is legitimate, so you'll just end up getting *more* spam.

If you do get spam despite these precautions, the good news is that Windows Mail, Outlook 2003, and Outlook 2007 all come with a Junk E-mail feature that can help you cope. (Outlook Express does not have a Junk E-mail feature, unfortunately.) Junk E-mail is a *spam filter*, which means that it examines each incoming message and applies sophisticated tests to determine whether the message is spam. If the tests determine that the message is probably spam, the program exiles the email to a separate Junk E-mail folder. It's not perfect

TIP If you create web pages, never put your email address on a page because spammers use *crawlers* that harvest addresses from web pages. If you must put an address on a page, hide it using some simple JavaScript code:

```
    <script
language="JavaScript"
type="text/javascript">
    <!--
    var add1 = "webmaster"
    var add2 = "@"
    var add3 = "whatever.com"
    document.write(add1 +
➥add2 + add3)
    //-->
    </script>
```

(no spam filter is), but with a bit of fine-tuning it can be a very useful weapon against spam.

What do I mean by fine-tuning? I mean using the program's Junk E-mail options to adjust the settings to suit the way you work and the type of mail you receive. Use the following techniques to view the Junk E-mail options:

- **Windows Mail**—Select Tools, Junk E-mail Options.
- **Outlook 2007 and Outlook 2003**—Select Tools, Options, click the Preferences tab, and then click Junk E-mail.

Figure 8.10 shows the Windows Mail Junk E-mail Options dialog box.

FIGURE 8.10

The Junk E-mail Options dialog box displayed by Windows Mail.

You can use three standard techniques to fine-tune your spam filter:

- **Set the Junk E-mail protection level**—Use the settings on the Options tab to set the protection level. A high protection level means that the program aggressively marks messages as spam. That may sound good, but filtering spam is a trade-off between protection and convenience. That is, the stronger the protection you use, the less convenient the filter becomes, and vice versa. This inverse relationship is the result of a filter phenomenon called a *false positive*—a legitimate message that the filter has pegged as spam and has moved to the Junk E-mail folder. The stronger the protection level, the more likely it is that false positives will occur, so the more time you must spend checking the Junk E-mail folder for legitimate messages that need to be rescued.

- **Designate safe senders**—If you use the Low or High junk email protection level, you can reduce the number of false positives by letting the mail programs know about the people or institutions that regularly send you mail. By designating these addresses as Safe Senders, you tell the program to leave their incoming messages in your Inbox automatically and never redirect them to the Junk E-mail folder. You can add individual email addresses of the form *someone@somewhere.com*, or domain names of the form *@somewhere.com*. Use the settings in the Safe Senders tab to do this.

- **Block people who send spam**—If you notice that a particular address is the source of much spam or other annoying email, the easiest way to block the spam is to block all incoming messages from that address. You can do this using the Blocked Senders list, which watches for messages from a specific address and relegates them to the Junk E-mail folder. Use the settings in the Blocked Senders tab to do this.

These are all useful methods, but many people forget that Windows Mail and Outlook 2007 (not Outlook 2003, unfortunately) also offer two more useful features that enable you to handle spam with an international flavor:

- **Spam that comes from a particular country or region**—If you receive no legitimate messages from that country or region, you can treat all messages from that location as spam. Windows Mail and Outlook 2007 do this by using the *top-level domain* (*TLD*), which is the final suffix that appears in a domain name. There are two types: a generic top-level domain, such as com, edu, or net; and a country code top-level domain, such as ca (Canada) and fr (France). Windows Mail and Outlook 2007 use the latter to filter spam that comes from certain countries.

- **Spam that comes in a foreign language**—If you don't understand a language, you can safely treat all messages that appear in that language as spam. The character set of a foreign language always appears using a special encoding unique to that language. (An *encoding* is a set of rules that establishes a relationship between the characters and their representations.) Windows Mail and Outlook 2007 use that encoding to filter spam in a specified language.

With the Junk E-mail Options dialog box open, use the following steps to configure these aspects of your spam filter:

1. Display the International tab.
2. To filter spam based on one or more countries, click the Blocked Top-
   Level Domain List button. You see the Blocked Top-Level Domain List
   dialog box, shown in Figure 8.11.

FIGURE 8.11

*Use the Blocked Top-Level Domain List dialog box to select the country domains that you
want to treat as spam.*

3. Activate the check box beside each of the countries you want to filter.
4. Click OK.
5. To filter spam based on one or more languages, click the Blocked
   Encodings List button. You see the Blocked Encodings List dialog box,
   shown in Figure 8.12.

FIGURE 8.12

Use the Blocked Encodings List dialog box to select the languages that you want to treat as spam.

6. Activate the check box beside each of the languages you want to filter.

7. Click OK.

8. Click to put the new filter settings into effect.

Maintaining Your Privacy on the Web

Back in 1999, Sun Microsystems CEO Scott McNealy growled at a group of reporters, "You have zero privacy anyway. Get over it." It's a famous line that manages to be both grim and glib at the same time, but is it true? That depends. If you use Internet Explorer (or any other browser) with the standard configuration and without performing any kind of maintenance, then, yes, you basically have no privacy online. A person who sits down at your computer can tell with just a few mouse clicks where you've been and what you did while you were there; companies can track your movements; marketers (or stalkers) can find out just about anything about you.

However, if you configure Internet Explorer in a certain way, if you manage what your computer saves about your online sessions, and if you know the right tools to use, you can most definitely troll the online waters with almost complete privacy. This chapter takes you through a few tweaks that show you what you need to know and do.

Cover Your Tracks by Deleting Your Browsing History

Easy

You might think that the biggest online privacy risks are sitting out "there" in cyberspace, but that's not true. Your biggest risk is actually sitting right under your nose, so to speak: it's Internet Explorer. That's because Internet Explorer (just like Firefox, Safari, and any other web browser) saves tons of information related to your online activities. So the first step in covering your online tracks is to manage the information that Internet Explorer stores.

As you surf the Web, Internet Explorer maintains what it calls your *browsing history*, which consists of the following five data types:

- **Temporary Internet files**—This is Internet Explorer's cache, and it consists of copies of text, images, media, and other content from the pages you've visited recently. Internet Explorer stores all this data so that the next time you view one of those pages, it can retrieve data from the cache and display the site much more quickly. This is clearly a big-time privacy problem because it means that anyone can examine the cache to learn where you've been surfing.

- **Cookies**—This is Internet Explorer's collection of cookie files, which are small text files that sites store on your computer. I discuss cookies in more detail later in this chapter, but for now it's enough to know that although most cookies are benign, they can be used to track your activities online.

- **History**—This is a list of addresses of the sites you've visited, as well as each of the pages you visited within those sites. By default, Internet Explorer stores 20 days' worth of history. Again, this is a major privacy accident just waiting to happen, because anyone sitting at your computer can see exactly where you've been online over the past 20 days.

- **Form data**—This refers to the AutoComplete feature, which stores the data you type in forms and then uses that saved data to suggest possible matches when you use a similar form in the future. For example, if you use a site's Search box frequently, Internet Explorer remembers your search strings and displays strings that match what you've typed, as shown in Figure 9.1. (Press the down-arrow key to select the one you want, and then press Enter.) This is definitely handy, but it also means that anyone else who uses your computer can see your previously entered form text.

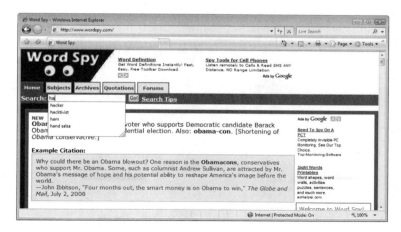

FIGURE 9.1

Internet Explorer's AutoComplete feature suggests previously entered text that matches what you've typed so far.

- **Passwords**—This is another aspect of AutoComplete, and Internet Explorer uses it to save form passwords. For example, if you enter a username and a password on a form, Internet Explorer asks if you want to save the password. If you click Yes, Internet Explorer stores the password and enters it automatically the next time you fill in the form (provided you enter the same username). Again, this is nice and convenient, but it's really just asking for trouble because it means that someone sitting down at your computer can log on to a site, a job made all the easier if you activated the site option to save your username!

Fortunately, you can plug any and all of these privacy holes by deleting the data. Even better, Internet Explorer 7 makes it much easier to delete your browsing history. In previous versions, you had to make separate deletions for cache files, cookies, visited URLs, saved form data, and saved passwords. In Internet Explorer 7, you perform these steps:

1. Select Tools, Delete Browsing History to display the Delete Browsing History dialog box shown in Figure 9.2.

NOTE If you don't want Internet Explorer to save your form data, passwords, or neither, select Tools, Internet Options, select the Content tab, and then click Settings in the AutoComplete group. In the AutoComplete Settings dialog box, deactivate the Forms check box to stop saving form data. If you no longer want to save form passwords, deactivate the User Name and Passwords on Forms check box. Click OK in all open dialog boxes.

FIGURE 9.2
Use the Delete Browsing History dialog box to delete some or all of your Internet Explorer 7 browsing history.

2. Click Delete Files and then click Yes to remove all files from the Internet Explorer cache, located in the following folder:

Windows Vista—`%UserProfile%\AppData\Local\Microsoft\`
`Windows\Temporary Internet Files`

Windows XP—`%UserProfile%\Local Settings\Temporary Internet Files`

> **TIP** If you just want to delete certain cookies—for example, those from advertisers—open the Cookies folder and delete the files individually.

3. Click Delete Cookies and then click Yes to remove all the cookies from the following folder:

Windows Vista—
`%UserProfile%\AppData\Roaming\Microsoft\Windows\Cookies`

Windows XP—
`%UserProfile%\Cookies`

4. Click Delete History and then click Yes to remove the list of websites you've visited, which resides as files in the following folder:

> **TIP** If you want to delete history from a certain site, day, or week, click Favorites Center (or press Alt+C), and click History to display the History list. If you want to delete just a few sites, open the appropriate History branch, and then, for each site, right-click the site and then click Delete. If you want to delete a number of sites, right-click the appropriate day or week and then click Delete. Click Yes when Internet Explorer asks you to confirm.

Windows Vista—
```
%UserProfile%\AppData\Local\
Microsoft\Windows\History
```
Windows XP—`%UserProfile%\`
`Local Settings\History`

NOTE If you want to clean house, you can click Delete All to erase everything in one shot.

5. Click Delete Forms and then click Yes to remove your saved form data.

6. Click Delete Passwords and then click Yes to remove your saved passwords.

7. Click Close.

WINDOWS MEDIA PLAYER PRIVACY OPTIONS

When you use Windows Media Player to play content from an Internet site, the program communicates certain information to the site, including the unique ID number of your copy of Windows Media Player. This allows content providers to track the media you play, and they might share this data with other sites. So, although the Player ID does not identify you personally, it might result in sites sending you targeted ads based on your media choices. If you do not want such an invasion of privacy, you can instruct Windows Media Player not to send the Player ID. Press Alt+F and then select Tools, Options. In the Options dialog box, display the Privacy tab and make sure that the Send Unique Player ID to Content Providers check box is deactivated. (However, remember that some content sites *require* the Player ID before you can play any media. For example, a site might request the ID for billing purposes. In that case, you should read the site's privacy statement to see what uses it makes of the ID.) Also deactivate the I Want to Help Make Microsoft Software and Services Even Better… check box to avoid sending your Windows Media Player usage data to Microsoft. You should also deactivate the Save File and URL History in the Player check box if you don't want other people who use your computer to see the media files and sites that you play and visit.

Clear the Address Bar List Without Also Clearing Your History List

Medium

Another part of Internet Explorer's AutoComplete feature involves the web addresses that you type into the Address bar. As I discussed in Chapter 4, "Terrific Web Tweaks," when you start typing a URL into the Address bar, Internet Explorer displays a list of addresses that match what you've typed. If you see the one you want, use the arrow keys to select it, and then press Enter to surf to it.

> **NOTE** You can configure Internet Explorer to not save the web addresses that you type. Select Tools, Internet Options, select the Content tab, and then click Settings in the AutoComplete group. In the AutoComplete Settings dialog box, deactivate the Web Addresses check box to stop saving typed URLs. Click OK in all open dialog boxes.

➡ **See** "Become an Address Bar Guru," **p. 39**.

That's mighty convenient, but not very private because other people who have access to your PC can also see those addresses. So another good privacy tweak is to clear the Address bar list so that no URLs appear as you type.

One way to clear the Address bar list is to clear the history files, as described in the previous section. That is, you select Tools, Delete Browsing History, and then click Delete History.

That works well, but it also means that you lose all your browsing history. That may be exactly what you want, but you may prefer to preserve the history files. In this section I show you a script tweak that removes the Address bar URLs but lets you save your history.

First, note that Internet Explorer stores the last 25 typed URLs in the following Registry key (see Figure 9.3):

`HKCU\Software\Microsoft\Internet Explorer\TypedURLs`

You can therefore clear the Address bar list by closing all Internet Explorer windows and deleting the settings `url1` through `url25` in this key. Listing 9.1 presents a script that does this for you.

> **NOTE** See Chapter 37, "Running Scripts," to learn how to run this script. The file containing the script in Listing 9.1—`DeleteTypedURLs.vbs`—is available from my website at http://mcfedries.com/cs/content/TweakItFreakIt.aspx.

FIGURE 9.3

The last 25 addresses you typed into the Address bar are stored in the TypedURLs *Registry key.*

Listing 9.1   A Script That Deletes Internet Explorer's Typed URLs

```
Option Explicit
Dim objWshShell, nTypedURLs, strRegKey, strURL, i
Set objWshShell = WScript.CreateObject("WScript.Shell")
On Error Resume Next
'
' First determine the number of typed URLs in the Registry
'
nTypedURLs = 0
strRegKey = "HKCU\Software\Microsoft\Internet Explorer\TypedURLs\"
Do While True
    '
    ' Read the next typed URL
    '
    strURL = objWshShell.RegRead(strRegKey & "url" & nTypedURLs + 1)
    '
    ' If we get an error, it means we've read all
    ' the typed URLs, so exit the loop
    If Err <> 0 Then
        'nTypedURLs = nTypedURLs - 1
        Exit Do
    End If
    nTypedURLs = nTypedURLs + 1
Loop
```

continues

Listing 9.1   Continued

```
'
' Run through the typed URLs
'
For i = 1 to nTypedURLs
    '
    ' Delete the Registry setting
    '
    objWshShell.RegDelete strRegKey & "url" & i
Next 'i
objWshShell.Popup "Finished deleting " & nTypedURLs & _
                  " typed URLs", , "Delete Typed URLs"
```

This script begins by running through all the settings in the TypedURLs key, and counts them as it goes. This is necessary because there may not be the full 25 typed URLs in the key, and if you try to delete a nonexistent Registry key, you get an error. With the number of typed URLs in hand, the script then performs a second loop that deletes each Registry setting.

Cover Your Online Tracks by Deleting Your Google Web History

Medium

It's a Google world out there, and we all spend big chunks of our day using one Google service or another, from Search to Gmail to Google Docs to Google Groups. We use "the Google" so much because the company is very good at what it does, we get the results we want, and you can't beat the price—free!

However, because we use Google so much, it necessarily means that Google knows an awful lot about us. It knows what we search for, which YouTube videos we watch, which newsgroups we frequent, and through services such as Gmail (email), Picasa (online photo sharing), Docs (online documents), and Blogger (blogs), it has access to tons of our personal data.

No one will blame you if you're more than a little nervous about one company knowing so much about you. And when in the summer of 2008 a judge ordered Google to hand over its YouTube user records to Viacom as part of a lawsuit, you now have the specter of the government and corporations having the capability to coerce your online profile from Google.

For services such as Gmail and Picasa, the answer is simple: either don't use those services, or don't use them all under a single Google account. The latter is becoming an increasing popular Google technique: create one account for Gmail, another for Google Docs, yet another for Blogger, and so on. It's a lot harder to manage, of course, but it prevents Google from sharing data between services, and it prevents Google from consolidating all your data into a larger profile of you. (Note, however, that Google has made some recent moves that might prevent you from using multiple Google accounts on the same computer.)

Google's Web History service is another story because it can be incredibly useful. Unlike Internet Explorer's 20-day history, Google's Web History stores all your history—your searches and the pages you visit—for as long as you surf. So if you visited a site a month ago and would like to go back, Internet Explorer can't help you, but Google Web History can.

Of course, having a record of *all* our online activity in one place (one potentially subpoena-able place, to boot) is a privacy nightmare. So how do you reconcile the convenience and intrusiveness of Web History?

The easiest way is to temporarily prevent Web History from tracking your online life. The next time you plan to visit a site that you don't want tracked, use either of the following techniques to temporarily shut off Web History:

- **Sign out from your Google account**—This works because Google tracks your web history only when you're signed in. Go to any Google page and click the Sign Out link in the upper-right corner. Google signs out of your account and returns you to the same page.

- **Pause the Web History service**—Go to www.google.com/history, and sign in if you see the login screen. In the list of links on the left, click Pause. When you're done surfing, return to your Web History page and click Resume.

What if you forget to sign out and Google has tracked some activity that you don't want to appear in your web history? You can remove those items by following these steps:

1. Go to www.google.com/history.
2. Sign in to your account.
3. Click the Remove Items link.
4. Navigate to the history page that has the item or items you want to delete.
5. Activate the check box beside each item.
6. Click Remove. Google removes the items from your history.

NOTE If you want to trash your entire history, click the Clear Entire Web History link.

TIP If you use the Google toolbar, you may also want to clear the recent search terms that appear in the Search box. Pull down the Search box list and click Clear History.

If you don't have a Google account, you might think you're safe, but that's not the case. Google adds cookies to your PC to track your searches. It's not as comprehensive as Web History, but Google is still monitoring your activity. To prevent this, block Google from adding cookies to your computer, as described in the next section.

Keep a Site's Hands Off Your PC by Blocking Cookies

Medium

A *cookie* is a small text file that's stored on your computer. Websites use them to "remember" information about your session at that site: shopping cart data, page customizations, usernames, passwords, and so on.

No other site can access your cookies, so they're generally safe and private under most—but definitely not all—circumstances. To understand why cookies can sometimes compromise your privacy, you have to understand the different cookie types that exist:

- **Temporary cookie**—This type of cookie lives just as long as you have Internet Explorer running. Internet Explorer deletes all temporary cookies when you shut down the program.

- **Persistent cookie**—This type of cookie remains on your hard disk through multiple Internet Explorer sessions. The cookie's duration depends on how it's set up, but it can be anything from a few seconds to a few years.

- **First-party cookie**—This is a cookie set by the website you're viewing.

- **Third-party cookie**—This is a cookie set by a site other than the one you're viewing. Advertisers that have placed an ad on the site you're viewing create and store most third-party cookies.

These cookie types can compromise your privacy in two ways:

- A site might store *personally identifiable information*—your name, email address, home address, phone number, and so on—in a persistent first- or third-party cookie and then use that information in some way (such as filling in a form) without your consent.

- A site might store information about you in a persistent third-party cookie and then use that cookie to track your online movements and activities. The advertiser can do this because it might have (for example) an ad on dozens or hundreds of websites, and that ad is the mechanism that enables the site to set and read their cookies. Such sites are supposed to come up with *privacy policies* stating that they won't engage in surreptitious monitoring of users, they won't sell user data, and so on.

To help you handle these scenarios, Internet Explorer implements a privacy feature that gives you extra control over whether sites can store cookies on your machine. To check out this feature, select Internet Explorer's Tools, Internet Options command, and then display the Privacy tab, shown in Figure 9.4. You set your cookie privacy level by using the slider in the Settings group.

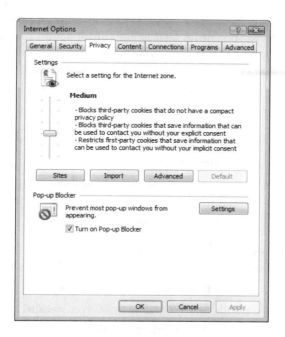

FIGURE 9.4

In the Internet Options dialog box, use the Privacy tab to manage your cookies.

That's fine on a broad level, but you can fine-tune your cookie management by preventing specific sites from adding cookies to your computer. In the previous section, for example, you learned that you can prevent Google from tracking your search activity by preventing it from adding cookies to your PC. You might also want to block ad sites such as doubleclick.net.

Here are the steps to follow in Internet Explorer to block a site from adding cookies:

1. Select Tools, Internet Options.
2. Display the Privacy tab.
3. Click Sites.
4. Use the Address of Website text box to type the site domain.
5. Click Block.
6. Repeat steps 4 and 5 to add all the sites you want blocked.
7. Click OK in the open dialog boxes.

Surf Anonymously with a Proxy Server

Medium

A big part of surfing privately involves not leaving a trail of digital bread-crumbs in your wake. The most obvious way you leave a trail is by accessing any website. The site's web server records all the pages you visit in the server log, and those log entries include important details such as your IP address (technically, the IP address of your network's router or gateway) and the web browser that you're using.

To prevent this, you need to put something between you and the web server, and that something is a site called an *anonymous proxy server* (also called just an *anonymizer*). As the name implies, this type of site lets you surf anony-mously by acting as a proxy on your behalf. Here's the basic procedure:

1. You tell the anonymous proxy server which site you want to see.

2. The anonymizer contacts the site and requests the data.

3. The site sends the data to the anonymizer.

4. The anonymizer passes the data along to your web browser.

The web server doesn't know a thing about you, so none of your data gets stored in the server logs, and your privacy is protected.

There are two ways to use an anonymous proxy:

■ Use a public anonymous proxy server website.

■ Configure your web browser to use an anonymous proxy server.

Using a Web Proxy

An anonymous proxy server website—also called a *web proxy*—is a good way to go if you want to anonymize only some of your web surfing. The idea is that you navigate to the anonymous proxy site, perhaps set a few options, and then enter the URL of the website you want to view. There are commercial web prox-ies where you pay so much per month, but there are also a few free web proxies available. What's the catch? There are a couple: the web proxy will probably serve up a few ads, and your bandwidth is usually throttled, so the surfing tends to be on the slow side. Here are two web proxies that I recommend:

■ **Proxify**—This site probably has the best reputation of all the anony-mous proxy sites. As you can see in Figure 9.5, it offers lots of security options and even has prefab settings to optimize for speed, security, and compatibility. See proxify.com.

■ **The Cloak**—This site also has a good reputation and offers lots of options for customizing the proxy (see Figure 9.6), although it's a bit slower than Proxify. See the-cloak.com.

FIGURE 9.5

The Proxify anonymous proxy server site.

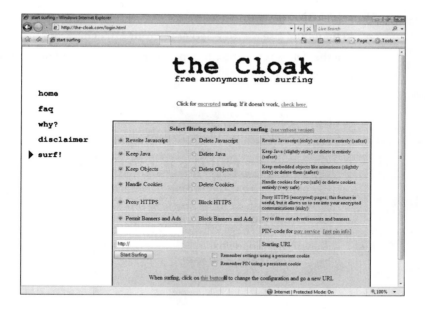

FIGURE 9.6

The Cloak anonymous proxy server site.

Configuring Internet Explorer to Use a Proxy Server

Web proxies are fine if you just want to be anonymous part-time. However, if you always want to be anonymous, it's a hassle to always go back and forth with the web proxy. A more convenient method is to get the IP address of an anonymous proxy server and then configure Internet Explorer to always surf using that proxy.

Here are a couple of sites that offer lists of free proxy servers:

- **Public Proxy Servers**—www.publicproxyservers.com/page1.html
- **AtomInterSoft**—www.atomintersoft.com/free_proxy_list

Make a note of the IP address and port of the proxy server you want to use. (If you see an address in the form 123:45:67:89:80, it means that the IP address is 123.45.67.89 and the port is 80.) Follow these steps to set up the proxy server in Internet Explorer:

1. Select Tools, Options.
2. Display the Connections tab.
3. Click LAN Settings.
4. Activate the Use a Proxy Server for Your LAN check box.
5. Use the Address text box to type the proxy server's IP address, as shown in Figure 9.7.

FIGURE 9.7

Use the controls in the Proxy Server group to configure a proxy server for Internet Explorer.

6. Use the Port text box to type the proxy server's port.
7. Activate the Bypass Proxy Server for Local Addresses check box.
8. Click OK in all the open dialog boxes.

Tweaking Windows for Safe and Fun Family Use

If you have children who share your computer (how brave of you!), or if you're setting up a computer for the kids' use, it's wise to take precautions regarding the content and programs that they can access. Locally, this might take the form of blocking access to certain programs (such as your financial software) and setting time limits on when the computer is used. If the computer has Internet access, you might also want to allow only specific sites and prevent file downloads.

All this sounds daunting, but the Parental Controls in Windows Vista make things a bit easier by offering an easy-to-use interface that lets you set all the aforementioned options and lots more, as you'll see in this chapter. (Note that you get Parental Controls only in the Home Basic, Home Premium, and Ultimate editions of Windows Vista.)

Get Control by Turning on Parental Controls

Vista

Easy

Before you can do anything with Parental Controls, you need to create a standard user account for each child who uses the computer:

1. Select Start, Control Panel.

2. Click Add or Remove User Accounts and then enter your UAC credentials. The Manage Accounts window appears.

3. Click Create a New Account. The Create New Account window appears.

4. Type the user's name, be sure the Standard Account option is activated, and then click Create Account.

When that's done, you get to Parental Controls by selecting Start, Control Panel, and then clicking the Set Up Parental Controls link. Enter your UAC credentials to get to the Parental Controls window, and then click the user you want to work with to get to the User Controls window.

You should activate two options here (see Figure 10.1):

- **Parental Controls**—Click the On, Enforce Current Settings option. This enables the Windows Vista Web Filter, and the Time Limits, Games, and Allow and Block Specific Programs links in the Settings area.

- **Activity Reporting**—Click the On, Collect Information About Computer Usage option. This tells Vista to track system events such as blocked logon attempts and attempted changes to user accounts, system date and time, and system settings.

FIGURE 10.1

The User Controls page enables you to set up web, time, game, and program restrictions for the selected user.

Keep Your PC Safe with a List of Allowed Programs

Easy

You set up your kids with standard user accounts, and the good news is that Vista security is structured in such a way that standard users can't do much overall harm to a computer. However, that doesn't mean you should give your kids the run of the PC. There are plenty of executable files lurking on a typical Windows Vista system, and the vast majority of them should be off-limits. However, anything can happen with an overly curious or fumble-fingered child at the keyboard.

> **NOTE** Actually, the list doesn't include every application on the PC: it bypasses all the games that are installed (including the games that come with Windows Vista). To restrict games, return to the User Controls window, click Games, and then click Block or Allow Specific Games.

To prevent mishaps or confusion caused by starting an improper program, you can configure a child's parental controls so that he or she can start only specific programs. Here are the steps to follow:

1. In the User Controls window, click Allow and Block Specific Programs to display the Application Restrictions window.

2. Activate the *User* Can Only Use the Programs I Allow option (where *User* is the name of the user you're working with). Vista displays a list of all the executable files on the computer.

3. Activate the check box beside each program you want to allow the user to start, as shown in Figure 10.2.

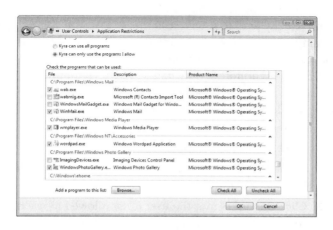

FIGURE 10.2

Activate the check box beside each application that it's okay for the user to start.

4. If Vista missed a program, click Browse, use the Open dialog box to select the application's executable file, and then click Open. Vista adds the program to the list.

5. Click OK.

If the child attempts to start any other program, he or she sees a dialog box like the one shown in Figure 10.3.

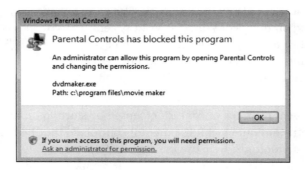

FIGURE 10.3
If an application isn't on the list of allowed programs, the child sees a dialog box like this.

Maintain Balance by Enforcing Computer Time Limits

Easy

As I'm sure you know, if you give a kid access to a computer, he or she will stay on the computer all day and all night. That sort of obsessive behavior doesn't exactly lead to a balanced life, so I'm sure you nag your kids to get off the computer and go play outside (or read a book or whatever). If you're sick of nagging, you can tweak your parental controls to let Windows Vista be the Bad Cop for a change. Specifically, you can configure time limits that determine when, in one-hour blocks, a user is allowed access to the computer. During blocked hours, the child either can't log on, or the child is automatically logged off when the time comes.

Follow these steps to set up time limits for a child:

1. In the User Controls window, click Time Limits to display the Time Restrictions window.

2. Click the hours that the user is *not* allowed to use the computer. (You can also click and drag over several consecutive time blocks.) Windows Vista uses blue to show the times when the user is blocked from using the computer, as shown in Figure 10.4.

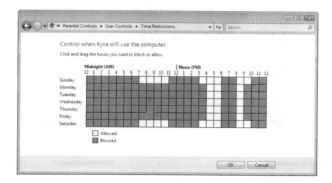

FIGURE 10.4

Use the Time Restrictions window to specify the times that the user is blocked from using the computer.

   3. Click OK.

   If the child attempts to log on during a restricted time, he or she sees the message shown in Figure 10.5.

FIGURE 10.5

If a user attempts to log on during a blocked time, the logon fails with the message shown here.

If the child is already logged on, the Parental Controls icon appears in the notification area. He or she can move the mouse pointer over the icon to see how much time is left, as shown in Figure 10.6. (When there's a minute left, a fly-out message appears, warning the user that time is short.) When that time runs out, Windows Vista hides the user's session and displays the logon screen.

NOTE You might think that Vista logs the user off at the end of the allowed time, but that's not the case. Instead, Vista leaves the user's session running in the background. This is important, because it means that the user doesn't lose unsaved changes in any running programs. Instead, the next time the user is able to log on, Vista is kind enough to restore the user's programs and documents exactly as they were before.

FIGURE 10.6

The child can monitor how much time is left by hovering the mouse pointer over the Parental Controls icon in the notification area.

Let Kids Surf Safely with a List of Allowed Websites

Easy

The web is a dangerous place even for experienced users, so it's no place to send a child without some kind of adult supervision. Of course, you can't hover over your kids every second that they're online, so how do you ensure they're surfing safely? You can take advantage of the Windows Vista Web Filter that's part of Parental Controls. Although you can use this feature to block web data based on content, for younger children it's a lot easier to just provide them with a list of allowed websites.

Here's how to set this up:

1. In the User Controls window, click Windows Vista Web Filter to display the Web Restrictions window.
2. Activate the Block Some Websites or Content option.
3. Click Edit the Allow and Block List link to open the Allow or Block Specific Websites window.
4. Use the Website Address text box to type in the URL of a site you want to allow.
5. Click Allow. Windows Vista adds the URL to the Allowed Websites list, as shown in Figure 10.7.
6. Repeat steps 4 and 5 for each site you want to allow.
7. Activate the Only Allow Websites Which Are on the Allow List check box.
8. Click OK to return to the Web Restrictions window.
9. Click OK.

FIGURE 10.7

The sites you add appear in the Allowed Websites list.

As you can imagine, it's a tad tedious to enter a bunch of allowed sites by hand. To make your life easier, you can import lists of allowed or blocked sites.

First, create a new text file and change the extension to Web Allow Block List (for example, MyURLs.Web Allow Block List). Open the file and add the following text to start:

```
<WebAddresses>
</WebAddresses>
```

Between these lines, add a new line for each site using the following format:

```
<URL AllowBlock="1">address</URL>
```

Replace *address* with the site URL. Here's an example:

```
<WebAddresses>
<URL AllowBlock="1">http://www.goodcleanfun.com</URL>
<URL AllowBlock="1">http://www.wholesomestuff.com</URL>
<URL AllowBlock="1">http://www.cuteanimals.com</URL>
<URL AllowBlock="1">http://www.educationalandfun.com</URL>
</WebAddresses>
```

Follow these steps to import the addresses:

1. In the User Controls window, click Windows Vista Web Filter to display the Web Restrictions window.

2. Click Edit the Allow and Block List link to open the Allow or Block Specific Websites window.

3. Click Import, use the Open dialog box to select the text file, and then click Open. Windows Vista adds the sites to the Allowed Websites list.

4. Click OK to return to the Web Restrictions window.

5. Click OK.

If the child tries to navigate to some other page, he or she sees the message shown in Figure 10.8.

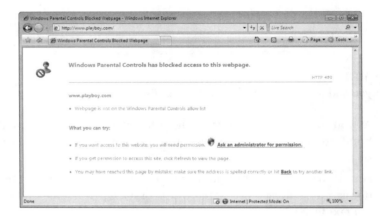

FIGURE 10.8
If a site's not on the Allowed Websites list, your kid can't get there from here.

Keep the Online World at Bay by Blocking File Downloads

Easy

File downloads on the Web pose a number of problems for young users. The major concern, of course, is that a file might be harboring spyware, a virus, or some other malware. This sort of content shouldn't make it through Vista's regular defenses (Internet Explorer protected mode, User Account Control, and Windows Defender), but why take chances? Even if a download is benign, unrestricted downloading could fill up the computer's hard drive or even incur extra bandwidth charges from your ISP.

To prevent these scenarios, follow these steps to use Parental Controls to prevent a user from downloading any files:

1. In the User Controls window, click Windows Vista Web Filter to display the Web Restrictions window.

    2. Activate the Block File Downloads check box.

    3. Click OK.

If the user clicks a download link, he or she sees the dialog box shown in Figure 10.9.

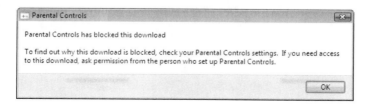

FIGURE 10.9

If the child tries to download a file from the web, Parental Controls blocks the download and displays this message.

More User Account Tweaks

User accounts may seem like simple things, but there's a lot more to them than meets the eye. For example, you know that in Windows Vista all standard users must enter administrator credentials to perform actions such as installing certain programs or modifying system settings, but did you know that you can disable all elevation prompts for those users? Did you know that you can disable all user accounts (except your own, of course)? Did you know that you can use the built-in Guest account as an easy way to give someone temporary (and limited) access to your computer? Did you know that it's possible to find out who is logged on to another computer on your network?

All these tasks are very doable, and the tweaks in this chapter show you how.

Prevent Elevation for All Standard Users

Medium

At the heart of the Windows Vista security model is the User Account Control (UAC), which uses a principle called the *least-privileged user*. The idea behind this is to create an account level that has no more permissions than it requires. Such accounts are prevented from editing the Registry and performing other administrative tasks. However, these users can perform day-to-day tasks such as installing programs (as long as they don't change any system settings).

In Windows Vista, the least-privileged user concept arrives in the form of a new account type called the standard user. This means that Vista has three basic account levels:

- **Administrator account**—This built-in account can do anything to the computer.

- **Administrators group**—Members of this group (except the Administrator account) run as standard users but are able to elevate their privileges when required just by clicking a button in a dialog box.

- **Standard users group**—These are the least-privileged users, although they, too, can elevate their privileges when needed.

If you're running as a standard user and attempt a task that requires administrative privileges, Vista uses an extra level of protection. That is, instead of just prompting you for consent, it prompts you for the credentials of an administrator, as shown in Figure 11.1. If your system has multiple administrator accounts, each one is shown in this dialog box. Type the password for any administrator account shown, and then click Submit.

FIGURE 11.1

When a standard user launches a task that requires administrative privileges, Windows Vista displays this dialog box to ask for administrative credentials.

Notice, too, that Windows Vista switches to *secure desktop* mode: it darkens the screen and it prevents you from doing anything else with Vista until you give your credentials or cancel the operation.

There are two problems with this:

NOTE These steps require the Group Policy Editor, which is available only with Vista Business, Vista Enterprise, and Vista Ultimate. If you're not running one of these versions, normally I'd show you how to modify the Registry to get the same effect. Unfortunately, the policy value that we tweak here doesn't have a Registry equivalent for security reasons.

- Standard users almost never have the proper credentials to elevate an action.

- The combination of the sudden appearance of the User Account Control dialog box and the change into secure desktop mode is confusing for many users, particularly the inexperienced.

These two problems mean that in most cases it would be better if a standard user didn't get prompted to elevate their privileges. Instead, it would be better to display an Access Denied message and let the user move on from there.

You can use the Group Policy Editor to set this up. Here are the steps to follow:

1. Select Start, type `gpedit.msc` into the Search box, and then press Enter. The User Account Control dialog box appears.

2. Enter your administrator's credentials to continue. The Group Policy Editor appears.

3. Open the Computer Configuration branch.

4. Open the Windows Settings branch.

5. Open the Security Settings branch.

6. Open the Local Policies branch.

7. Click the Security Options branch.

8. Double-click the User Account Control: Behavior of the Elevation Prompt for Standard Users policy.

9. In the list, choose Automatically Deny Elevation Requests, as shown in Figure 11.2.

10. Click OK to put the new setting into effect.

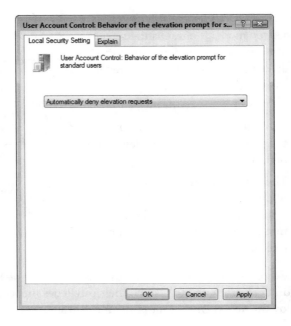

FIGURE 11.2
Open the User Account Control: Behavior of the Elevation Prompt for Standard Users policy and choose Automatically Deny Elevation Requests.

Now when a standard user attempts something that requires elevated privileges, he or she just sees a simple dialog box like the one shown in Figure 11.3. Vista doesn't switch into secure desktop mode, and the user only has to click OK to continue.

NOTE The dialog box the user sees varies depending on the program or service that requires elevation. In each case, however, the user's only choice is to click OK.

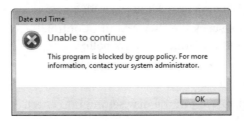

FIGURE 11.3
When standard users are denied elevation requests, they see a simple dialog box when they attempt an administrator-level task.

Close Off Your Computer by Disabling All Other Users

Medium

If you've got other user accounts on your computer, there may be times when you don't want anyone else to use the computer for a while. For example, perhaps the hard drive is getting full and you don't want anyone using the machine until you add more capacity. Similarly, if you have an account set up for a child and that child violates the rules you've set for using the computer, you might want to temporarily disable the account as punishment.

Whatever the reason, you need some way of disabling all other user accounts. The standard Windows user account tools don't give you any direct way of doing this, but it's possible to make it happen by digging far below the Windows surface.

Follow these steps to delete one or more user accounts:

1. Select Start, type `lusrmgr.msc` into the Search box, and then press Enter. (In Windows XP, select Start, Run to open the Run dialog box, type `lusrmgr.msc`, and then click OK.)

2. In Vista, the User Account Control dialog box appears, so enter your UAC credentials to continue. The Local Users and Groups snap-in appears.

3. Click Users. Windows displays a list of the users on your system, as shown in Figure 11.4.

FIGURE 11.4
Use the Local Users and Groups snap-in to disable user accounts.

4. Double-click the account you want to disable. The account's Properties dialog box appears.

5. Activate the Account Is Disabled check box.

6. Click OK to return to the Local Users and Groups window.

NOTE When you disable an account, Windows indicates this by adding a downward pointing arrow to the account icon, as shown in Figure 11.4 with the Administrator and Guest accounts (which are disabled by default in Windows Vista).

7. Repeat steps 4 to 6 to disable the other accounts you want to block.

8. Select File, Exit to close the Local Users and Groups snap-in.

When an account is disabled, Windows doesn't include an icon for it in the logon screen, so there's no way for the user to log on to his or her account. When you're ready to give others access to the PC, repeat the preceding steps, except deactivate the Account Is Disabled check box for each account.

Use the Guest Account to Give Folks Temporary Access

Medium

What do you do if you have someone visiting your place and that person wants to, for instance, surf the Web or access some media on your computer? You could allow the person to log on using an existing account, but that might not be reasonable because of privacy or security concerns. You could set up a user account for that person, but that seems like overkill, particularly for a person on a short visit.

A better solution is to enable the Guest account and allow your visitor to log on under that account. Follow these steps to enable the Guest account:

1. Press Windows Logo+R to open the Run dialog box, type `control nusrmgr.cpl`, and click OK.

2. In Windows Vista, click the Manage Another Account link and then enter your UAC credentials to continue. The User Accounts window appears.

3. Click the Guest account icon. Windows asks if you want to turn on the Guest account.

4. Click Turn On (Vista) or Turn On the Guest Account (XP). Windows activates the Guest account.

Your guest is now free to use your computer safely:

- In the Windows Vista or Windows XP Home logon screen (see Figure 11.5), click the Guest icon.

- In the Log On to Windows dialog box, type `Guest` into the User Name text box and click OK.

> **CAUTION** You should probably rename the Guest account if you're going to leave it activated for a while. See Chapter 7, "Keeping the Bad Guys at Bay."

FIGURE 11.5
With the Guest account enabled, you see an icon for the account in the Windows Vista (and Windows XP Home) logon screen.

Determine Who Is Logged On

Easy

How do you know who's logged on to a Vista machine? For example, what if you're sitting down at another person's computer and you're not sure who's logged on and what privileges they have?

No problem. The WHOAMI command gives you information about the user who is currently logged on to the computer:

```
WHOAMI [/UPN ¦ /FQDN ¦ LOGONID] [/USER ¦ /GROUPS ¦ /PRIV] [/ALL] [/FO
Format]
```

/UPN	(Domains only) Returns the current user's name using the user principal name (UPN) format.
/FQDN	(Domains only) Returns the current user's name using the fully qualified domain name (FQDN) format.

> **TIP** WHOAMI is built into Windows Vista, but for Windows XP you need to download and install the Windows XP Service Pack 2 Support Tools from http://tinyurl.com/6xrl7 (which points to http://www.microsoft.com/downloads/details.aspx?FamilyID=49ae8576-9bb9-4126-9761-ba8011fabf38).

`/LOGONID`	Returns the current user's security identifier (SID).
`/USER`	Returns the current user-name using the *computer\user* format.
`/GROUPS`	Returns the groups of which the current user is a member.
`/PRIV`	Returns the current user's privileges.
`/ALL`	Returns the current user's SID, username, groups, and privileges.

TIP My command is actually two commands in one, thanks to the DOSKEY && operator, which lets you run multiple commands on a single line.

NOTE The file containing the script in Listing 11.1 — `WhoIsLoggedOn.vbs`—is available from my website at http://mcfedries.com/cs/content/TweakItFreakIt.aspx.

`/FO Format`   The output format, where *format* is one of the following values:

   `table`   The output is displayed in a row-and-column format, with headers in the first row and values in subsequent rows.

   `list`   The output is displayed in a two-column list, with the headers in the first column and values in the second column.

   `csv`   The output is displayed with headers and values separated by commas. The headers appear on the first line.

For example, start a Command Prompt session on the computer (in Vista, select Start, type **command** into the Search box, and then press Enter; in XP, select Start, Run, type **cmd**, and click OK) and enter the following command:

`whoami /all /fo list > whoami.txt&&start whoami.txt`

This command redirects the current user's SID, username, groups, and privileges to a file named whoami.txt using the list format, and then opens the file.

If you want to know who's logged on to a computer on your network, use the script in Listing 11.1.

Listing 11.1   A Script That Determines Who Is Currently Logged On to a Remote Computer

```
Option Explicit
Dim strComputer, objWMI, colSystem, objComputer, strUserName
'
' This script uses WMI to connect to a remote computer
```

```
' and get the username of the logged on user.
'
' Get the computer name
'
strComputer = InputBox("Type the computer name:", "Who Is Logged On?")
'
' Make sure we have a name before proceeding
'
If strComputer <> "" Then
    '
    ' Get the WMI interface
    '
    Set objWMI = GetObject("winmgmts:{impersonationLevel=impersonate}!\\" & _
                strComputer & "\root\cimv2")
    '
    ' Return the computer system
    '
    Set colSystem = objWMI.ExecQuery _
        ("Select * from Win32_ComputerSystem")
    '
    ' Access the remote computer's data
    '
    For Each objComputer in colSystem
        '
        ' Parse the user name (which is returned as COMPUTER\USER)
        '
        strUserName = objComputer.UserName
        strUserName = Mid(strUserName, InStr(strUserName, "\") + 1)
        '
        ' Display the user
        '
        WScript.Echo "The current user on " & _
                    objComputer.Name & " is "& strUserName
    Next
End If
```

This script first asks for the name of the computer. It then uses Windows Management Instrumentation (WMI) to return the remote system, which returns the UserName property (the current user's username) and the Name property (the computer's name). This data is then displayed in a dialog box like the one shown in Figure 11.6.

FIGURE 11.6

An example of the dialog box displayed by the script in Listing 11.1.

CHAPTER 12

Taking Advantage of the Administrator Account

The security problems in Windows XP were well documented and much lampooned. Why was XP such a security nightmare? There are a few culprits, but for my money the biggest by far was that most users were running Windows XP with administrator-level permissions. Administrators can do *anything* to a Windows machine, including installing programs, adding devices, updating drivers, installing updates and patches, changing Registry settings, running high-level administrative tools such as Group Policy Editor, and creating and modifying user accounts. This is convenient, but it leads to a huge problem: Any malware that insinuates itself onto the system will also be capable of operating with administrative permissions, thus enabling the program to wreak havoc on the computer and just about anything connected to it.

This was an issue before XP, and the XP programmers tried to solve the problem by creating a second-tier account level called the *limited user*, which had only very basic permissions. Unfortunately, there were three gaping holes in this "solution":

- XP prompted you to create one or more user accounts during setup, but it didn't force you to create one. If you skipped this part, XP started under the Administrator account.

- Even if you elected to create users, the setup program didn't give you an option for setting the account security level. Therefore, any account you created during XP's setup was automatically added to the Administrators group.

- If you created a limited user account, you probably didn't keep it for long because XP hobbled the account so badly that you couldn't use it to do anything but the most basic computer tasks. You couldn't even install most programs because they generally require write permission for the %SystemRoot% folder and the Registry, and limited users lacked that permission.

In Windows Vista, the limited user is gone, and in its place is the least-privileged user, which I talked about in Chapter 11, "More User Account Tweaks."

➤ **See** "Prevent Elevation for All Standard Users," **p. 125**.

In Vista, users are either standard users or administrators, but both types run with standard user privileges. If a user needs to perform an advanced operation such as running the Registry Editor, the user needs to elevate his or her privileges: a standard user must enter an administrator's username and password, whereas an administrator need only click Continue in the UAC dialog box.

What are these users elevating to? They are elevated to the built-in Administrator account, which on a Vista system is all-powerful and can do *anything* to the computer. That's why Vista hides the Administrator account and makes it relatively difficult to access. However, many tweaks require at least temporary use of this account (or, at least, its privileges), and this chapter shows you a few ways to take advantage of this account.

Activate the Administrator Account

Medium

One of the confusing aspects about Windows Vista is that the Administrator account seems to disappear after the setup is complete. That's because, for security reasons, Windows Vista doesn't give you access to this all-powerful account. I should say it doesn't give you *easy* access to this account. The Welcome screen doesn't include an option to choose the Administrator, and no option exists anywhere in the Control Panel's user account windows to enable this account to log on.

That's probably just as well because it keeps most users much safer, but it's annoying for those of us who might occasionally require the Administrator account. For example, tools such as the Windows Automated Installation Kit require that you be logged on with the Administrator account.

Fortunately, you can activate the Administrator account in several ways. Here's a quick look at two of them:

- **Using the Local Security Policy Editor**—Select Start, type `secpol.msc`, press Enter, and then enter your UAC credentials. In the Local Security Policy Editor, open the Local Policies, Security Options branch, and then double-click the Accounts: Administrator Account Status policy. Click Enabled and then click OK.

- **Using the Local Users and Groups snap-in**—Select Start, type `lusrmgr.msc`, press Enter, and then enter your UAC credentials. In the Local Users and Groups snap-in, click Users and then double-click Administrator. In the Administrator Properties dialog box, deactivate the Account Is Disabled check box, as shown in Figure 12.1, and then click OK.

FIGURE 12.1

One way to activate the Administrator account is to use the Local Users and Groups snap-in to open the Administrator Properties dialog box.

These methods suffer from a serious drawback: they don't work in all versions of Windows Vista, in particular Vista Home Basic and Vista Home Premium.

Fortunately, we haven't exhausted all the ways to activate Vista's Administrator account. Here's a method that works with *all* versions of Vista:

1. Select Start, type `command`, right-click Command Prompt, and then click Run as Administrator. The User Account Control dialog box appears.

2. Enter your UAC credentials to continue.

3. At the command line, enter the following command:

   ```
   net user Administrator
   /active:yes
   ```

That's it! Log off and you'll now see the Administrator account in the logon screen, as shown in Figure 12.2.

CAUTION Right now your freshly activated Administrator account has *no* password! Log on as the Administrator and immediately use Control Panel to give the account a strong password.

NOTE When you're done with the Administrator account, be sure to disable it again for security. At an Administrator command prompt, enter the follow command:

```
net user Administrator
/active:no
```

FIGURE 12.2

When you activate the Administrator account, an icon for that account appears in the logon screen.

➜   With the Administrator account active, it's a good idea to rename it; **see** "Rename Built-In Accounts for Better Security," **p. 71**.

Make the Administrator Account More Secure

Medium

If you want to run a lean installation of Windows Vista, you might want to limit the number of user accounts on the system. In fact, you might prefer to use only the built-in accounts: Administrator and Guest. That's fine, but if you're using Administrator as your day-to-day account, you might someday regret not having the extra protection of User Account Control watching out for you.

Fortunately, it's possible to configure some versions of Vista (Business, Enterprise, and Ultimate) to run the Administrator account in *admin approval mode*, which means you see the UAC credential prompts just like any other administrator account.

Here's how to turn on admin approval mode for the Administrator account:

1. Select Start, type `secpol.msc`, and press Enter. If you're currently using an account other than Administrator, the User Account Control dialog box appears.

2. Enter your UAC credentials. The Local Security Policy Editor appears.

3. Open the Local Policies, Security Options branch.

4. Double-click the User Account Control: Admin Approval Mode for the Built-In Administrator Account policy.

5. Click Enabled, as shown in Figure 12.3.

6. Click OK.

FIGURE 12.3

Enable the User Account Control: Admin Approval Mode for the Built-In Administrator Account policy to bring the Administrator account under UAC protection.

Run Command Prompt as the Administrator Automatically

Medium

Lots of Windows Vista tweaks require an elevated Command Prompt session. For example, to use the CONVERT utility to convert a drive to NTFS (as described in Chapter 7, "Keeping the Bad Guys at Bay") requires an elevated command prompt. Similarly, the BCDEDIT tool (see Chapter W3, "Creating Your Own Custom Startup") requires the Administrator account.

➜   **See** "Max Out Security by Encrypting Important Data," **p. 79**.

➜   **See** "Edit the Windows Boot Manager," in the online chapter "Creating Your Own Custom Startup."

As I show you in Chapter 36, "Running the Command Prompt," getting yourself an elevated command line is a relatively simple matter of right-clicking Command Prompt, clicking the Run as Administrator command, and then entering your UAC credentials.

➜   **See** "Running Command Prompt as the Administrator," **p. 427**.

That's not a big deal if you require an elevated command prompt only once in a blue moon, but if it's something you do regularly, it's a hassle to track down the Command Prompt in the Start menu's layers and do the right-click thing. Even if you pin Command Prompt to the main Start menu, you still have to right-click and then click Run as Administrator, and at least half the time you're either going to forget to do this, or you're not going to realize that whatever you're doing requires elevated privileges, and you have to bail out and start again. Finally, this doesn't help you if you use CMD.EXE (Command Prompt's executable file) in other contexts. For example, you learn how to tweak Windows to open any folder in a command prompt session in Chapter 23, "Handy File and Folder Tweaks." The right-click thing doesn't work with that tweak, so you can use it to open any folder in an elevated command prompt session.

To avoid these hassles, it's possible to configure Windows Vista to *always* open Command Prompt in an elevated session. Here are the steps to follow:

1. Select Start, type **regedit**, and press Enter. The User Account Control dialog box appears.

2. Enter your UAC credentials to open the Registry Editor.

> **NOTE** If you don't feel comfortable editing the Registry, there's a file containing the necessary changes—RunCommandPromptElevated.reg—on my website at http://mcfedries.com/cs/content/TweakItFreakIt.aspx.

3. Navigate to the following key:

   HKEY_CURRENT_USER\Software\Microsoft\Windows NT\CurrentVersion\
   ➥AppCompatFlags\Layers

4. Select Edit, New, String Value. The Registry Editor creates a new value
   in the Layers key.

5. Type the following and press Enter (modify the Windows location if
   yours is installed somewhere other than C:\Windows):

   C:\Windows\System32\cmd.exe

6. Double-click the entry you just created. The Edit String dialog box
   appears.

7. Type **RUNASADMIN** and click OK. Figure 12.4 shows the Registry Editor
   with this new setting in place.

FIGURE 12.4
*Modifying the Windows Vista Registry to always run Command Prompt with elevated privi-
leges.*

Run a Script as the Administrator

Medium

When you run scripts in Windows Vista, you may on occasion need to run
those scripts under the auspices of the Administrator account. For example, in
Chapter 34, "Tweaking Windows with the Registry Editor," I show you a script
that toggles the Registry Editor between disabled and enabled, and that script
must be run under the Administrator account.

➜ **See** "Preventing Other Folks from Messing with the Registry," **p. 406**.

Another example is the script that extracts logon failures that I showed you in
Chapter 7. In that example, the technique I used was to start an elevated
command prompt session and run the script from there. That works, but it's a

bit of a hassle. If you run a lot of
Administrator scripts, you'd probably prefer something a lot more direct.

➜   **See** "Sniff Out Logon Failures," **p. 72.**

I'm happy to report that a much more
direct method is available. You can tweak
the Vista file system to display a Run as
Administrator command when you right-
click a VBScript file. Click that command, enter your UAC credentials, and
your script runs with Administrator privileges.

NOTE If you don't feel like
modifying the
Registry by hand, there's a file containing the necessary changes—
VBSFile_RunAsAdminisrator.
reg—on my website at http://
mcfedries.com/cs/content/TweakIt
FreakIt.aspx.

Here's what you do:

1. Select Start, type **regedit**, and press Enter. The User Account Control
   dialog box appears.
2. Enter your UAC credentials to open the Registry Editor.
3. Navigate to the following key:

   HKEY_CLASSES_ROOT\VBSFile\Shell

4. Select Edit, New, Key, type **RunAs**, and press Enter.
5. With the new runas key selected, select Edit, New, Key, type **Command**,
   and press Enter.
6. In the Command key, double-click the (Default) to open the Edit String
   dialog box.
7. Type the following value and click OK (modify the Windows location if
   yours is installed somewhere other than C:\Windows):

   "C:\Windows\System32\WScript.exe" "%1" %*

8. Select Edit, New, String Value. The Registry Editor creates a new value
   in the Layers key.
9. Type **IsolatedCommand** and press Enter.
10. Double-click the entry you just created. The Edit String dialog box
    appears.
11. Type the following value and click OK (again, modify the Windows
    location if yours is installed somewhere other than C:\Windows):

    "C:\Windows\System32\WScript.exe" "%1" %*

Figure 12.5 shows the modified Registry. With these tweaks in place, right-click
a VBScript file and you see the Run as Administrator command, as shown in
Figure 12.6.

FIGURE 12.5

Tweaking the Windows Vista Registry to add the Run as Administrator command to the short-cut menu of any VBScript file.

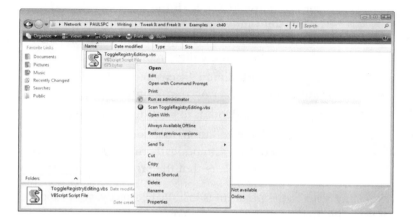

FIGURE 12.6

Right-clicking a VBScript file reveals the new Run as Administrator command.

Install and Run an Older Program as the Administrator

Medium

Programs born P.V. (pre-Vista) don't know a thing about User Account Control, of course, so many of them assume they'll be installed with Administrator privileges. That wasn't a big deal in XP and earlier, but Windows Vista isn't too happy with most of these programs. You'll know that's the case when you get a UAC credentials prompt not only when you install the program, but also every time you *run* the program. This is seriously annoying, but fortunately there's a way to work around it.

First you need to uninstall the program. Once that's done, follow these steps to install it:

1. Locate the executable file that runs the installation program:

   - If you downloaded the installation program, open the folder that contains the download.

   - If you downloaded a Zip archive, extract the files and then open the folder you used for the extraction.

   - If the program comes on a CD or DVD, insert the disc. If the AutoPlay window appears, close it. Select Start, Computer, right-click the disc, and then click Explorer to open the disc's root (top) folder.

> **TIP** If you don't see a likely candidate for the installation program, look for a folder named Setup or Install. If you see more than one possibility, look for a file named autoplay.inf, right-click the file, click Open With, and then click Notepad. In the file, look for the [autorun] section and read the Open line:
>
> [autorun]
> Open=setup.exe

2. Right-click the installation executable and then click Run as Administrator. The User Account Control dialog box appears.

3. Enter your UAC credentials to continue with the installation.

4. At the end of the installation, look for a check box or other option that, when enabled, automatically runs the program. Be sure to *deactivate* this option to ensure that the program doesn't start right away.

Now that your rogue program is installed correctly, your next step is to launch it correctly. Here's what you have to do:

1. Locate the file that starts the program. You can use any of the following:

   - The program's executable file, which you'll find in the folder where you installed the program (look in C:\Program Files).

   - The program's icon in the Start menu's All Programs submenu.

   - The program's icon on the desktop or the Quick Launch toolbar (if you opted to create shortcuts in either place).

2. Right-click the file and then click Run as Administrator. The User Account Control dialog box appears.

3. Enter your UAC credentials to continue starting the program.

CHAPTER 13

Crucial Password Hacks

Computer security is a remarkably fragile thing. You can erect firewalls, encrypt communications, even physically lock your laptop, but in most security situations, there's only one thing sitting between an intruder and your network or computer: a password. In other words, your precious data, your private thoughts, your confidential memos, your secret ideas are protected by just a measly few characters.

That doesn't seem like much of a barrier when you look at it in such a stark light, but it's actually not as bad as all that. Or I should say that it's not as bad as all that *provided* you have a password that's up to the job. A good strong password that can't be guessed at, figured out, or hacked means you've set up an all-but-impenetrable barrier that will keep your data and systems safe.

This chapter is devoted to achieving this optimal password state. You learn not only how to create strong passwords, but also how to enforce good password hygiene among the people whose computing lives you're responsible for.

Bulletproof Your Password

Easy

When you first install or start Windows Vista or Windows XP, the administrator-level account you create doesn't require a password. Given all the security concerns of the past few years, this is more than a little odd. If you didn't bother assigning a password to this account, you should fix this gaping security hole as soon as possible. In fact, it's a good idea to assign passwords to *all* your user accounts on *all* your network computers.

However, it's not enough to just use any old password. You can improve the security of Windows—and, hence, of your entire network—by making each password robust enough that it is impossible to guess and is impervious to software programs designed to try different password combinations. Such a password is called a *strong* password. Ideally, you want to build a password that provides maximum protection while still being easy to remember.

Lots of books will suggest absurdly fancy password schemes (I've written some of those books myself), but there are really only three things you need to know to create strong-like-bull passwords:

- **Use passwords that are at least 8 characters long**—Shorter passwords are susceptible to programs that just try every letter combination. You can combine the 26 letters of the alphabet into about 12 million 5-letter word combinations, which is no big deal for a fast program. If you bump things up to 8-letter passwords, however, the total number of combinations rises to 200 *billion*, which would take even the fastest computer quite a while. If you use 12-letter passwords, as many experts recommend, the number of combinations goes beyond mind-boggling: 90 *quadrillion*, or 90,000 trillion!

- **Mix up your character types**—The secret to a strong password is to include characters from the following categories: lowercase letters, uppercase letters, numbers, and symbols. If you include at least one character from three (or, even better, all four) of these categories, you're well on your way to a strong password.

> **TIP** How will you know whether the password you've come up with fits the definition of *strong*? One way to find out is to submit the password to an online password complexity checker. (If you're the least bit paranoid about these things, consider submitting a password that's only similar to the one you want to use.) I recommend Microsoft's (http://tinyurl.com/cpjh4 or http://www.microsoft.com/protect/yourself/password/checker.mspx), but a Google search on "password complexity checker" will reveal many others.

■ **Don't be too obvious**—Because forgetting a password is inconvenient, many people use meaningful words or numbers so that their password will be easier to remember. Unfortunately, this means that they often use extremely obvious things such as their name, the name of a family member or colleague, their birth date, their Social Security number, or even their system username. Being this obvious is just asking for trouble.

MANAGING MULTIPLE LOGINS

If you read books or websites devoted to security, almost every single one will offer the same two bits of password advice:

- Use a different password for every site or account that requires one.
- Don't write down your passwords.

If you're like me, you probably have dozens of logins: email accounts, social networking sites, blogging tools, and on and on. Sorry, but nobody with a life can manage dozens of different passwords, and anyone who goes that far can't possibly remember them all, so they must be written down. In other words, the sage advice of the security gurus isn't worth spit in the real world.

My solution is to come up with a small set of password tokens—short (4 to 6 characters long) strings of letters or numbers that you can easily remember. Here's a sample set: Mgmt, Feist, Sloan, 1357, 2468. Combine these tokens to create your passwords: Mgmt1357, Sloan2468, and so on. How do you remember? Assign a symbol to each token. For example: ! for Mgmt, * for Fiest, ^ for Sloan, # for 1357, and ## for 2468. Now, for each site and account, write down (go ahead, it's okay) the symbols that correspond to the tokens you used for the password. If a site's password is Mgmt1357, write down the site name followed by !#; if an account's password is Sloan2468, write down the account name followed by ^##.

Set a Minimum Password Length and Strength

Medium

Okay, so you know how to create a strong password, and you can certainly pass along that information to the other people in your home or business, but how can you be sure that they'll take up the strong password gospel?

The truth is you can't, and surveys of password use over the years have been remarkably consistent: most users are lazy and they prefer to use simple passwords that are easy to remember. If the user operates a standalone PC, it's their funeral. But it's more likely these days that the user is part of a network, and a brain-dead password puts not only that PC at risk, but it puts the entire network at risk.

If it's *your* network you're worried about, you can take matters into your own hands and set up password policies that ensure your users protect their PCs with strong passwords. There are two policies you can implement:

- **Minimum Password Length**—This policy sets the minimum number of characters for the password. You enter a value that represents the number of characters, and that value can be as high as 14 or as low as 1. (If you use 0, it means no password is required.) A good choice here is 8.

- **Password Must Meet Complexity Requirements**—If you enable this policy, Windows examines each new password and accepts it only if it meets the following criteria: It doesn't contain all or part of the person's username; it's at least six characters long; and it contains characters from three of the following four categories: uppercase letters, lowercase letters, digits (0–9), and nonalphanumeric characters (such as $ and #).

NOTE If you set the Minimum Password Length policy to a value between 0 and 5, and you enable the Password Must Meet Complexity Requirements policy, the latter policy takes priority and the minimum password length is six characters. If you set the Minimum Password Length policy to a value between 7 and 14, and you enable the Password Must Meet Complexity Requirements policy, the former policy takes priority and Windows uses its value as the minimum password length.

NOTE These steps require the Local Security Policy Editor, which is available only with Vista Business, Vista Enterprise, Vista Ultimate, and XP Professional. There's no other way to specify password strength, but you can set a minimum password length using Command Prompt, as I discuss as I discuss later in this section.

Follow these steps to implement these policies:

1. Log on to the computer you want to work with.

2. In Windows Vista, select Start, type `secpol.msc`, press Enter, and then enter your administrator's credentials to continue. (In XP, select Start, Run, type `secpol.msc`, and then click OK.) The Local Security Policy Editor appears.

3. Open the Account Policies branch.

4. Click the Password Policy branch.

5. Double-click the Minimum Password Age policy to open its property sheet.

6. Use the Password Must Be at Least spin box to set the minimum number of characters in any password, as shown in Figure 13.1, and then click OK.

7. Double-click the Password Must Meet Complexity Requirements policy.

8. Click Enabled and then click OK.

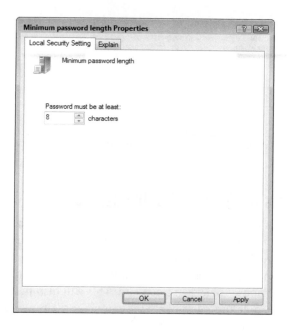

FIGURE 13.1

In the Minimum Password Length policy property sheet, use the spin box to set the minimum number of characters in any password.

You can also set the minimum password length at the command prompt, which is great if you're working on a Vista Home, Vista Home Premium, or XP Home machine. Here's how:

1. Log on to the computer you want to work with.

2. In Windows Vista, select Start, type **cmd.exe**, right-click cmd.exe in the results, click Run as Administrator, and then enter your administrator's

CAUTION These passwords have no effect on any existing passwords. They apply only when you set a password on a new account or when you change a password on an existing account.

credentials to continue. (In XP, select Start, Run, type **cmd.exe**, and then click OK.) The Command Prompt window appears.

3. Enter the following command, changing *n* to the minimum length you want to use:

```
net accounts /maxpwlen:n
```

With these policies in effect, if users try to change their password to something weak, they see the dialog box shown in Figure 13.2.

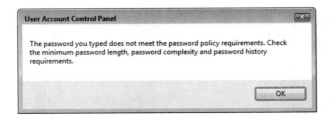

FIGURE 13.2
Users see a dialog box like this one if their new password isn't up to snuff.

Require Users to Change Their Passwords

Medium

When you create a user on a Windows system, it's a good idea to assign a password to the new account. You could just ask the user to use that password (and, as you see at the end of this section, it's possible to prevent the user from changing the password). However, most people are more comfortable if they can choose their own password. This will also help you in the long run because people are more likely to remember their own password, so you'll get fewer "I forgot my password!" calls.

One common practice is to assign a standard password—usually the word password or the person's username—and then tell the user to change it. That's fine, but can you be sure the user will do that? No, of course not! Therefore, you can rest easier at night by forcing the user to do so.

A quick tweak of the user's account is all you need here:

1. In Windows Vista, select Start, type **lusrmgr.msc**, press Enter, and then enter your administrator's credentials to continue. (In XP, select Start, Run, type **lusrmgr.msc**, and then click OK.) The Local Users and Groups snap-in appears.

2. Click Users.

3. Double-click the user you want to work with.

4. If the Password Never Expires check box is activated, click it to deactivate it.

5. Activate the User Must Change Password at Next Logon check box, as shown in Figure 13.3.

NOTE These steps require the Local Users and Groups snap-in, which is available only with Vista Business, Vista Enterprise, Vista Ultimate, and XP Professional. No workaround exists for Vista Home, Vista Home Premium, or XP Home.

FIGURE 13.3

To force a user to change a temporary password, activate the User Must Change Password at Next Logon check box.

6. Click OK.

The next time the user logs on, he'll see a message that he is required to change his password. The user must click OK and then enter his new password.

If you want to bypass the Local Users and Groups snap-in, you can perform the same operation with the script shown in Listing 13.1.

NOTE The file containing the script in Listing 13.1—ExpirePassword.vbs—is available from my website at http://mcfedries.com/cs/content/TweakItFreakIt.aspx.

Listing 13.1   A Script That Expires a User's Password to Force a Password Change

```
Option Explicit
Dim objWshNetwork, strComputer, strUser, objUser
'
' Get the Network object
'
Set objWshNetwork = CreateObject("WScript.Network" )
'
' Get the name of the current computer
'
strComputer = objWshNetwork.ComputerName
'
' Get the user
'
strUser = InputBox("Type the name of the user:")
'
' Make sure we have a name before proceeding
'
If strUser <> "" Then
    Set objUser = GetObject("WinNT://" & strComputer & "/" & strUser)
    '
    ' Expire the user's password
    '
    objUser.Put "PasswordExpired", 1
    '
    ' Put the new setting into effect
    '
    objUser.SetInfo
    '
    ' Display a message
    '
    WScript.Echo "The password for " & objUser.FullName & " is now
expired."
End If
```

This script prompts for the username, returns the user as an object, and then sets the user object's PasswordExpired property to True. Note that you must run this script as the Administrator, as described in Chapter 12, "Taking Advantage of the Administrator Account."

➜   **See** "Run a Script as the Administrator," **p. 141.**

PREVENTING USERS FROM CHANGING THEIR PASSWORDS

If you've gone to the trouble of supplying a user with a strong password, you may not want him or her to change it and possibly compromise security. There are a couple of ways you can set this up. To use the Local Users and Groups snap-in, follow steps 1 to 3 in this section, and then activate the User Cannot Change Password check box. You can also apply this tweak from the command line. In Windows Vista, select Start, type **cmd.exe**, right-click cmd.exe in the results, click Run as Administrator, and then enter your administrator's credentials to continue. (In XP, select Start, Run, type **cmd.exe**, and then click OK.) Enter the following command:

```
net user username /passwordchg:no
```

Be sure to replace *username* with the name of the user.

Prevent People from Reusing Old Passwords

Medium

In the previous tweak I showed you how to force a user to change his or her password at the next logon. Ah, but you may have noticed that there's a rather large fly in this particular soup: the user might just enter the same password! You'd think that Windows would see that and prevent the user from doing this but, no, Windows just blithely "changes" the password and allows the user to log on. Dumb!

To prevent this, you need to implement a policy called Enforce Password History. This policy determines the number of old passwords that Windows stores for each user. By "remembering" previous passwords, Windows is able to prevent a user from reusing an old password. For example, if you set this value to 10, the user can't reuse a password until he or she has used at least 10 other passwords.

Follow these steps to implement this policy:

1. Log on to the computer you want to work with.

2. In Windows Vista, select Start, type **secpol.msc**, press Enter, and then enter your administrator's credentials to continue. (In XP, select Start,

NOTE These steps require the Local Security Policy Editor, which is available only with Vista Business, Vista Enterprise, Vista Ultimate, and XP Professional. For other versions of Vista and XP, you can enforce password history using Command Prompt, as I discuss next.

Run, type `secpol.msc`, and then click OK.) The Local Security Policy Editor appears.

3. Open the Account Policies branch.

4. Click the Password Policy branch.

5. Double-click the Enforce Password History policy to open its property sheet.

6. Use the Keep Password History for X Passwords Remembered spin box to set the number of unique passwords the user must enter, as shown in Figure 13.4, and then click OK. Enter a number between 0 and 24.

7. Click OK.

FIGURE 13.4
In the Enforce Password History Properties sheet, use the spin box to set the number of pass-words that Windows saves for each user.

You can also enable password history at the command prompt, which is great if you're working on a Vista Home, Vista Home Premium, or XP Home machine. Here's how:

1. Log on to the computer you want to work with.

2. In Windows Vista, select Start, type `cmd.exe`, right-click cmd.exe in the results, click Run as Administrator, and then enter your administrator's

credentials to continue. (In XP, select Start, Run, type `cmd.exe`, and then click OK.) The Command Prompt window appears.

3. Enter the following command, changing *n* to the number of passwords you want Windows to save:

```
net accounts /uniquepw:n
```

With this policy in effect, if users try to reuse a password that's stored in their password history, they see the message shown in Figure 13.5.

FIGURE 13.5

Users see this message if they try to reuse an old password that's saved in their password history.

Recover from a Forgotten Password

Vista

Medium

Few things in life are as frustrating as a forgotten password. To avoid this headache, Windows Vista offers a couple of precautions that you can take now in case you forget your password.

The first precaution is called the password hint, which is a word, phrase, or other mnemonic device that can help you remember your password. To see the hint in the Welcome screen, type any password and press Enter. When Vista tells you the password is incorrect, click OK. Vista redisplays the Password text box with the hint below it.

The second precaution you can take is the Password Reset Disk. This is a USB flash drive or floppy disk that enables you to reset the password on your account without knowing the old password. To create a Password Reset Disk, follow these steps:

> **TIP** To add a password hint to an account, press Windows Logo+R to open the Run dialog box, type `control nusrmgr.cpl`, and click OK. Click the Manage Another Account link and then enter your UAC credentials to continue. Click the user, click Change the Password, enter the existing password (twice), and then fill in the Type a Password Hint text box.

1. Log on as the user for whom you want to create the disk.

2. Press Windows Logo+R to open the Run dialog box, type `control nusrmgr.cpl`, and click OK.

3. In the Tasks pane, click Create a Password Reset Disk. This launches the Forgotten Password Wizard.

4. Insert the flash drive or floppy disk. (If you're going the floppy route, note that you'll need a blank, formatted disk.)

5. Click Next. The Create a Password Reset Disk dialog box appears.

6. Select the drive that contains the flash disk, or drive A if you're using a floppy disk.

7. Click Next. The Current User Account Password dialog box appears.

8. Type the current user's password and click Next. Windows Vista creates the password reset disk.

9. Click Next.

10. Click Finish.

The password reset disk contains a single file named `Userkey.psw`, which is an encrypted backup version of your password. Be sure to save this disk in a secure location and, just to be safe, don't label the disk. If you need to use this disk, follow these steps:

1. Start Windows Vista normally.

2. When you get to the Welcome screen, leave your password blank and press the Enter key. Windows Vista will then tell you the password is incorrect.

3. Click OK.

4. Click the Reset Password link.

5. In the initial Password Reset Wizard dialog box, click Next.

6. Insert the password reset disk, select the drive, and click Next.

7. In the Reset the User Account Password dialog box (see Figure 13.6), type a new password (twice), type a password hint, and click Next.

8. Click Finish.

FIGURE 13.6

You can use a password reset disk to recover from a forgotten password.

CHAPTER

14

General Performance Tweaks

Our computers are never as fast as we'd like them to be, and it's a rare day when you're not twiddling your thumbs waiting for Windows to complete some task. Part of the reason for this is that, let's face facts, we're spoiled. Computers perform most tasks in a fraction of the blink of an eye, and the majority of the rest take at most a few seconds. So when something takes *10* seconds (groan!) or even *20* seconds (#$%^@! computer!), impatience sets in. The wait *seems* interminable, but we're talking about a vanishingly small amount of time in the overall scheme of things.

Too philosophical? I thought as much. Not to worry, there are lots of ways you can speed up Windows. There's nothing you can do to make Windows perform every task in a fraction of the blink of an eye, but there's plenty you can do to shave a few seconds here and a few seconds there, as the tweaks in this chapter show.

IN THIS CHAPTER

- Start Faster by Disabling the Windows Startup GUI
- Save Time by Logging On Automatically
- Speed Up a Program by Changing Its Execution Priority
- Open Files and Folders with a Click
- Disable Services for Faster Performance
- Make Windows Shut Down Services Faster

Start Faster by Disabling the Windows Startup GUI

Easy

Windows startup is always frustratingly slow, and I'm afraid there's not a lot you can do to change that. Windows just naturally takes an awfully long time to pull itself up by its own bootstraps. Every little bit helps, however, and in this tweak I show you how to shave a couple of seconds of your boot times by disabling the otherwise useless graphics that Windows displays as part of its setup routine.

> **NOTE** You should also activate the No GUI Boot check box if Windows hangs while switching video modes for the progress bar, or if the display of the progress bar is garbled.

Here are the steps to follow to boot Windows without graphics:

1. In Windows Vista, select Start, type `msconfig`, press Enter, and then enter your UAC credentials. (In Windows XP, select Start, Run to open the Run dialog box, type `msconfig`, and then click OK. The System Configuration Utility window appears.

2. Select the Boot tab.

3. Activate the No GUI Boot check box, as shown in Figure 14.1. This tells Windows not to load the VGA display driver that is normally used to display the progress bar during startup.

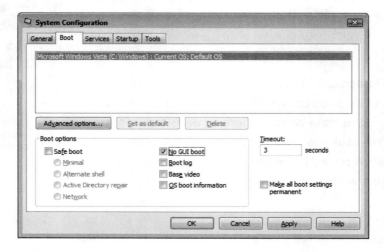

FIGURE 14.1

In the System Configuration Utility's Boot tab, activate the No GUI Boot check box.

4. Click OK. Windows tells you that the new configuration requires a reboot.

5. Save your work, shut down your running programs, and then click Restart.

➔ You can also speed up Windows boots by disabling some of the programs that launch automatically at startup. **See** "Prevent Programs from Starting Automatically," **p. 388**.

Save Time by Logging On Automatically

Medium

In Chapter 13, "Crucial Password Hacks," I argued that a password is all that stands between you and an intruder trying to get his grubby hands on your data. With a strong password associated with your user account, any snoop with hands-on access to your computer will be thwarted at the Windows logon screen because he doesn't know, can't guess, and can't hack your password.

In this tweak, we throw all that out the window! That is, I'm going to show you how to configure Windows to log your account onto the computer automatically. This means you bypass the logon screen and get access to the desktop without any interaction on your part.

This is a faster way to boot because you bypass having to enter your password, and it's a more convenient way to boot because you can turn on your computer first thing, go grab a coffee or whatever, and then sit right down to your desktop when you get back.

On the downside, this tweak has a couple of negatives:

- If *you* get direct post-boot access to your desktop, so will anyone else. That is, anyone can sit down at your computer, turn it on, and then start messing with your stuff after the boot smoke clears.

- If you have other users on your computer, they can't log on from system startup, unless you hold down Shift while Windows boots (see the Tip that follows).

However, if security isn't a big deal for you, and if you're the only user of your PC, by all means set up an automatic logon, as described in the following steps:

1. In Windows Vista, select Start, type `control userpasswords2`, press Enter, and then enter your UAC credentials. (In Windows XP, select Start, Run to open the Run dialog box, type `control userpasswords2`, and then click OK. The User Accounts dialog box appears.

2. Display the Users tab.

3. Click your username (or the name of whichever user you want to automatically log on).

4. Deactivate the Users Must Enter a User Name and Password to Use this Computer check box, as shown in Figure 14.2.

FIGURE 14.2

Use the User Accounts dialog box to configure an automatic logon.

5. Click OK. The Automatically Log On dialog box appears. The username you clicked in step 3 is filled in automatically.

6. Type the user's password into the Password and Confirm Password text boxes.

7. Click OK.

The next time you start your PC, Windows logs on your account automatically.

TIP If you have other accounts on your system, you can still log on one of them at startup if need be. Restart your computer and, after the various BIOS messages are done, press and Hold the Shift key. This tells Windows to bypass the automatic logon and display the logon screen.

Speed Up a Program by Changing Its Execution Priority

Medium

Windows treats all programs equally, but there's a tweak you can perform to make Windows treat some programs as more equal than others. That is, you can improve the performance of a program by adjusting the priority given to the program by your computer's processor. The processor enables programs to run by doling out thin slivers of its computing time to each program. These time slivers are called *cycles* because they are given to programs cyclically. For example, if you have three programs running—A, B, and C—the processor gives a cycle to A, one to B, another to C, and then another to A again. This cycling happens quickly, appearing seamless when you work with each program.

> **TIP** To bypass the Windows Security screen, either press Ctrl+Shift+Esc, or right-click an empty section of the taskbar and click Task Manager.

The *base priority* is the ranking that determines the relative frequency with which a program gets processor cycles. A program given a higher frequency gets more cycles, which improves the program's performance. For example, suppose that you raise the priority of program A. The processor might give a cycle to A, one to B, another to A, one to C, another to A, and so on.

Follow these steps to change a program's priority:

1. Launch the program you want to work with.

2. Press Ctrl+Alt+Delete to open the Windows Security screen and then click the Start Task Manager link.

3. Display the Processes tab.

4. Right-click your application's process to display its shortcut menu.

5. Click Set Priority, and then click (from highest priority to lowest) Realtime, High, or Above Normal, as shown in Figure 14.3. Task Manager warns you that changing a program's priority could cause system instability.

6. Click Change Priority (in Windows XP, click Yes).

> **TIP** After you've changed the priority of one or more programs, you might forget the values that you have assigned to each one. To help, you can view the priority for all the items in the Processes tab. Click View and then click Select Columns to display the Select Columns dialog box. Activate the Base Priority check box and click OK. This adds a Base Priority column to the Processes list.

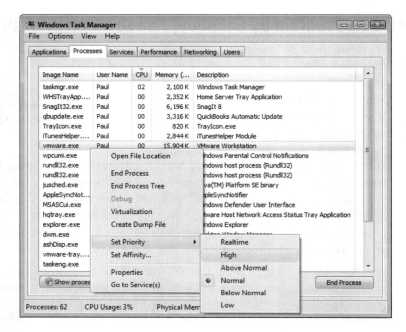

FIGURE 14.3
To speed up a program, set it base priority to Realtime, High, or Above Normal.

Open Files and Folders with a Click

 You can open files and folders more quickly and consistently by customizing Windows to open items with a single mouse click instead of a double-click.

Easy

Double-clicking isn't a difficult skill to learn, but it can be hard to master. Even experienced mouse users—particularly when they're in a hurry—get their timing incorrect or move the mouse slightly so that the double-click doesn't take. So opening files and folders with a single-click is not only faster but also more efficient. This has the added advantage of making Windows more consistent; for example, you already open items on the Start menu with a single-click.

Yet another advantage you get with configuring single-clicking is that it makes Windows more weblike:

- **"Clickable" Windows objects look like web page links**—In most web pages, links have two main characteristics: the link text appears under-lined, and when you position the mouse over a link, the mouse pointer changes to a small hand with a pointing finger. You get the same effect when you turn on single-clicking: icon titles and filenames are underlined, and the mouse pointer changes to a hand when you position it over an icon or filename.

CAUTION Until you get used to the new single-click metaphor (which doesn't take long), you'll occasionally lapse into the old ways and try to select an object by clicking it. This, of course, launches the object, which can have disastrous consequences. For example, if you accidentally launch a registration (.reg) file, it will update the Windows Registry, which could lead to problems.

- **You single-click to launch icons and programs**—Web page links require just a single click to activate them, and single-clicking brings the same idea to Windows. That is, you can launch icons and files by single-clicking them instead of the usual double-clicking required in the classic Windows interface.

- **You select objects by hovering the mouse over them**—You normally select an object by clicking it. With single-clicking turned on, you select an object by positioning the mouse pointer over the object for a second or two (this is called *hovering* over the object). To select multiple objects, hover over the first object to select it, then hold down Ctrl and hover over each of the rest of the objects. If the objects are contiguous, hover over the first object, then hold down Shift and hover over the last object.

To control these settings, follow these steps:

1. In Windows Vista, select Start, type `control folders`, and press Enter. (In Windows XP, select Start, Run to open the Run dialog box, type `control folders`, and then click OK. The Folder Options dialog box appears.

2. Select the General tab.

3. Activate the Single-Click to Open an Item (Point to Select) check box, as shown in Figure 14.4. By activating this settings, you're telling Windows that single-clicks launch objects, and hovering selects objects.

4. Choose how Windows underlines objects:

   - **Underline Icon Titles Consistent with My Browser Settings**—If you activate this option, Windows underlines icon and file links the same way that Internet Explorer is set up to underline web page links. This usually means that Windows underlines everything that's clickable. This is often a good way to go at the beginning, because it gives you a strong visual clue that single-clicking is activated, so you'll be less likely to launch icons and files accidentally.

FIGURE 14.4
In the Folder Options dialog box, activate the Single-Click to Open an Item (Point to Select) check box.

> ■ **Underline Icon Titles Only When I Point at Them**—If you activate this option, Windows doesn't underline any clickable objects until you point at one. This is a good choice after you get used to single-clicking, because it gives you a cleaner interface and having only one thing underlined at a time makes it more obvious which object you're clicking or selecting.

   5. Click OK to put the new settings into effect.

Disable Services for Faster Performance

Medium

Windows comes with dozens of programs called *services* that operate behind the scenes and perform essential tasks either on their own or in support of other programs or Windows features. Because services are software, they run in memory and so take up a small chunk of your system's resources. Any one service doesn't affect performance all that much, but load up a bunch of them and your PC slows down noticeably.

Windows understands this, so many services don't run automatically at startup. Instead, the services run only when you or a program requests them. So you can improve Windows performance by doing two things:

- Prevent Windows from automatically starting some services at boot time.

- Prevent Windows from starting other services that you don't need.

In both cases, you do this by disabling those services that you don't (or *think* you don't) need. First, here are the general steps to follow to disable a service:

1. Select Start, type **services.msc**, press Enter, and then enter your UAC credentials. (In Windows XP, select Start, Run, type **services.msc**, and click OK). The Services window appears.

2. Double-click the service you want to disable.

3. In the General tab, drop down the Startup Type list and select Disabled, as shown in Figure 14.5.

FIGURE 14.5

Open a service and then choose Disabled in the Startup Type list.

4. Click OK.

That's easy enough, but the hard part is knowing which services are okay to disable. To help out, Table 14.1 presents a list of the Windows services that you may be able to disable. None of these services are required by other services, so disabling any

NOTE Whether you see many of the services in Table 14.1 depends on which version of Windows you're running. For example, you don't see many of these services if you're using Vista Home Basic, Vista Home Premium, or XP Home.

of these won't break something else. However, I suggest caution: disable one at a time, reboot, and make sure Windows seems to be operating normally. Also, if your PC is part of a corporate network, you might want to get permission or guidance from your IT department before disabling any services.

Table 14.1   Windows Services You Might Consider Disabling

Service	Startup Type	Disable If...
Application Management	Manual	You don't deploy software using Group Policy.
Block Level Backup Engine Service	Manual	You don't use Windows Vista's built-in Backup service.
Certificate Propagation	Manual	You don't use smart cards.
Computer Browser	Automatic	You're willing to refresh the Network window by hand (because this service looks for network computers automatically).
Desktop Window Manager Session Manager	Automatic	You don't use Vista's Aero theme.
DFS Replication	Manual	You don't need to synchronize folders on multiple servers or across a network.
Diagnostic Policy Service	Automatic	You don't need Windows components to access the built-in diagnostic services (problem detection and troubleshooting).
Diagnostic Service Host	Manual	Same as above.
Diagnostic System Host	Manual	Ditto.
Distributed Transaction Coordinator	Manual	You're not running software that requires transaction processing (which is restricted to big-time corporate services such as transactional databases).
Fax	Manual	You don't use your PC for faxing.
Health Key and Certificate Management	Manual	You don't use any software that requires X.509 cryptographic certificates.
IKE and AuthIP IPsec Keying Modules	Automatic	You don't use high-end Internet security protocols.
Internet Connection Sharing (ICS)	Disabled	You don't allow other computers to share your Internet connection.
IP Helper	Automatic	You don't use the latest version of the Internet Protocol (IPv6), which is almost certainly the case (IPv4 still being the standard).
IPsec Policy Agent	Automatic	You don't implement any group policies that require Internet Protocol security (IPsec).

Service	Startup Type	Disable If...
KtmRm for Distributed Transaction Coordinator	Automatic	You don't use databases or other resources that require the Microsoft Distributed Transaction Coordinator (which is needed only by corporate systems).
Link-Layer Topology Discovery Mapper	Manual	You never use Vista's Network Map feature.
Microsoft iSCSI Initiator Service	Manual	You don't use any remote SCSI devices.
Microsoft Software Shadow Copy Provider	Manual	You don't need to access the volume shadow copies (essentially, file and folder snapshots) to revert objects to a previous state.
Net.Tcp Port Sharing Service	Disabled	You don't (or your applications don't) need to share TCP ports.
Netlogon	Manual	You don't use a domain controller.
Network Access Protection Agent	Manual	Your network doesn't have a server that implements Network Access Protection.
Offline Files	Automatic	You never use network files while not connected to the network.
Parental Controls	Manual	You don't use Vista's Parental Controls feature.
Peer Name Resolution Protocol	Manual	You don't use collaborative applications such as Windows Meeting Space.
Peer Networking Grouping	Manual	Same as above.
Peer Networking Identity Manager	Manual	Ditto.
Performance Logs and Alerts	Manual	You don't use performance logs and alerts.
PnP-X IP Bus Enumerator	Manual	You don't mind that Windows doesn't show external network devices automatically.
PNRP Machine Name Publication Service	Manual	You don't run any programs that require the Peer Name Resolution Protocol.
Print Spooler	Automatic	You don't print.
Problem Reports and Solutions Control Panel Support	Manual	You don't use Vista's Problem Reports and Solutions feature.
Program Compatibility Assistant Service	Automatic	You don't run applications using compatibility mode.
Quality Windows Audio Video Experience	Manual	You don't stream audio or video on your home network.
ReadyBoost	Automatic	You don't use Vista's ReadyBoost feature.
Remote Registry	Manual	You don't need to allow network computers to connect to your PC's Registry.

Continues

Table 14.1   Continued

Service	Startup Type	Disable If...
Security Center	Automatic	You don't need to use the Security Center to monitor your PC's security status.
Smart Card	Manual	You don't use smart cards.
Smart Card Removal Policy	Manual	Same as above.
SNMP Trap	Manual	Your network doesn't use any Simple Network Management Protocol (SNMP) programs.
SuperFetch	Automatic	You don't want Windows to use the SuperFetch cache to improve performance (as described in Chapter 1, "Vital Performance Tweaks").

➤   **See** "Boost Vista Performance Using a Flash Drive," **p. 10**.

Service	Startup Type	Disable If...
Tablet PC Input Service	Automatic	Your computer isn't a TabletPC.
Task Scheduler	Automatic	You don't use Task Scheduler.
Themes	Automatic	You don't use themes to customize your PC.
TPM Base Services	Manual	You don't use Vista's BitLocker drive encryption.
Windows Backup	Manual	You don't use Windows Backup.
Windows CardSpace	Manual	You don't use a CardSpace digital ID.
Windows Defender	Automatic	You use an antispyware program other than Windows Defender.
Windows Error Reporting Service	Automatic	You don't send error data to Microsoft.
Windows Media Center Extender Service	Disabled	You don't use a Media Center Extender device.
Windows Media Center Receiver Service	Manual	You don't use Windows to play TV or radio signals.
Windows Media Center Scheduler Service	Manual	You don't use Media Center to record TV shows.
Windows Media Center Service Launcher	Automatic	You've disabled the previous two services. (This service launches the previous two services at startup if your computer has a TV tuner card.)
Windows Media Player Network Sharing Service	Manual	You don't share your Media Player library.
Windows Search	Automatic	You don't use Vista's desktop search engine (or you use another, such as Google Desktop Search).
WMI Performance Adapter	Manual	You don't have any network programs that use Windows Management Instrumentation (WMI) to performance data.

Make Windows Shut Down Services Faster

Medium

If it seems to take Windows forever to shut down, the culprit might be all those services that it has running because Windows has to shut down each service one by one before it can shut down the PC. In each case, Windows waits a certain amount of time for the service to close, and if it hasn't closed in that time, Windows kills the service. It's that waiting for services to shut themselves down that can really bring the shutdown process to its knees.

However, most services shut down as soon as they get the command from Windows. So although it's polite of Windows to give some services a bit of extra time, it's really wasted time because in most cases Windows is just going to have to kill those slow services anyway. So in that case, you should tweak Windows to tell it to kill services faster. Here's how:

1. Select Start, type **regedit**, press Enter, and then enter your UAC credentials. (In Windows XP, select Start, Run, type **regedit**, and click OK.) The Registry Editor appears.

2. Navigate to the following key:

   `HKLM\SYSTEM\CurrentControlSet\Control`

3. Double-click the `WaitToKillServiceTimeout` setting.

4. Reduce the value from 20000 to 1000.

5. Click OK.

> **TIP** You can also reduce the amount of time that Windows waits before killing running applications at shutdown. In the Registry Editor, navigate to the following key:
>
> `HKCU\Control Panel\Desktop`
>
> Double-click the `WaitToKillAppTimeout` setting. (If you don't see this setting, select Edit, New, String Value, type **WaitToKillAppTimeout**, and click OK.) Change the value to **5000**, and click OK.

Streamlining the Start Menu

The whole purpose of the Start menu is, as its name implies, to start things, particularly programs and documents. Yes, you can also launch these objects via shortcut icons on the desktop, but that's not a great alternative because windows cover the desktop most of the time. So, if you want to get something going in Windows, the vast majority of the time you're going to have to do it via the Start menu. The good news is that the Start menu is wonderfully flexible and geared, in fact, to launching objects with as few mouse clicks or keystrokes as possible. To get to that state, however, you have to work with a few relatively obscure options and settings, which you'll learn about in this chapter.

Pin a Program to the Start Menu for Easy Access

Easy

The left side of the Start menu displays the *favorite programs list*, which includes the shortcut icons for the nine programs that you've used most frequently, plus the Internet and E-mail icons at the top. The latter two are fixed in place, so this part of the Start menu is called the *pinned programs list*.

The Start menu's list of favorite programs is such a time-saving feature that it can be frustrating if a program drops off the list. Another aggravation is that the icons often change position because Windows displays the programs in order of popularity. When you display the Start menu, this constant shifting of icons can result in a slight hesitation while you look for the icon you want. (This is particularly true if you've expanded the maximum number of icons.) Contrast both of these problems with the blissfully static nature of the pinned programs list's Internet and E-mail icons, which are always where you need them, when you need them.

You can get the same effect with other shortcuts by adding—or *pinning*—them to the pinned programs list. To do this, first open the Start menu and find the shortcut you want to work with. Then you have two choices:

- Right-click the shortcut and then click Pin to Start Menu.
- Drag the shortcut and drop it in the pinned programs list.

You can also use this technique to pin shortcuts residing on the desktop to the pinned programs lists. If you decide later that you no longer want a shortcut pinned to the Start menu, right-click the shortcut and then click Unpin from Start Menu.

TIP To expand the number of icons that Windows displays in the Start menu, right-click Start, click Properties, and then click the Customize button that's beside the Start Menu option. Use the Number of Recent Programs to Display spin box to specify the number of favorite programs you want to display. If you don't think you have enough screen space to display all the icons, deactivate the Large Icons option (in Vista, it's at the bottom of the list of Start menu features). This significantly reduces the amount of space each icon takes up on the Start menu.

TIP When you display the Start menu, you can select an item quickly by pressing the first letter of the item's name. If you add several shortcuts to the pinned programs list, however, you might end up with more than one item that begins with the same letter. To avoid conflicts, rename each of these items so that they begin with a number. For example, renaming "Backup" to "1 Backup" means you can select this item by pressing 1 when the Start menu is displayed. (To rename a Start menu item, right-click the item and then click Rename.)

Convert Start Menu Links to Menus

Easy

The right side of the Start menu contains a number of built-in Windows features, which are set up as links. That is, you click an item, and a window or a program runs in response. That's fine for items such as Search or Help and Support, but it's not very efficient for an item such as Control Panel where you're usually looking to launch a specific icon. It seems wasteful to have to open the Control Panel window, locate the icon, launch it, and then close Control Panel.

A better approach is to convert a link into a menu of items that would normally display in a separate window. For example, the Control Panel item could display a menu of its icons. One of the nicer features in Windows is that it's easy to convert many of the Start menu links into menus. Here are the required steps:

1. Right-click the Start menu and then click Properties to display the Taskbar and Start Menu Properties dialog box.

2. Select the Start Menu tab, make sure the Start Menu option is activated, and then click the Customize button to its right to open the Customize Start Menu dialog box.

3. In Windows XP, select the Advanced tab.

4. In the list of Start menu items, find the following items and activate the Display as a Menu option:

   Computer (My Computer in XP)

   Control Panel

   Documents (My Documents in XP)

   Games (Vista only)

   Music (My Music in XP)

   Personal folder (your username)

   Pictures (My Pictures in XP)

   Network Connections (XP only)

5. Activate the Favorites Menu check box to add a menu of your Internet Explorer favorites to the Start menu.

6. In the Start Menu Items group, find the System Administrative Tools item and activate the Display on the All Programs Menu and the Start Menu option. This gives you an Administrative Tools menu that offers shortcuts to features such as Computer Management, Device Manager, System Configuration, and the Local Security Policy editor.

7. (XP only) Make sure that the List My Most Recent Documents check box is activated. This adds the My Recent Documents menu to the Start menu, which displays the last 15 documents that you worked with.

> **CAUTION** If other people have access to your user account, you might want to bypass showing the Recent Items (in Vista) or My Recent Documents (in XP) menu for privacy reasons.

8. Click OK to return to the Taskbar and Start Menu Properties dialog box.

9. (Vista only) Make sure that the Store and Display a List of Recently Opened Files check box is activated. This adds the Recent Items menu to the Start menu, which displays the last 15 documents that you worked with.

10. Click OK.

Make the Start Menu Appear More Quickly

Medium

If you're into the instant gratification thing, this tweak's for you. When you press the Windows Logo key, you might notice a slight delay before the Start menu appears. You also get delays when you hover the mouse over a menu item within the Start menu system. If you want your menus to appear right away, your wish is Windows' command. Here's what you do:

1. Select Start, type `regedit`, press Enter, and then enter your UAC credentials. (In Windows XP, select Start, Run, type `regedit`, and click OK.) The Registry Editor appears.

2. Navigate to the following key:

    HKCU\Control panel\Desktop

3. Double-click the MenuShowDelay setting.

4. Reduce the value from 400 to 5.

5. Click OK.

6. Restart your PC to put the new setting into effect.

Prevent the Start Menu from Highlighting New Programs

Easy

One of the hardest things that novice Windows users have to figure out is where things end up on their systems. When they download a program, extract a file from an archive, or save a document attached to an email message, the resulting file ends up *somewhere*, and new users often have trouble finding it. This is also true when novices install a program. The setup routine seems to proceed without any fuss, but when it's over the inexperienced user is often left staring at the same old desktop (unless the installation program added a desktop icon), with no clue about where the installed program "went."

Windows attempts to solve this mystery by highlighting new additions to the Start menu, as shown in Figures 15.1 and 15.2. Novices can then follow the highlights to locate their new program. This is a useful idea, and it seems to help the inexperienced, and anything that makes Windows less impenetrable to the uninitiated is okay in my books.

FIGURE 15.1
Windows XP lets users know when new programs have been added to the Start menu.

FIGURE 15.2

Both Windows Vista (shown here) and Windows XP highlight newly added Start menu items.

However, it's not always okay on *my* PC. Like me, you may find the Start menu highlights annoying, distracting, and unnecessary because as an experienced user you *know* where programs go when you install them. Fortunately, you can configure Windows to not highlight new programs on the Start menu. It won't make you a more efficient Windows user, but it will make you a happier Windows user.

Here are the steps to follow:

1. Right-click the Start menu and then click Properties to display the Taskbar and Start Menu Properties dialog box.

2. Select the Start Menu tab, make sure the Start Menu option is activated, and then click the Customize button to its right to open the Customize Start Menu dialog box.

3. In Windows XP, select the Advanced tab.

4. Click to deactivate the Highlight Newly Installed Programs check box. (In Vista, you find this check box in the list of Start menu items.)

5. Click OK to return to the Taskbar and Start Menu Properties dialog box.

6. Click OK.

Get Rid of Start Menu Icons You Don't Use

Medium

The right side of the Start menu is loaded with predefined links to built-in components such as your user folder, Documents, Pictures, Control Panel, Help and Support, and more. If there are any of these links that you don't use, it's possible to configure Windows to remove them from the Start menu. This gives you a custom Start that's less cluttered and easier to navigate.

Here are the steps to follow to remove unused icons from your Start menu:

1. Select Start, type **gpedit.msc**, press Enter, and then enter your UAC credentials. (In Windows XP, select Start, Run, type **gpedit.msc**, and click OK.) The Group Policy Editor appears.

2. Open the User Configuration branch.

3. Open the Administrative Templates branch.

4. Click the Start Menu and Taskbar branch.

5. Double-click the policy you want to work with:

   ■ Remove All Programs list from the Start menu

   ■ Remove and prevent access to the Shut Down, Restart, Sleep, and Hibernate commands (Vista)

   ■ Remove and prevent access to the Shut Down command (XP)

   ■ Remove Default Programs link from the Start menu.

   ■ Remove Documents icon from Start Menu

   ■ Remove Favorites menu from Start Menu

   ■ Remove frequent programs list from the Start Menu

   ■ Remove Games link from Start Menu

   ■ Remove Help menu from Start Menu

> **NOTE** These steps require the Group Policy Editor, which is available only with Vista Business, Vista Enterprise, Vista Ultimate, and XP Professional. If you're not running one of these versions, I'll show you how to perform the same tweaks using the Registry.

- Remove Logoff on the Start Menu
- Remove Music icon from Start Menu
- Remove Network Connections from Start Menu
- Remove Network icon from Start Menu
- Remove Pictures icon from Start Menu
- Remove pinned programs list from the Start Menu
- Remove Recent Items menu from Start Menu
- Remove Run menu from Start Menu
- Remove Search Computer link
- Remove Search link from Start Menu
- Remove the "Undock PC" button from the Start Menu
- Remove user folder link from Start Menu

6. Click Enabled and then click OK.

7. Repeat steps 5 and 6 to implement other Start menu policies as needed.

8. Log off and then log back on to put the policies into effect.

If you prefer (or need) to implement these policies via the Registry, first open the Registry Editor (in Vista, click Start, type `regedit`, press Enter and enter your UAC credentials; in XP, select Start, Run, type `regedit`, and click OK). Navigate to the following key:

```
HKCU\Software\Microsoft\Windows\CurrentVersion\Policies\Explorer
```

(If you don't see the `Explorer` key, click the `Policies` key, select Edit, New, Key, type `Explorer`, and press Enter.)

For each policy you want to implement, you need to follow these steps:

1. Select Edit, New, DWORD (32-bit) Value.

2. Type the policy name and press Enter.

3. Press Enter to open the new Registry value.

4. Type `1` and click OK.

Table 15.1 lists the Start menu policies and their equivalent Registry settings.

Table 15.1   Start Menu Policies and Their Registry Equivalents

Start Menu Policy	Registry Setting
Remove All Programs list from the Start menu	NoStartMenuMorePrograms
Remove and prevent access to the Shut Down, Restart, Sleep, and Hibernate commands	NoClose

Start Menu Policy	Registry Setting
Remove Default Programs link from the Start menu	NoSMConfigurePrograms
Remove Documents icon from Start Menu	NoSMMyDocs
Remove Favorites menu from Start Menu	NoFavoritesMenu
Remove frequent programs list from the Start Menu	NoStartMenuMFUprogramsList
Remove Games link from Start Menu	NoStartMenuMyGames
Remove Help menu from Start Menu	NoSMHelp
Remove Logoff on the Start Menu	StartMenuLogOff
Remove Music icon from Start Menu	NoStartMenuMyMusic
Remove Network Connections from Start Menu	NoNetworkConnections
Remove Network icon from Start Menu	NoStartMenuNetworkPlaces
Remove Pictures icon from Start Menu	NoSMMyPictures
Remove pinned programs list from the Start Menu	NoStartMenuPinnedList
Remove Recent Items menu from Start Menu	NoRecentDocsMenu
Remove Run menu from Start Menu	NoRun
Remove Search Computer link	NoSearchComputerLinkInStartMenu
Remove Search link from Start Menu	NoFind
Remove the "Undock PC" button from the Start Menu	NoStartMenuEjectPC
Remove user folder link from Start Menu	NoUserFolderInStartMenu

Remember to log off and then log back on to put the policies into effect.

TIP To prevent a program from appearing on the Start menu's frequent programs list, open the Registry Editor and display the following key:

`HKCR\Applications\`*`program.exe`*

Here, *program.exe* is the name of the program's executable file. (If the key doesn't exist, create it.) Create a string value called `NoStartPage` (you don't need to assign a value to it). Restart Windows to put the new setting into effect.

Speeding Up Your Web Surfing

We all spend huge chunks of our day online, and much of that time is spent prowling the Web for treasure troves of information or entertainment. If you've got all the time in the world, your web surfing safaris can be leisurely affairs where you drift from site to site as the mood and links take you. However, it's much more likely that you're looking to *save* time, not waste it. If that's the case, you've come to the right chapter. Here you learn quite a few tweaks for ramping up your web surfing speed. Some of these mods make you more efficient (such as searching directly from the Address bar), whereas others are designed to make web surfing faster (such as using OpenDNS and maintaining your own DNS database). Either way, if time's short, these tweaks will help you surf more.

Use Any Search Engine from the Address Bar

Medium

To search from the Internet Explorer Address bar, first type your search text. As you type, Internet Explorer adds `Search for "text"` below the Address bar, where *text* is your search text. When you've finished your search text, use the Down arrow key to select the `Search for` item and then press Enter. Alternatively, precede your search text with the word **go**, **find**, or **search**, or with a question mark (**?**), as in these examples:

```
go vbscript

find wmi

search neologisms

? registry
```

Address bar–based searching with the search text preceded by a keyword such as go or ? is often the quickest route for simple searches. Unfortunately, you're limited to using Internet Explorer's default search engine. But what if you regularly use several search engines, depending on the search text or the results you get? In that case, it's still possible to set up Address bar searching for any number of other search engines.

To see how this works, let's run through an example. Follow these steps to set up Address bar searching for Google:

1. Select Start, type **regedit**, press Enter, and then enter your UAC credentials. (In Windows XP, select Start, Run, type **regedit**, and click OK.) The Registry Editor appears.

2. Navigate to the following key:

   `HKCU\Software\Microsoft\Internet Explore\SearchURL`

3. Create a new subkey. The name of this subkey will be the text that you enter into the Address bar before the search text. For example, if you name this subkey google, you'll initiate an Address bar search by typing **google** *text*, where *text* is your search text.

4. Select the new subkey and double-click its (Default) value for editing.

5. Type the URL that initiates a search for the search engine, and specify **%s** as a placeholder for the search text. For Google, the URL looks like this:

   `http://www.google.com/search?q=%s`

6. You also have to specify the characters or hexadecimal values that Internet Explorer substitutes for characters that have special meaning within a query string: space, pound sign (#), percent (%), ampersand (&), plus (+), equal (=), and

> **TIP** I suggest using subkey names that are as short as possible to minimize typing. For example, I use the name g for my Google key (meaning that I can search by typing **g** *text* into the Address bar).

question mark (?). To do this, add the following settings to the new sub-key (note that these values work with all search engines):

Name	Type	Data
<space>	REG_SZ	+
#	REG_SZ	%23
%	REG_SZ	%25
&	REG_SZ	%26
+	REG_SZ	%2B
=	REG_SZ	%3D
?	REG_SZ	%3F

Figure 16.1 shows a completed example. The text that you type into the Address bar before the search string—that is, the name of the new subkey—is called the *search prefix*.

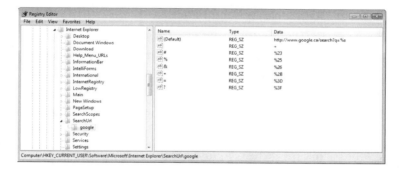

FIGURE 16.1

A sample search prefix for the Google search engine.

How do you know the proper URL to use for a search engine? Go to the search engine site and run a search with a single word. When the results appear, examine the URL in the Address bar, which usually takes the following general form:

```
ScriptURL?QueryString
```

Here, `ScriptURL` is the address of the site's search script and `QueryString` is the data sent to the script. In most cases, you can just copy the URL and substitute %s for your search text when you set up your search prefix. I often experiment with reducing the query string to the minimum necessary for the search to execute properly. For example, a typical Google search might produce a URL such as the following:

```
http://www.google.com/search?rls=ig&hl=en&q=mcfedries&btnG=Search
```

In the query string, each item is separated by an ampersand (&), so I delete one item at a time until either the search breaks or I'm down to the search text (q=mcfedries in the earlier query string). To save you some legwork, the following are the minimal search URLs for a number of search sites:

All the Web:

http://www.alltheweb.com/search?query=%s&cat=web

AltaVista:

http://www.altavista.com/web/results?q=%s

AOL Search:

http://search.aol.com/aolcom/search?query=%s

Ask.com:

http://www.ask.com/web?q=%s

Encarta (Dictionary only):

http://encarta.msn.com/encnet/features/dictionary/DictionaryResults.
➥aspx?search=%s

Encarta (General):

http://encarta.msn.com/encnet/refpages/search.aspx?q=%s

Excite:

http://msxml.excite.com/info.xcite/search/web/%s

Live.com:

http://www.live.com/?q=%s

Lycos:

http://search.lycos.com/default.asp?query=%s

Technorati:

http://www.technorati.com/search/%s

Yahoo:

http://search.yahoo.com/bin/search?p=%s

Create a Custom Search Provider

Medium

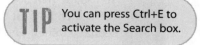

TIP You can press Ctrl+E to activate the Search box.

If you're using Internet Explorer 7, the Address bar isn't the only way to search. Besides dealing with a search engine site directly, Internet Explorer 7 also lets you run searches from the Search box, which appears to the right of the Address bar. Enter your search term in the Search box and then press Enter or click Search (you can also press Alt+Enter to open the results in a new tab).

By default, Internet Explorer initially submits the search text to the Windows Live search engine. (The default search engine is also the one that Internet Explorer uses for the Address bar AutoSearch.) If you want access to other search engines—or *search providers*, as Internet Explorer insists on calling them—via the Search box, follow these steps:

1. Click the drop-down arrow to the right of the Search box.
2. Click Find More Providers. Internet Explorer displays a web page with links to various search engines, as shown in Figure 16.2.

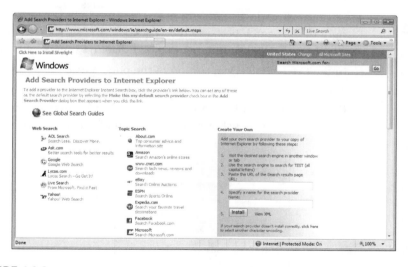

FIGURE 16.2
Internet Explorer offers a list of search providers that you can add to the Search box.

3. Click the link for the search engine you want to add. The Add Search Provider dialog box appears.
4. If you want Internet Explorer to use this search engine as the default, activate the Make This My Default Search Provider check box.
5. Click Add Provider.

To use the new search engine, drop down the Search box list to see a list of the search engines, and then click the one you want to use.

That's fine, but what if the search engine you really want to use isn't listed? That's not even remotely a problem because you can create a custom search provider for just about any search tool.

Here are the steps to follow:

1. Navigate to the search engine or site you want to use.

2. Run a search using TEST (all-caps) as the search string.

3. Copy the resulting URL from the Address bar.

4. Click the drop-down arrow to the right of the Search box and then click Find More Providers. Internet Explorer displays the list of providers.

5. In the Create Your Own section of the page, paste the address from step 3 into the URL text box.

6. Use the Name text box to specify the name that appears in the Search box list. Figure 16.3 shows an example that's ready to go.

> **TIP** You can change the default search engine at any time. Drop down the Search box list and then click Change Search Defaults. In the Change Search Defaults dialog box, click the search engine you want to use and then click Set Default. Click OK to put the new setting into effect.

> **NOTE** The example in Figure 16.3 is the search URL from my Word Spy website. Here's the full URL:
>
> `http://www.wordspy.com/`
> `scripts/search.asp?q=TEST`

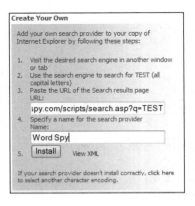

FIGURE 16.3

Use the Create Your Own section to create a custom search provider.

7. Click Install. The Add Search Provider dialog box appears.

8. If you want Internet Explorer to use this search engine as the default, activate the Make This My Default Search Provider check box.

9. Click Add Provider.

Make Tabs More Efficient

Easy

Like Firefox, Opera, Safari, and quite a few other browsers, Internet Explorer 7 finally brought tabbed browsing to Microsoft's flagship browser. You can open up to about 50 tabs in each window, which ought to be enough for anybody. One of the nicest features of tabs is that Internet Explorer supplies each tab with its own execution thread, which means that you can start a page loading in one tab while reading downloaded page text in another tab. You can also specify multiple home pages that load in their own tabs when you start Internet Explorer, as described in Chapter 4, "Terrific Web Tweaks."

➜   **See** "Load Multiple Home Pages at Startup," **p. 37**.

Tabs are only as useful as they are easy to use, and Internet Explorer does a good job of smoothing the transition to tabbed browsing. One way that it does this is by giving you a satisfying variety of methods to use for opening a page in a new tab. There are six in all:

- **Hold down Ctrl and click a link in a web page**—This creates a new tab and loads the linked page in the background.

- **Use the middle mouse button (if you have one) to click a link in a web page**—This creates a new tab and loads the linked page in the background.

- **Type the page URL into the Address bar and then press Alt+Enter**—This creates a new tab and loads the page in the foreground.

- **Click the New Tab button (or press Ctrl+T) to display a blank tab**—Type the page URL into the Address bar and then press the Enter key. This loads the page in the foreground.

- **Click and drag a web page link or the current Address bar icon and drop it onto the New Tab button**—This creates a new tab and loads the page in the foreground.

- **Click a link in another program**—This creates a new tab and loads the linked page in the foreground.

Opening a page in the background in a new tab when you Ctrl+click a link is useful if you want to keep reading the current page. However, I find that most of the time I want to read the new page right away. If you have a fast connection, the page loads quickly enough that the delay between clicking and reading is usually minimal.

In such cases, you can tell Internet Explorer to switch to the new tab automatically when you Ctrl+click a link:

> **TIP** While you've got the Tabbed Browsing Settings dialog box on the go, you should also make sure that the Open New Tabs Next to the Current Tab check box is activated. This is more efficient because otherwise (that is, if you deactivate this check box) Internet Explorer opens each new tab at the end of the current tab list, so you might have to scroll the tabs to return to your original page.

1. Select Tools, Internet Options to open the Internet Options dialog box.

2. Display the General tab.

3. Click Settings in the Tabs group to open the Tabbed Browsing Settings dialog box.

4. Activate the Always Switch to New Tabs When They Are Created check box.

5. Click OK in each open dialog box to put the new setting into effect.

Speed Up Web Surfing with OpenDNS

Easy

When you type a web address (for example, http://www.microsoft.com/windows) into any browser, the domain part of that address (www.microsoft.com) gets translated into a number called an *IP address* (such as 207.46.197.32) that uniquely points to the server located at www.microsoft.com. A connection is established between your own IP address and the server's IP address, and you see the website's data.

The association between an Internet node (such as a web server) and its unique IP address is maintained by the *Domain Name System* (*DNS*), and the conversion of a domain name into an IP address is handled by a *DNS server*. Chances are you currently use your ISP's DNS server to handle this so-called *domain name resolution*. This likely works well, but your ISP probably has only a server or two handling DNS requests, so at times your surfing may get bogged down as the DNS server tries to handle large workloads.

You can eliminate these inevitable DNS delays by switching to OpenDNS, a company that does nothing but domain name resolution. OpenDNS is faster because it maintains a collection of datacenters in the United States and Europe, and each datacenter is home to multiple servers that do nothing but resolve domain names into IP addresses. This means that OpenDNS can handle just about any workload with no lag, so your web surfing is never slowed down waiting for DNS to resolve.

This is the point where you wait for the painful news about how much such a wonderful service will cost you. No need to sit down for this, because OpenDNS is completely free! They make money by showing ads any time you accidentally type a non-existent domain name. Sweet!

> **TIP** You might think you see those ads each time you enter an address with a typo, but that's not necessarily so. OpenDNS looks out for common errors such as typing .cmo instead of .com, and will correct those errors automatically.

Even better, you don't have to sign up for anything, download anything, or send away for specialized equipment. Instead, you only have to configure your DNS settings to use the main OpenDNS server addresses:

208.67.222.222

208.67.220.220

(You can sign up for a free OpenDNS account, and that enables you to filter content, block domains, create URL shortcuts, and more. See www.opendns.com for more info.)

The easiest way to set up your computers for the OpenDNS servers is to configure your router to use the servers. That way, your entire network uses OpenDNS automatically. How you do this depends on the router, but you first need to access the router's setup pages. Here are the general steps to follow:

> **NOTE** Here are some common default IP addresses used by router manufacturers:
>
> Belkin   192.168.2.1
>
> D-Link   192.168.0.1
>
> Linksys   192.168.1.1
>
> Netgear   192.168.1.1

1. Start any web browser.

2. In the Address bar, type the router address, and then press Enter. See your device documentation for the correct address, but in most cases the address is either http://192.168.1.1 or http://192.168.0.1. You usually see a Connect dialog box.

3. Type the default username and password. Note that in most cases

> **TIP** If you're not sure which username and password to use, try **admin** for both. If that doesn't work, leave the username blank and try either **admin** or **password** for the password. If you still can't get in, see whether your device is listed in the Default Password List maintained at http://www.phenoelit-us.org/dpl/dpl.html.

you need to enter only the password; again, see the device documentation for the logon details.

4. Click OK. The router's setup page appears.

From here, look for the router's Internet connection settings. For example, Figure 16.4 shows the Internet Connection Settings page for my network's D-Link router. Notice at the bottom of the page I've configured the router to use the OpenDNS servers.

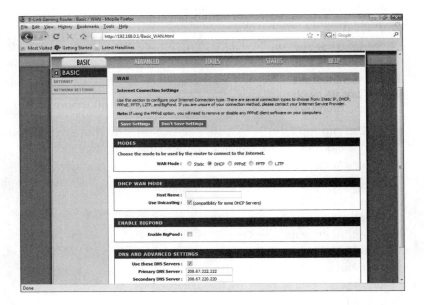

FIGURE 16.4
Configure your router to use the OpenDNS servers.

If you don't have access to your router, of if you'd prefer to try OpenDNS on a single PC as a test, you need to configure that computer's DNS settings.

Here are the steps to follow in Windows Vista:

1. Select Start, Control Panel.

2. Under Network and Internet, click the View Network Status and Tasks link. The Network and Sharing Center appears.

3. Click Manage Network Connections. The Network Connections window appears.

4. Right-click the network connection you use to access the Internet, click Properties, and then enter your UAC credentials. The connection's Properties dialog box appears.

5. In the Networking tab, click Internet Protocol Version 4 (TCP/IPv4) and then click Properties. The Internet Protocol Version 4 (TCP/IPv4) Properties dialog box appears.

6. Activate the Use the Following DNS Server Addresses option.

7. In the Preferred DNS Server address box, enter 208.67.222.222. (To enter this address, type **208**, type **67**, type a dot (.), type **222**, and then type **222**.)

8. In the Alternate DNS Server address box, enter 208.67.220.220. Figure 16.5 shows the completed dialog box.

FIGURE 16.5

Configure your Windows Vista Internet connection to use the OpenDNS servers.

9. Click OK in all the open dialog boxes.

10. Restart your computer to put the new settings into effect.

Here are the steps to follow in Windows XP:

1. Select Start, All Programs, Accessories, Communications, Network Connections. The Network Connections window appears.

2. Right-click the network connection you use to access the Internet, and then click Properties. The connection's Properties dialog box appears.

3. In the General tab, click Internet Protocol (TCP/IP) and then click Properties. The Internet Protocol (TCP/IP) Properties dialog box appears.

4. Activate the Use the Following DNS Server Addresses option.

5. In the Preferred DNS Server address box, enter 208.67.222.222. (To enter this address, type **208**, type **67**, type a dot (.), type **222**, and then type **222**.)

6. In the Alternate DNS Server address box, enter 208.67.220.220.

7. Click OK in all the open dialog boxes.

8. Restart your computer to put the new settings into effect.

Access Common Sites Faster

OpenDNS is faster than using your ISP's DNS servers, but it still requires querying a remote database. To avoid the lag time associated with resolving domain names remotely, you can set up your own DNS database on your Windows PC.

Easy

First, you need to determine the IP address of those sites that you access most often. Here's how:

1. Select Start, type **cmd**, and press Enter. (In Windows XP, select Start, Run to open the Run dialog box, type **cmd**, and click OK.) The Command Prompt appears.

2. Type **ping**, a space, and then the domain name of the site you want to work with.

3. Press Enter. Windows sends a packet to the server to see if it responds.

4. Make a note of the IP address that appears in the response.

5. Repeat steps 2–4 for other sites you want to work with.

When you run the ping command, you see output that looks like this:

```
C:\Users\Paul>ping wordspy.com

Pinging wordspy.com [209.34.176.37] with 32 bytes of data:

Reply from 209.34.176.37: bytes=32 time=38ms TTL=112
Reply from 209.34.176.37: bytes=32 time=37ms TTL=112
Reply from 209.34.176.37: bytes=32 time=38ms TTL=112
Reply from 209.34.176.37: bytes=32 time=38ms TTL=112
```

```
Ping statistics for 209.34.176.37:
    Packets: Sent = 4, Received = 4, Lost = 0 (0% loss),
Approximate round trip times in milli-seconds:
    Minimum = 37ms, Maximum = 38ms, Average = 37ms
```

The domain name gets resolved to its IP address, and `ping` uses that address to send the ping packets to the server. The `ping` command displays the IP address in the results (209.34.176.37 in the preceding example).

To make use of this data, you need to set up a database that maps IP addresses to their corresponding domain names. You do that using a text file named `hosts` (no extension) that comes with all Windows Vista and XP computers.

Follow these steps to open the `hosts` file in Windows XP:

1. Select Start, Run (or press Windows Logo+R) to open the Run dialog box.

2. Type the following command into the Open text box:

   notepad %systemroot%\System32\drivers\etc\hosts

3. Click OK. The `hosts` file opens in Notepad.

Windows Vista requires elevated permissions to edit any file in the `%SystemRoot%` folder or any of its subfolders. Therefore, you need to follow these steps to open `hosts` in Notepad:

1. Select Start, type **cmd**, and then press Ctrl+Shift+Enter. This runs the selected item with elevation, so the User Account Control dialog box appears.

2. Enter your UAC credentials to continue.

3. At the command prompt, type the following:

   notepad %systemroot%\System32\drivers\etc\hosts

4. Press Enter. The `hosts` file opens in Notepad.

With the `hosts` file open, start a new line at the end of the file. Then enter the mapping using the following general format:

IP   DomainName

Here, replace *IP* with the IP address returned by the `ping` command, and replace *DomainName* with the domain name associated with the IP address. Here are some examples:

```
209.34.176.37    wordspy.com
207.46.197.32    microsoft.com
64.233.187.99    google.com
```

Giving Windows a Makeover

A *time suck* is any activity that uses up large amounts of time. One of the great time sucks of our age is Windows and its all-but-innumerable options for customizing the interface. You can fiddle with the fonts, dabble with the desktop, and customize the colors till your mouse arm aches and the sound of your deadlines whooshing by is but a distant memory.

I keep my customizations in check by applying a simple rule in advance: If the interface tweak won't make me more productive or efficient, I move on to more useful pursuits. Harsh? Perhaps, but I *never* miss a deadline!

So in this chapter and the next you won't find any cute customizations. We're all business as I show you a half dozen tweaks that should make your work with Windows easier and more efficient.

Hide Some (or Even All) Notification Area Icons

Vista

XP

Medium

For most people, the notification area on the right side of the taskbar is either really useful or is a complete waste of otherwise useful taskbar space. You're more likely to fall into the latter camp if your notification area is bristling with icons, as shown in Figure 17.1.

FIGURE 17.1

An out-of-control notification area.

If your notification area is threatening to take over the taskbar, or if you find you never use some or all of the icons, this tweak shows you how to reduce the space used by the notification area.

To get started, right-click an empty part of the taskbar, and then click Properties to open the Taskbar and Start Menu Properties dialog box. In Windows Vista, display the Notification Area tab (see Figure 17.2); in Windows XP, display the Taskbar tab.

FIGURE 17.2

In Windows Vista, use the Notification Area tab to customize the notification area.

To help reduce notification area clutter and make this part of the taskbar more useful, you can do two things:

- Activate the Hide Inactive Icons check box. When this check box is activated, Windows hides notification area icons that you haven't used for a while. This gives the taskbar a bit more room to display program buttons, so leave this option activated if you don't use the notification area icons all that often.

- (Windows Vista only) In the System Icons group, deactivate the check box for each icon you don't use: Clock, Volume, Network, or Power (enabled on notebooks only).

- (Windows XP only) Deactivate the Show the Clock check box to remove the clock from the notification area.

If your notification area is crowded with icons, it's inefficient to display all the icons if you use only a few of them. Instead of showing them all, activate the Hide Inactive Icons check box and click Customize. You now have a couple of choices:

- For the icons you use often, click the item's Behavior column and then click Show in the list that appears. This tells Windows to always display the icon in the notification area.

- For icons you never use, click Hide, instead, which tells Windows to never display the icon in the notification area.

To minimize the amount of screen real estate used by the notification area, you must do three things:

1. Deactivate all the system icons.
2. Activate the Hide Inactive Icons check box.
3. Set every icon's Behavior value to Hide.

This works well enough, but it suffers from a couple of problems: Windows still shows the "chevron" that you click to display the hidden icons; and you'll probably need to keep hiding icons as you install new applications.

If that all sounds like way to much work, you can disable the notification area entirely by following these steps:

1. Select Start, type `gpedit.msc`, press Enter, and then enter your UAC credentials. (In Windows XP, select Start, Run, type `gpedit.msc`, and click OK.) The Group Policy Editor appears.

2. Open the User Configuration branch.

3. Open the Administrative Templates branch.

> **NOTE** These steps require the Group Policy Editor, which is available only with Vista Business, Vista Enterprise, Vista Ultimate, and XP Professional. If you're not running one of these versions, I'll show you how to perform the same tweaks using the Registry.

4. Click the Start Menu and Taskbar branch.

5. Double-click the Hide the Notification Area policy, click Enabled, and then click OK.

6. Double-click the Remove Clock from the System Notification Area policy, click Enabled, and then click OK.

7. Log off and then log back on to put the policy into effect.

If you prefer (or need) to implement this policy via the Registry, first open the Registry Editor (in Vista, click Start, type **regedit**, press Enter and enter your UAC credentials; in XP, select Start, Run, type **regedit**, and click OK). Navigate to the following key:

```
HKCU\Software\Microsoft\Windows\CurrentVersion\Policies\Explorer
```

(If you don't see the `Explorer` key, click the `Policies` key, select Edit, New, Key, type **Explorer**, and press Enter.)

Now follow these steps:

1. Select Edit, New, DWORD (32-bit) Value.

2. Type **NoTrayItemsDisplay** and press Enter.

3. Press Enter to open the `NoTrayItemsDisplay` setting, type **1**, and then click OK.

4. Select Edit, New, DWORD (32-bit) Value.

5. Type **HideClock** and press Enter.

6. Press Enter to open the `HideClock` setting, type **1**, and then click OK.

7. Log off and then log back on to put the policies into effect.

Get Control of Taskbar Grouping

Medium

Taskbar grouping means that when the taskbar fills up with buttons, Windows looks for programs that have multiple open windows, and it consolidates those window icons into a single button, as shown in Figure 17.3. The number on the left side of the button tells you how many windows are open. To access one of these grouped windows, you click the button and then click the window you want.

NOTE Taskbar grouping works only with applications that support a multiple document interface (MDI), where each open window or document is really a process that's running under a single application. For example, each open Windows Explorer window is a process of the `explorer.exe` application, and each Internet Explorer window is a process of the `iexplore.exe` application. Taskbar grouping doesn't work with single-document applications such as Notepad and WordPad.

FIGURE 17.3

When the taskbar gets filled with buttons, Windows groups similar windows into a single button, as shown here with Windows Explorer and Internet Explorer.

The grouping feature makes it easier to read the name of each taskbar button, but the price is a slight efficiency drop because it takes two clicks to activate a window instead of one. If you don't like this trade-off, you can disable the grouping feature by following these steps:

> **TIP** You can close all of a group's windows at once by right-clicking the group button and then clicking Close Group.

1. Right-click the taskbar and then click Properties.

2. Display the Taskbar tab.

3. Deactivate the Group Similar Taskbar Buttons check box.

4. Click OK.

Alternatively, you can tweak the grouping feature to suit the way you work. You do this by tweaking the Registry, as detailed in the following steps:

> **TIP** Another way to prevent grouping is to give the taskbar more room to display buttons. The easiest way to do that is to resize the taskbar by dragging its top edge up until the taskbar expands. If this doesn't work, the taskbar is probably locked. Unlock it by right-clicking the taskbar and then clicking Lock the Taskbar.

1. Select Start, type **regedit**, press Enter, and then enter your UAC credentials. (In Windows XP, select Start, Run, type **regedit**, and click OK.) The Registry Editor appears.

2. Navigate to the following key:

   HKCU\Software\Microsoft\Windows\CurrentVersion\Explorer\Advanced\

3. Select Edit, New, DWORD (32-bit) Value.

4. Type **TaskbarGroupSize** and then press Enter.

5. Press Enter to open the TaskbarGroupSize setting for editing.

6. Use the Value Data text box to enter one of the following values:

■ **0** —When the grouping kicks in (that is, when the taskbar gets full), Windows groups the buttons from only the applications that you have used the least.

■ **1** —When the grouping kicks in, Windows groups the buttons from only the application that has the most windows open. If a second application surpasses the number of open windows in the first application, the second application's windows are grouped as well (that is, the first application's windows remained grouped).

■ ***x*** —Windows groups any application that has at least *x* windows open, where *x* is a number between 2 and 99. Note that the grouping occurs even if the taskbar is not full.

7. Log off and then log back on to put the new setting into effect.

Turn Off Vista's Aero Interface

Easy

A lot of the prerelease and post-release Vista hoopla was centered on the new Aero interface, which offers plenty of eye candy:

■ **Aero Glass**—This is the new look of Vista's windows, controls, and other elements. The "Glass" part means that for systems with relatively high-end graphics capabilities, the Vista window title bars and borders have a transparency effect.

■ **Window thumbnails**—These are scaled-down versions of windows and documents. For supported file types, these thumbnails are "live," which means they reflect the current content of the window or document. For example, in folder windows, the icon for a PowerPoint presentation shows the first slide, and an icon for an image file shows the image. Similarly, a Windows Media Player thumbnail shows live content, such as a running video.

■ **Flip and Flip 3D**—When you hold down Alt and press Tab, Vista displays not an icon for each open window, but a thumbnail for each window. Each time you press the Tab key, Vista "flips" to the next window (hence the name of this new feature: Flip). You can also press Windows Logo+Tab to organize the open windows in a 3D stack. Pressing the arrow keys or scrolling the wheel mouse flips you from one window to another (this feature is called Flip 3D).

■ **Taskbar thumbnails**—The live thumbnails idea also extends to the taskbar. If you mouse over a taskbar button, Vista displays a live thumbnail for the window associated with the button.

Except for the glass effect (which seems completely useless to me), these Aero features are worthwhile additions to the interface. Or perhaps I should say they're worthwhile additions *provided* you have a powerful graphics card is stuffed with lots of graphics RAM. Otherwise, even if the video card is capable of running Aero, it may not run Aero *well*, and that can slow you down.

TIP If, like me, you love Aero but hate Aero Glass, turn it off! Right-click the desktop, click Personalize, and then click Window Color and Appearance. In the Window Color and Appearance page, deactivate the Enable Transparency check box, and then click OK.

If Aero is acting like an anchor on your system's graphics, shut it off by following these steps:

1. Right-click the desktop and then click Personalize. The Personalization window appears.

2. Click Window Color and Appearance.

3. Click Open Classic Appearance Properties for More Color Options. The Appearance Settings dialog box appears.

4. Select Windows Vista Basic, as shown in Figure 17.4.

FIGURE 17.4

To get rid of Aero, choose the Windows Vista Basic color scheme.

5. Click OK to put the new interface color scheme into effect.

Useful Interface Tweaks

In this chapter, we continue to improve the efficiency of Windows by tweaking the interface. I start you off with a couple of easy tweaks that make the cursor easier to find and improve the readability of Windows text. The third tweak is more ambitious as I show you how to configure your PC to support not one, not two, but *three* monitors. That may sound like a lot, but it's the setup I use, and I'll never go back to anything less because it's just so darned efficient.

Widen the Blinking Cursor to Make It Easier to See

Easy

If you're running Windows on a smallish notebook screen, or on a display where you've cranked up the resolution, you may have noticed a not insignificant problem: the blinking insertion point cursor is often devilishly difficult to see because it's so tiny. That's a drag because it means you often have to waste precious time hunting down the cursor.

The problem is that the cursor is only one pixel wide, which is a pretty narrow object to find on a small or high-res screen. To fix that, you can widen the cursor to make it easier to spot.

Here are the steps to follow in Windows Vista to widen the cursor:

1. Select Start, type **access**, and press Enter. (In XP, select Start, Run, type **access.cpl**, and click OK.) The Ease of Access Center appears.

2. Click Make the Computer Easier to See.

3. Use the Set the Thickness of the Blinking Cursor list to choose the cursor width you want. Windows Vista shows a preview of the new cursor width, as shown in Figure 18.1.

TIP Another thing that makes the cursor hard to locate is when the blink rate is too slow. At the slowest blink rate, the cursor disappears from the screen for a second or two, so it's pretty tough to spot in a field of text. To ensure your cursor is blinking at a decent rate, select Start, type **control keyboard**, and press Enter. (In XP, select Start, Run, type **control keyboard**, and click OK.) In the Keyboard Properties dialog box, display the Speed tab and use the Cursor Blink Rate slider to set the blink rate. On my systems, I drag the slider all the way to the right to get the fastest rate.

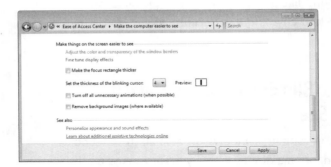

FIGURE 18.1
When you select a width from the Set the Thickness of the Blinking Cursor list, the cursor width appears in the Preview box.

4. Click Save to put the new setting into effect.

Here are the steps to follow in Windows XP to widen the cursor:

1. Select Start, Run, type **access.cpl**, and click OK. The Accessibility Options dialog box appears.

2. Select the Display tab.

3. In the Cursor Options group, drag the Width slider to the right to widen the cursor.

4. Click OK to put the new setting into effect.

Make Text Easier to Read by Adjusting the Font Size

Easy

Running Windows at a high resolution is useful because it means you can fit more items on the screen because everything appears smaller. The downside is that, depending on the resolution, some fonts may be too small to read comfortably.

You can solve this problem by increasing the dots per inch (DPI) setting in Windows. The default is 96 DPI, which means that Windows uses 96 pixels (dots) for every inch of screen space. (Physical measurements are relative to the screen resolution, so a one-inch line may not actually be one inch long on your screen.)

> **TIP** The Ease of Access Center (or the Accessibility Options in XP) has lots of options that are handy for all users. One of my favorites is Toggle Keys, which sounds a tone when you press Caps Lock, and that serves as a useful warning for all those times you press Caps Lock accidentally. (You also hear a tone when you press Num Lock or Scroll Lock.) In Vista, open the Ease of Access Center, click Make the Keyboard Easier to Use, activate the Turn on Toggle Keys check box, and then click Save. In XP, open the Accessibility Options, display the Keyboard tab, activate the use ToggleKeys check box, and then click OK. Note that Toggle Keys uses your PC's internal (motherboard) speaker, so if your computer doesn't have one, Toggle Keys won't work.

For example, a line that is meant to be one inch long will be drawn using 96 pixels. However, if you increase the DPI setting, the line appears longer. For example, if you change the DPI to 120, Windows Vista will scale the screen to use 120 pixels to create the same line. In other words, if you scale the DPI setting up, everything on the screen appears larger, including the text, which makes it easier to read.

Follow these steps to increase the DPI value in Windows Vista:

1. Right-click the desktop and then click Personalize. The Personalization window appears.

2. Click Adjust font size (DPI). The User Account Control dialog box appears.

3. Enter you UAC credentials to continue. The DPI Scaling dialog box appears.

4. If you want to go with 120 DPI, activate the Larger Scale (120 DPI) option, and then skip to step 7. Otherwise, click Custom DPI to display the Custom SPI Setting dialog box, shown in Figure 18.2.

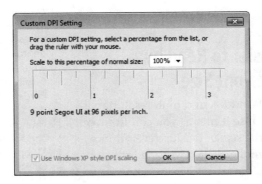

FIGURE 18.2
Use the Custom DPI Setting dialog box to set the DPI to a percentage of the default scaling.

5. Use the Scale to this Percentage of Normal Size control to either select a predefined percentage or type a custom percentage (a number between 100 and 500). You can also click and drag the ruler to set the percentage.

6. Click OK to return to the DPI Scaling dialog box.

7. Click OK. Windows Vista tells you that you must restart your computer for the change to take effect.

8. Close any documents and programs you have open.

9. Click Restart Now. Windows Vista restarts and puts the new font scaling into effect.

Follow these steps to increase the DPI value in Windows XP:

1. Right-click the desktop and then click Properties. The Display Properties dialog box appears.

2. Display the Settings tab.

3. Click Advanced.

CAUTION It's possible to scale the DPI beyond your screen resolution, which means that parts of the display no longer fit on the screen. This can make it impossible to see the entire Start menu or all the controls in a dialog box. To avoid this, scale back the DPI or increase your screen resolution to compensate.

4. Display the General tab.

5. If you want to go with 120 DPI, use the DPI Setting list to select the Large Size (120 DPI) option, and then skip to step 8. Otherwise, use the DPI Setting list to select Custom Setting to display the Custom SPI Setting dialog box.

6. Use the Scale to this Percentage of Normal Size control to select a pre-defined percentage. You can also click and drag the ruler to set the percentage.

7. Click OK to return to the DPI Scaling dialog box.

8. Click OK. Windows XP tells you that you must restart your computer for the change to take effect.

9. Close any documents and programs you have open.

10. Click Restart Now. Windows Vista restarts and puts the new font scaling into effect.

Run Windows with Three or More Monitors

Hard

Most tweaks aimed at improving productivity accomplish their goal by saving you a few seconds here and a few seconds there. Do that a few dozen times a day, and you're finishing your day a half hour earlier than usual. Improvements to productivity are almost always marginal, but you occasionally come across a new way of doing things that offers a radical increase in efficiency. Over the past few years, study after study has shown that you can greatly improve your productivity by doing one thing: adding a second monitor to your system. That makes a ton of sense when you think about it, because you can have whatever you're working on displayed on one monitor, and your reference materials (or your email client or whatever) on the second monitor. If that's the way you want to go, there are lots of video cards out there with dual outputs (either a VGA port and a DVI port, or dual DVI ports) that can drive two monitors.

However, I want to crank things up a notch in this tweak and go for not two, but *three* monitors! This is the setup I use in my office, and it rocks. I have Word on one monitor, reference materials or whatever on a second monitor, and Outlook on the third. It's almost scary how productive this setup makes me.

How does this work? The secret is that you have to install a second video card on your system. However, you can't just plop any old video card in there and hope things will work. Instead, you need to use video cards that come with dual-GPU (graphics processing unit) support. Both ATI and NVIDIA offer dual-GPU technologies:

■ **ATI CrossFire**—ATI's dual-GPU technology is called *CrossFire*. To use it, you need a motherboard with a CrossFire-compatible chipset and two free PCI Express slots that are designed for CrossFire, as well as two CrossFire-capable video cards from the same Radeon chipset family (for example, two Radeon X1950 cards from any manufacturer). Figure 18.3 shows two video cards connected with a CrossFire bridge. To learn more about CrossFire-compatible equipment, see http://ati.amd.com/technology/crossfire/.

FIGURE 18.3

Two ATI video cards connected with a CrossFire bridge.

■ **NVIDIA SLI**—NVIDIA's dual-GPU technology is called *scalable link interface (SLI)*. To use it, you need a motherboard with an SLI-compatible chipset and two free PCI Express slots designed for SLI, as well as two SLI-capable video cards that use the same NVIDIA chipset (for example, two GeForce 8800 GTS cards from any manufacturer). To learn more about SLI-compatible equipment, see http://sg.slizone.com/.

Each of these video cards has two output ports, so you have a total of four ports to use. After you get the cards installed, you run VGA or DVI cables from three of those ports (or four, if you want to go all the way and use four monitors) to the corresponding ports on your monitors. When you next start Windows, install the video card drivers. Note that if you're using Windows Vista, you'll likely see a message similar to the one shown in Figure 18.4. Click the message and then look for the option that enables either CrossFire or SLI.

NOTE If all this sounds like a bunch of graphics gobbledygook to you, or if you're not comfortable with the idea of installing a video card, I've got just the solution. My book *Build It. Fix It. Own It.* (Que 2008) explains all these technologies in easy-to-understand language, and shows you step-by-step how to install things like video cards. For more info, see www.mcfedries.com/cs/content/BuildItFixItOwnIt.aspx.

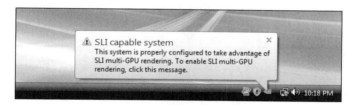

FIGURE 18.4

Click this message to enable (in this case) SLI on your PC.

Now you're ready to configure Windows to extend the desktop across all your monitors. Here are the steps to follow:

1. Make sure all your monitors are connected and turned on.

2. Open the display settings:

   ■ **Windows Vista**—Right-click the desktop, click Personalize, and then click Display Settings. Figure 18.5 shows the Display Settings dialog box that appears. The four icons represent the four output ports of the video cards.

   ■ **Windows XP**—Right-click the desktop, click Properties, and then click the Settings tab.

3. Click the icon for the monitor you want to add.

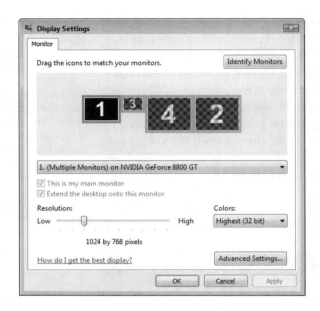

FIGURE 18.5

Use the Display Settings dialog box to configure your multiple-monitor setup.

4. Activate the Extend the Desktop Onto This Monitor check box.

5. Click Apply. Windows asks if you want to keep the new setting.

6. If you see the desktop on one of your monitors, it means it was added successfully, so click Yes; otherwise, click No and try another.

7. Repeat steps 3–6 to add your other monitors to the desktop.

8. Click and drag the monitor icons to the orientation you prefer. For example, you might want your main monitor (the monitor that holds the taskbar) in the middle and the other two monitors on either side. Figure 18.6 shows just such a setup: the main monitor (1) is flanked by the two other monitors (2 and 4).

> **TIP** If you're using four monitors, it doesn't matter which one you click. If you're only using three monitors, however, you still see four monitor icons, so how do you know which one to click? In general, Windows doesn't set the resolution on an empty port, so the smallest icon (number 3 in Figure 18.5) is usually the one to avoid.

> **TIP** Ideally, you should be able to move your mouse continuously across all the monitors. If you find that the mouse stops at the right edge of your left monitor, then it means you need to exchange the icons of the left and right monitors.

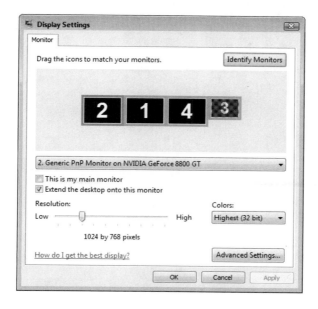

FIGURE 18.6

Click and drag the monitor icons into the arrangement you want.

9. Adjust the resolution for each monitor, as desired.

10. Click OK.

Useful and Fun Interface Mods

Throughout this book I've tried to provide you with tweaks that would, even in a small way, make your life with Windows Vista or XP easier, faster, more efficient, or more secure. In other words, my emphasis has been on practical tweaks rather than on frivolous ones. In this chapter I give in a teensy tiny bit to frivolity and show you some tweaks that I think are quite fun. However, my practical side refuses to wait in the wings, so although the first tweak is pure fun, you can use (if you want to, that is) the next two tweaks to boost your Windows efficiency, so they have more than a whiff of practicality about them.

Give Windows a Custom Logo

Medium

If you want to add a personal touch to your PC, you can tweak it to display a custom logo. In Windows XP, this logo appears in the General tab of the System Properties dialog box; in Windows Vista, the logo appears in Control Panel's System window.

Give Windows XP a Custom Logo

In a few places in this book, I ask you to
open up the Windows XP System Properties
dialog box to make a tweak or two to your
PC. In XP, here are the fastest ways to open
System Properties:

TIP   Customizing the General tab or System window isn't terribly useful for your individual machine, but if you build PCs for family, friends, and friends of friends, this is a great way to brand your creations.

- Press Windows Logo+Pause/Break.

- Click Start, right-click My Computer,
  and then click Properties.

- Select Start, Run, type **sysdm.cpl**, and click OK.

All three methods should land you on the General tab. (If not, click the
General tab to display it.) If you purchased your XP PC from a manufacturer,
chances are the company has customized the General tab with a logo and the
company name. For example, Figure 19.1 shows the General tab for my trusty
old ThinkPad; you can see that it displays the IBM logo, and it also says IBM
Corporation above the processor info. You can also click the Support
Information button to see a dialog box that displays technical support info
for IBM.

FIGURE 19.1

*Most manufacturers customize the System Properties General tab with a logo, company name,
and support information.*

Happily, the logo, company name, and even the support information are all fully customizable. You can also add a "model" name below the company, which could be your PC's actual model name, or perhaps a nickname.

Let's start with the logo. Here are the steps to follow:

1. Create a new logo or modify an existing logo so that the resulting image is no more than 180 pixels wide and no more than 114 pixels high.

2. Select File, Save As to open the Save As dialog box.

3. In the Save As Type (or File Type) list, choose 256 Color Bitmap.

4. In the File Name text box, type `oeminfo.bmp`.

5. Open the `%SystemRoot%\System32` folder.

6. Click Save.

7. If the program asks whether you want to replace the existing file, click Yes.

> **TIP** If your logo uses a solid background color, it will usually look best in the General tab if you hide that background. You do this by setting the background color to display as transparent, which lets the background of the General tab appear. Check the Help system of your graphics editor to see if the program supports transparency.

> **NOTE** If your system already has an `oeminfo.bmp` file, you might want to save a copy of it in case you want to restore it later on. Right-click the file, click Copy, then press Ctrl+V to paste a copy of the file.

Now follow these steps to customize the company name, model name, and support info:

1. Select Start, Run to open the Run dialog box.

2. Type `%systemroot%\system32` and then click OK.

3. If XP tells you that the files are hidden, click Show the Contents of This Folder.

4. You now have two ways to proceed:
   - If your General tab already has a custom company name and support info, locate the `oeminfo.ini` file and then double-click it to open it in Notepad.

- If you're creating custom info from scratch, select File, New, Text Document, type **oeminfo.ini**, press Enter, and then click Yes when XP asks you to confirm the extension change. Press Enter again to open the new file in Notepad.

> **NOTE** There doesn't seem to be any limit to the length of these lines. However, the Support Information dialog box is wide enough to display only about 76 characters, so if any of your lines are longer than that, people viewing the support information will need to use the horizontal scrollbar to read those lines.

5. For the company name and model name, add or edit the following lines:

```
[general]
Manufacturer=CompanyName
Model=ModelName
```

6. For the support info, add or edit the following lines:

```
[Support Information]
Line1=First line
Line2=Secondline
[etc.]
```

7. Select File, Save to save your work. Figure 19.2 shows a sample oeminfo.ini file.

FIGURE 19.2
A custom oeminfo.ini file.

The next time you open the System Properties dialog box, the General tab shows the custom logo, company name, and model name, as shown in Figure 19.3. Click the Support Information button to display your custom support text, as shown in Figure 19.4.

FIGURE 19.3

The General tab showing the custom logo, manufacturer, and model.

FIGURE 19.4

Click the Support Information button to see your custom support text.

Give Windows Vista a Custom Logo

Windows Vista still has the System Properties dialog box, but the General tab is gone. Instead, Vista offers the System window, which is part of Control Panel's System and Maintenance category. Here are the three easiest ways to display the System window:

- Press Windows Logo+Pause/Break.
- Click Start, right-click Computer, and then click Properties.
- Select Start, type **system**, and then click System in the search results.

Figure 19.5 shows an uncustomized version of the System window. You can add a logo to the System section, and you can add support information in a new section that appears below the System section.

FIGURE 19.5

In Windows Vista, you can add a custom logo and support information to the System window.

Let's start with creating the logo:

1. In Paint, create a new logo or modify an existing logo so that the resulting image is no more than 120 pixels wide and no more than 120 pixels high.

2. Select File, Save As to open the Save As dialog box.

3. In the Save As Type (or File Type) list, choose 256 Color Bitmap.

> **TIP** If your logo uses a solid background color, it will usually look best in the System window if you hide that background. You do this by setting the background color to display as transparent, which lets the background of the System window appear. Check the Help system of your graphics editor to see if the program supports transparency.

4. Give your logo any name you want, and save it in any folder you want.

5. Click Save.

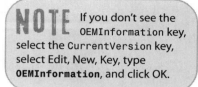

NOTE If you don't see the OEMInformation key, select the CurrentVersion key, select Edit, New, Key, type OEMInformation, and click OK.

Now follow these steps to customize the System window:

1. Select Start, type **regedit**, press Enter, and then enter your UAC credentials. Vista opens the Registry Editor.

2. Navigate to the following key:

   HKLM\Software\Microsoft\Windows\CurrentVersion\OEMInformation

3. Select File, New, String Value, type **Logo**, and press Enter. Press Enter again to open the new setting, and then type the full path to the logo file.

4. Select File, New, String Value, type **Manufacturer**, and press Enter. Press Enter again to open the new setting, and then type the company name you want to use.

5. Select File, New, String Value, type **SupportHours**, and press Enter. Press Enter again to open the new setting, and then type your support hours.

6. Select File, New, String Value, type **SupportPhone**, and press Enter. Press Enter again to open the new setting, and then type the support phone number.

7. Select File, New, String Value, type **SupportURL**, and press Enter. Press Enter again to open the new setting, and then type the support web address.

Figure 19.6 shows some sample values in the Registry, and Figure 19.7 shows how they customize the System window.

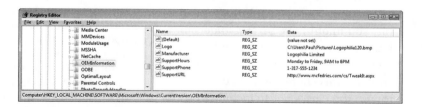

FIGURE 19.6

Custom OEM information in the Registry.

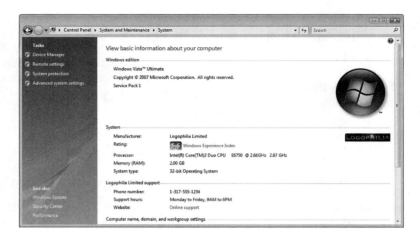

FIGURE 19.7
The System windows showing the custom logo and support info.

Customize the Places Bar for Easier Navigation

Medium

The left side of the standard Save As and Open dialog boxes in Windows XP, as well as the old-style Save As and Open dialog boxes in Windows Vista, include icons for several common locations:

- **Windows Vista**—Recent Places, Desktop, Computer, Network, and an icon for your main user profile folder, as shown in Figure 19.8.

- **Windows XP**—My Recent Documents, Desktop, My Documents, My Computer, and My Network Places.

The area that contains these icons is called the Places bar. If you have two or more folders that you use regularly (for example, you might have several folders for various projects that you have on the go), switching between them can be a hassle. To make this chore easier, you can customize the Places bar to include icons for each of these folders. That way, no matter which location you have displayed in the Save As or Open dialog box, you can switch to one of these regular folders with a single click of the mouse.

NOTE In Vista, if you display the Save As or Open dialog box and you see the Favorite Links pane instead, it means the application uses the updated dialog boxes. However, you can still customize the Favorite Links: to add a folder, drag it from the folder list and drop it inside the Favorite Links pane; to remove a custom shortcut from Favorite Links, right-click it, click Remove Link, and then click Yes when Vista asks you to confirm.

FIGURE 19.8

The Save As and Open dialog boxes display icons on the left for common locations.

Customizing the Places Bar via Group Policies

The easiest way to do this is via the Group Policy Editor, as shown in the following steps:

1. Select Start, type **gpedit.msc**, press Enter, and then enter your UAC credentials. (In Windows XP, select Start, Run to open the Run dialog box, type **gpedit.msc**, and then click OK.) The Group Policy Editor appears.

2. Open the User Configuration branch.

3. Open the Administrative Templates branch.

4. Open the Windows Components branch.

5. Open the Windows Explorer branch.

6. Open the Common Open File Dialog branch.

7. Double-click the Items Displayed in Places Bar policy.

8. Click Enabled.

9. Use the Item 1 through Item 5 text boxes to type the paths for the folders you want to display. These can be local folders or network folders, as shown in Figure 19.9.

> **NOTE** These steps require the Group Policy Editor, which is available only with Vista Business, Vista Enterprise, Vista Ultimate, and XP Professional. If you're not running one of these versions, I'll show you how to perform the same tweak using the Registry.

FIGURE 19.9
Open the Items Displayed in Places Bar policy, click Enabled, and then fill in the folder locations you want to use.

10. Click OK to put the policy into effect. Figure 19.10 shows an Open dialog box with icons for the folders from Figure 19.9 displayed in the Places bar.

FIGURE 19.10
The Open dialog box showing the custom Places bar.

Customizing the Places Bar via the Registry

If you don't have access to the Group Policy Editor, you can use the Registry Editor to perform the same tweak. Open the Registry Editor and navigate to the following key:

`HKCU\Software\Microsoft\Windows\CurrentVersion\Policies\`

Now follow these steps:

1. Select Edit, New, Key, type **comdlg32**, and press Enter.
2. Select Edit, New, Key, type **Placesbar**, and press Enter.
3. Select Edit, New, String Value, type **Place0**, and press Enter.
4. Press Enter to open the new setting, type the folder path, and then click OK.
5. Repeat steps 3 and 4 to add other places (named `Place1` through `Place4`). Figure 19.11 shows an example.

FIGURE 19.11

If your version of Windows doesn't come with the Group Policy Editor, you can still customize the Places bar using the Registry Editor.

Display Multiple Clocks for Different Time Zones

Easy

If you have colleagues, friends, or family members who work or live in a different time zone, it is often important to know the correct time in that zone. For example, you would not want to call someone at home at 9 a.m. your time if that person lives in a time zone that is three hours behind you. Similarly, if you know that a business colleague leaves work at 5 p.m. and that person works in a time zone that is seven hours ahead of you, you know that any calls you place to that person must occur before 10 a.m. your time.

If you need to be sure about the current time in another time zone, you can customize Windows Vista's date and time display to show not only your current time, but also the current time in the other time zone. Follow these steps:

1. Click the Clock icon and then click Change Date and Time Settings to display the Date and Time dialog box.

2. Click the Additional Clocks tab. Figure 19.12 shows a completed version of this tab.

FIGURE 19.12

Use the Additional Clocks tab to add one or two more clocks for different time zones in Windows Vista.

3. Activate the first Show This Clock check box.

4. Use the Select Time Zone list to click the time zone you want to display in the additional clock.

5. Use the Enter Display Name text box to type a name for the clock.

6. Repeat steps 4–6 for the second clock.

7. Click OK.

To see the clocks, click the time to display a fly-out similar to the one shown in Figure 19.13.

FIGURE 19.13

Click the time to see your additional clocks.

> **TIP** After you customize Windows Vista with the extra clocks, you normally click the time in the notification area to see the clocks. However, if you just hover the mouse pointer over the time, Windows Vista displays a banner that shows the current date, your current local time, and the current time in the other time zones.

Modding Music

In many modern households, music is now an all-digital affair where the CDs have been packed away and the tunes now exist as digital files playable only on a PC or a portable digital music device, such as an iPod or Zune. My own music collection has been all-digital for quite a while, and I wouldn't even consider going back to physical media.

Not that I eschew CDs altogether. I still purchase them for albums I really like because I get complete control over how I copy that music to my PC (pending whatever digital rights management hurdles have to be cleared).

Whether you're in the process of digitizing your music collection, or you're just copying the odd CD that comes your way, the first couple of tweaks in this chapter will be right up your alley because they show you some neat music copying tricks. You also learn how to share your media library over your network so that everyone can enjoy easy access to all that good tuneage.

Rip It Your Way with Custom Rip Settings

Medium

Windows Media Player comes with the welcome capability to copy (*rip* in the vernacular) tracks from an audio CD to your computer's hard disk. Although this process is straightforward (insert the CD and click the Rip button), you need to take into account several options *before* you start copying. These options include the location of the folder in which the ripped tracks will be stored, the structure of the track filenames, the file format to use, and the quality (bit rate) at which you want to copy the tracks. You control all these settings in the Rip Music tab of the Options dialog box (press Alt and then select Tools, Options to get there).

Selecting a Location and Filename Structure

The Rip Music to This Location group displays the name of the folder that will be used to store the copied tracks. By default, this location is %USERPROFILE%\Music in Windows Vista (it's %USERPROFILE%\My Music in Windows XP). To specify a different folder (for example, a folder on a partition with lots of free space), click Change and use the Browse for Folder dialog box to choose the new folder.

The default filenames that Windows Media Player generates for each copied track use the following structure:

`Track_Number Song_Title.ext`

Here, `Track_Number` is the song's track number on the CD, `Song_Title` is the name of the song, and `ext` is the extension used by the recording format (such as WMA or MP3). Windows Media Player can also include additional data in the filename, such as the artist name, the album name, the music genre, and the recording bit rate. To control which of these details the name incorporates, click the File Name button in the Rip Music tab to display the File Name Options dialog box, shown in Figure 20.1. Activate the check boxes beside the details you want in the filenames, and use the Move Up and Move Down buttons to determine the order of the details. Finally, use the Separator list to choose which character to use to separate each detail.

FIGURE 20.1

Use the File Name Options dialog box to specify the details you want in the filename assigned to each copied audio CD track.

Choosing the Recording File Format

Prior to version 10, Windows Media Player supported only a single file format: WMA (Windows Media Audio). This is an excellent music format that provides good quality recordings at high compression rates. If you plan to listen to the tracks only on your computer or on a custom CD, the WMA format is all you need. However, Windows Media Player 11 (which comes with Vista and is an upgrade in XP) supports a number of formats:

- **Windows Media Audio (WMA)**—This is Windows Media Player's default audio file format. WMA compresses digital audio by removing extraneous sounds that are not normally detected by the human ear. This results in high-quality audio files that are a fraction of the size of uncompressed audio.

- **Windows Media Audio Pro (WMA Pro)**—This version of WMA can create music files that are smaller than regular WMA and so are easier to play on mobile devices that don't have much room.

- **Windows Media Audio (variable bit rate)**—This version of WMA is a bit "smarter" in that it changes the amount of compression depending on the audio data: If the data is more complex, it uses less compression to keep the sound quality high; if the data is less complex, it cranks up the compression.

> **NOTE** If you're still using Windows Media Player 10 in XP, note that it supports only four of these formats: Windows Media Audio, Windows Media Audio (variable bit rate), Windows Media Audio Lossless, and MP3.

- **Windows Media Audio Lossless**—This version of WMA doesn't compress the audio tracks at all. This gives you the highest possible audio quality, but it takes up much more space (up to about 400MB per CD).

- **MP3**—This is a popular format on the Internet. Like WMA, MP3 compresses the audio files to make them smaller without sacrificing quality. MP3 files are generally about twice the size of WMA files, but more digital audio players support MP3 (although not many more, these days).

- **WAV**—This is an uncompressed audio file format that is compatible with all versions of Windows, even going back to Windows 3.0.

However, if you have an MP3 player or other device that might not recognize WMA files (although most do, unless you're one of the billions with an iPod), you should use the MP3 recording format.

Use the Format list in the Rip Music tab to choose the encoder you want to use. Note that if you select any Windows Media Audio format, the Copy Protect Music check box becomes enabled. Here's how this check box affects your copying:

- If Copy Protect Music is activated, Media Player applies a license to each track that prevents you from copying the track to another computer or to any portable device that is SDMI-compliant (SDMI is the Secure Digital Music Initiative; see www.sdmi.org for more information). Note, however, that you are allowed to copy the track to a writeable CD.

- If Copy Protect Music is deactivated, there are no restrictions on where or how you can copy the track. As long as you're copying tracks for personal use, deactivating this check box is the most convenient route to take.

Specifying the Quality of the Recording

The tracks on an audio CD use the CD Audio Track file format (`.cda` extension), which represents the raw (uncompressed) audio data. You can't work with these files directly because the CDA format isn't supported by Windows and because these files tend to be huge (usually double-digit megabytes, depending on the track). Instead, the tracks need to be converted into a Windows-supported format (such as

TIP
To save a bit of time, Media Player 11 offers a faster way to choose the format and audio quality. Point your mouse at the Rip tab and a downward-pointing arrow appears. Click the arrow to display a menu, and then select either Format (to select an audio file format) or Bit Rate (to select an audio quality).

MP3 or WMA). This conversion always involves compressing the tracks to a more manageable size. However, because the compression process operates by removing extraneous data from the file (that is, it's a *lossy* compression), there's a trade-off between file size and music quality. That is, the higher the compression, the smaller the resulting file, but the poorer the sound quality. Conversely, the lower the compression, the larger the file, but the better the sound quality. Generally, how you handle this trade-off depends on how much hard disk space you have to store the files and how sensitive your ear is to sound quality.

The recording quality is usually measured in kilobits per second (Kbps; this is called the *bit rate*), with higher values producing better quality and larger files, as shown in Table 20.1. To specify the recording quality, use the Audio Quality slider in the Rip Music tab. Move the slider to the right for higher-quality recordings, and to the left for lower quality.

Table 20.1   Ripping Bit Rates and the Disk Space They Consume

Kbps	KB/Minute	MB/Hour
32	240	14
48	360	21
64	480	28
96	720	42
128	960	56
160	1,200	70
192	1,440	84

Rip Music to a Network Location

Easy

When you rip music from an audio CD in Windows Media Player, the resulting digital audio files are stored in a subfolder of your user profile's Music folder (in Windows Vista) or My Music folder (in Windows XP). If you then want to give other people access to your music, you must share the music folder. That's not a big problem if you're dealing with one music folder, but what if you want to share music from several machines? Even if you go to the trouble of sharing all those other music folders, you're still left with the problem of trying to figure out which folder holds the music you want.

TIP If you have a machine running Windows Home Server, use the server's predefined Music shared folder to store your music. To learn more about Windows Home Server, see my book *Windows Home Server Unleashed*, published by Sams.

TIP In Windows Media Player 11, pull down the Rip menu and select More Options. The Options dialog box appears with the Rip Music tab selected.

A much better idea is to set up a music folder on a single network share and rip all music to that share.

Here are the steps to follow to change Media Player's rip location to a shared network folder:

1. If you haven't done so already, enable sharing on the network folder that you want to use.

2. In Windows Media Player, press Alt to display the menu bar, select Tools, Options, and then click the Rip Music tab.

3. In the Rip Music to This Location group, click Change to open the Browse for Folder dialog box.

4. Select the shared network folder that you created in step 1, and then click OK to return to the Options dialog box.

5. Click OK to put the new setting into effect.

Share Media Over Your Network

Easy

If you're using your Windows PC as the central storage location for your network's media files, you'll want to share that media with the rest of the users on your network. One way to do that is to share the media folders directly. However, Windows Media Player 11 gives you a second option: *media sharing*.

The idea behind media sharing is simple. As you might know, it can take quite a while to set up and customize a Media Player Library just the way you like it with playlists, album art, views, and other features. If you want other people to see and use the same setup, it's way too much work to configure each computer's Media Player separately. Fortunately, you don't have to bother with all that because the media sharing feature enables you to share your Media Player library with other network users or devices, just as you'd share a folder or a printer.

To activate media sharing, follow these steps:

1. On the Windows computer that you're using as a digital media hub, launch Windows Media Player by selecting Start, All Programs, Windows Media Player.

2. Pull down the Library tab's menu and select Media Sharing. The Media Sharing dialog box appears.

3. Click to activate the Share My Media check box, as shown in Figure 20.2.

NOTE If you're using a Windows XP system, you must upgrade to Windows Media Player 11 to use media sharing.

TIP After you run Media Player for the first time, Vista adds an icon for Media Player to the Quick Launch toolbar on the left side of the taskbar. For subsequent Media Player sessions, you can launch the program quickly by clicking that icon.

NOTE Another route to the Media Sharing dialog box is to press Alt, select Tools, Options (or pull down the menu for any other tab and select More Options) to open the Options dialog box. Display the Library tab and then click Configure Sharing.

FIGURE 20.2
Activate the Share My Media check box to turn on Media Player's media sharing feature.

4. Click OK. The User Account Control dialog box appears.

5. Enter your UAC credentials to continue. Media Player expands to show the devices connected to Media Player (see Figure 20.5, later in this section).

When computers or devices connect to your network, Media Player recognizes them and displays an icon in the notification area. Place your cursor over the icon to see the message `Windows Media Player found:` *computer*, where *computer* is the name of the new computer or device (see Figure 20.3). Double-click the message to open the Windows Media Player Library Sharing dialog box shown in Figure 20.4. Then click either Allow (if you want the computer or device to share your media) or Deny (if you don't).

FIGURE 20.3

Media Player displays this message when it detects a new computer or device connected to your network.

FIGURE 20.4

You can allow or deny other computers and devices access to your media library.

To control media sharing, display the Media Sharing dialog box again. This time, you see the configuration shown in Figure 20.5. The large box in the middle lists the network computers and devices that Media Player has detected. In each case, click an icon and then click either Allow or Deny. If you allow an item, you can also click Customize to specify exactly what you want to share based on three criteria: media types, star ratings, and parental ratings. Deactivate the Use Default Settings check box, and then use the controls to customize what you want to share.

> **NOTE** To control the default sharing settings, click the Settings button in the Media Sharing dialog box.

Denied   Not configured

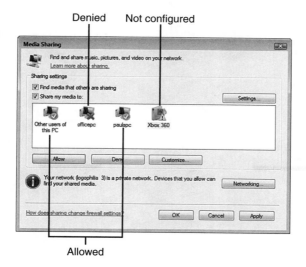

Allowed

FIGURE 20.5

Use the Media Sharing dialog box to allow or deny other network devices access to your Media Player library.

CHAPTER 21

Tweaking Photos

Our relationship with photography has gone from taking the occasional snapshot on vacation or at a party to practically documenting our lives. Why the switch? First, the advent of digital photography meant that the cost of taking a picture became negligible (assuming you didn't print the photo), so why not snap away at will? Second, cameras became our constant companions when they reached the point where they could be shoehorned into a mobile phone. You have your phone with you at all times, so now you have a camera full-time, as well, so why not snap away at will?

You can debate the pros and cons of living a life through a camera lens, but let's save that for the blogosphere. Here, our concern is handling the blizzard of digital photos that we all have to contend with these days. This chapter shows you a few tweaks that help you edit, manage, and share your digital photos.

Fix a Photo by Removing Red Eye

Easy

When you use a flash to take a picture of one or more people, in some cases the flash may reflect off the subjects' retinas. The result is the common phenomenon of *red eye*, where each person's pupils appear as red instead of black. (Some cameras come with a red eye reduction feature, which is usually a double flash: one to make the pupils contract before the shot and then another for the picture itself.)

If you have a photo where one or more people or animals have red eye because of the camera flash, you can use the Windows Vista Photo Gallery to improve the red eye and make your subjects look less crazed.

Here are the steps to follow:

1. Select Start, All Programs, Windows Photo Gallery to open the Windows Photo Gallery application.

2. Click the image that contains the red eye you want to remove.

3. Click Fix to open the Fix window.

4. Click the Zoom button and then use the slider to zoom in on the photo until you get a good look at the red eye. (If the red eye moves out of the view, click and drag the photo to pan the red eye into view.)

5. Click Fix Red Eye.

6. Click and drag your mouse to form a rectangle around the red eye, as shown in Figure 21.1. Windows Photo Gallery removes the red eye.

7. Repeat step 5 to fix any other examples of red eye in the photo.

8. Click Back to Gallery. Windows Photo Gallery applies the repairs.

NOTE If you're using Windows XP, you can remove red eye using the Windows Live Photo Gallery application, which works with XP Service Pack 2 or later. For more about Windows Live Photo Gallery, see "Stitch Multiple Photos into a Panorama," later in this chapter.

TIP If you need to pan the photo while the Fix Red Eye feature is activated, hold down Alt and then click and drag the photo.

CAUTION The Fix Red Eye feature is really just a color replacement feature. That is, it replaces red with black or dark grey. Therefore, when you drag the mouse, make sure the rectangle that you create covers only the red eye and not any other part of the image.

NOTE Windows Photo Gallery always keeps a backup copy of the original image, just in case. To undo all your changes (for example, if you think your friend looks better with red eyes!) and get the original image back, click the image and then click Fix. In the Fix window, open the Revert menu and then click Revert to Original (or press Ctrl+R).

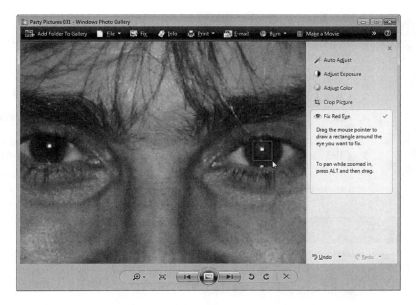

FIGURE 21.1

You can use Windows Photo Gallery's Fix Red Eye tool to remove red eye from a photo (as shown with the left eye in this image).

Crop a Photo to Get Rid of Unwanted Elements

Easy

Lots of digital photos are taken on the go, so often the framing of the subject leaves a bit to be desired. That is, the subject might be off to the side a bit, or the image might include surrounding elements that you don't want or need to see. Fortunately these framing gaffes aren't set in stone because you can use Vista's Windows Photo Gallery application to essentially "reframe" the photo:

- You can adjust the photo so that it shows only the photo subject.
- You can adjust the photo to remove elements around the edges that you don't want.

In both cases, you're removing material from the outer parts of the photo, a process called *cropping*. Vista's Windows Photo Gallery comes with a cropping tool, which you use to specify a rectangular area of a photo that you want to keep. Windows Photo Gallery discards everything outside of the rectangle.

NOTE If you're using Windows XP, you can crop images using the Windows Live Photo Gallery application, which works with XP Service Pack 2 or later. For more about Windows Live Photo Gallery, see "Stitch Multiple Photos into a Panorama," later in this chapter.

Here's how to crop a digital photo using Windows Photo Gallery:

1. Select Start, All Programs, Windows Photo Gallery to open the Windows Photo Gallery application.

2. Click the image you want to crop.

3. Click Fix to open the Fix window.

4. Click Crop Picture. Photo Gallery displays a cropping rectangle on the photo.

5. Click and drag a corner or side to define the area you want to keep, as shown in Figure 21.2. Remember that Photo Gallery keeps the area inside the rectangle.

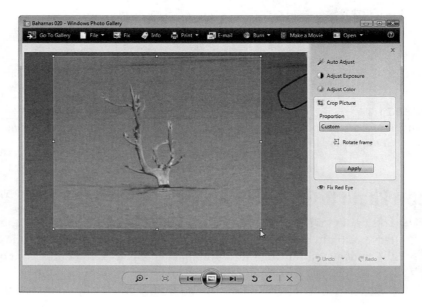

FIGURE 21.2

You can use Windows Photo Gallery's Crop Picture tool to crop out unwanted elements around the outside of a photo.

6. Click Apply. Photo Gallery crops the photo.

7. Click Back To Gallery.

NOTE If you want to crop a photo to achieve a particular aspect ratio—for example, 4×6 or 5×7—pull down the Proportion menu and choose the size you want. If you want to preserve the proportion but flip the sides of the cropping rectangle, click the Rotate Frame button.

Configure Custom Photo Import Names

Medium

When you need to import images from a device such as a digital camera, you can always connect the camera and then open the camera using the icon that appears in the Computer window. You can then move or copy the image from the camera to your PC using the standard cut (or copy) and paste techniques.

The only problem with that approach is that you end up with photos that use the existing filenames of the images. This is a problem because most cameras supply images with cryptic filenames, such as IMG_1083. These nondescriptive names can make it more difficult to find and work with images, particularly if you use the Details view in the Pictures folder.

To work around this problem, you can launch the import process from Windows Photo Gallery, which loads the Windows Picture and Video Import tool to perform the import. Crucially, this tool prompts you for an *event tag*—a word or short phrase—that describes the images you're importing. Windows Photo Gallery then uses this tag when it names the destination folder and the photos. For example, if you import on August 23, 2009 and you specify Cottage Vacation as the event tag, your imported images will be stored in a folder named 2009-08-23 Cottage Vacation, and the photos will be named Cottage Vacation 001, Cottage Vacation 002, and so on.

Even better, Windows Photo Gallery lets you customize the folder name using any of the following variations:

- Date Imported + Tag (the default)
- Date Taken + Tag
- Date Taken Range + Tag
- Tag + Date Imported
- Tag + Date Taken
- Tag + Date Taken Range
- Tag

You can also opt to preserve the original photo filenames if you prefer to skip the tag step, and you can set up separate settings for cameras, scanners, and discs.

Follow these steps to configure custom photo import names:

1. In Windows Photo Gallery, select File, Options.
2. Select the Import tab, shown in Figure 21.3.

FIGURE 21.3

In the Windows Photo Gallery Options dialog box, use the Import tab to configure custom import folder and filenames.

3. In the Settings For list, choose the device you want to work with: Cameras, CDs and DVS, or Scanners.

4. If you want to import photos to a different folder, click Browse, use the Browse for Folder dialog box to choose the folder, and then click OK.

5. In the Folder Name list, choose the format you want to use for the destination folder name.

6. In the File Name list, choose the format you want to use for the imported file names.

7. If you don't want specify a tag before the import, deactivate the Prompt for a Tag on Import check box.

8. Repeat steps 3–7 to configure import settings for other devices you use.

9. Click OK.

Stitch Multiple Photos into a Panorama

Easy

When you're on vacation, it can be frustrating if you come upon a vista that just won't fit in a single photo. It could be a massive mountain range or a peaceful beach landscape, but a single shot just doesn't do it justice. The usual "solution" here is to take several consecutive photos at the same elevation and with the same settings, but each photo begins about where the previous one ends. That way, you can print the photos and mount them side by side, which at least gives you an approximation of the original grandeur.

This works, but it means you must print the photos, and the gap between each image is a bit distracting, particularly if you didn't line up the shot perfectly and so there's a bit of overlap between them.

You can overcome all of these problems by "stitching" the photos into a single digital photo called a *panorama*. No built-in Windows tool does this, but Microsoft has created an update to Windows Photo Gallery that does. It's called Windows Live Photo Gallery, and you can install it on Vista Home Basic, Home Premium, and Ultimate PCs, as well as any PC running Windows XP Service Pack 2 or later. Go to http://get.live.com/, and then install Windows Live Photo Gallery.

After the program is installed, select Start, All Programs, Windows Live Photo Gallery to launch it. Now follow these steps to stitch your photos into a panorama:

1. Select the photos you want to stitch together, as shown in Figure 21.4.

FIGURE 21.4

You can use Windows Live Photo Gallery to stitch multiple photos into a single panorama.

2. Select Make, Create Panoramic Photo. Windows Live Photo Gallery analyzes the images to see if they're suitable for a panorama. If they are, the program stitches them together and then displays the Save Panoramic Stitch dialog box.

3. Use the File Name text box to name the stitched image.

4. Select a different location, if necessary.

5. Click Save. Windows Live Photo Gallery displays the stitched panorama, as shown in Figure 21.5.

> **TIP** This book's Technical Editor, Terri Stratton, provides the following tips for shooting photos for panoramas:
>
> ■ Each photo must have a common element with the next photo being stitched.
>
> ■ In order not to create a long, very narrow panorama, be sure to shoot above and below the target shot, again including a common element. This will give you a much better panoramic photo with a better proportion.
>
> ■ Be prepared to crop the final composite since the stitched shot is usually ragged on the edges. If you've missed one section of the shot, it can ruin the entire shot.
>
> ■ I've found that it really helps to extend the shots into areas that you don't want in the shot, both above, below and to each side. This gives you a better option of getting the panorama that you want after cropping.

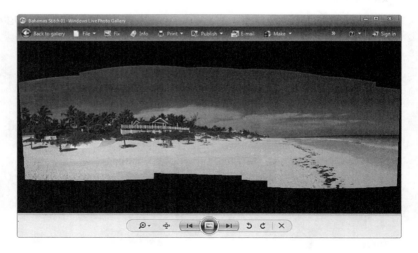

FIGURE 21.5

The six photos in Figure 21.4 stitched into a single panorama.

Publish Photos to Your Flickr Account

Easy

If you've got a Flickr (www.flickr.com) account for sharing your photos, you've probably experienced a common frustration: You use one program to import your photos, another to edit them, and then a third (your web browser or Flickr Uploadr) to send those photos to Flickr. Wouldn't it be *much* easier to be able to import, edit, and upload photos from a *single* application?

Sure it would, and now you can. If you get Windows Live Photo Gallery (see the previous section), you can use it to not only import and edit photos, but you can also use it to upload photos directly to Flickr. Nice!

Here's how it works:

1. In Windows Live Photo Gallery, select the photo or photos you want to upload.

2. Select Publish, More Services, Publish on Flickr. Windows Live Photo Gallery tells you that it requires your authorization to publish to Flickr.

3. Click Authorize. Your web browser appears and you see the Yahoo! sign-in page.

4. Type your Yahoo! ID and Password and click Sign In. The Authorize Windows Live Photo Gallery page appears.

5. Click OK, I'll Allow It. Flickr configures your account to authorize Windows Live Photo Gallery.

6. Return to Windows Live Photo Gallery and click Next. You see the Publish on Flickr dialog box.

7. Use the Flickr Account list to select the Flickr account you want to use (if you have more than one).

8. Use the Photo Sets list to choose or create a Flickr photo set.

9. Use the Photo Size list to select the width of the photos.

10. Use the Permissions list to select who can see the photos.

11. Click Publish. Windows Live Photo Gallery uploads the photos to Flickr.

12. When the upload is complete, either click View Photos to access your Flickr account, or click Close.

> **NOTE** In the future, you can upload by choosing your photos, selecting Publish, Publish on Flickr, and then filling in the Publish on Flickr dialog box.

> **NOTE** To revoke the Windows Live Photo Gallery permission, log on to your Flickr account, click You, and then click Your Account. Click the Extending Flickr tab and, in the Account Links section, click Edit. Click the Remove Permission? link beside Windows Live Photo Gallery, activate the I Understand… check box, and then click Revoke Permissions.

CHAPTER 22

Customizing Video

With average hard drives now weighing in at hundreds of gigabytes and terabyte hard drives becoming more and more commonplace, we suddenly find ourselves in the unusual position of having a lot more hard disk space than we can use. This, of course, is but a temporary situation. Parkinson's Law of Data tells us that "data expands to fill the space available," so before long even terabyte drives will begin to seem cramped. How is that possible? One word: video. Movies and recorded TV shows are multigigabyte monsters that threaten to swamp even the largest hard disks.

This chapter can help prevent that from happening (or, realistically, slow it down a bit) by showing you how to record shows to a remote location, remove ads, and compress videos so they take up less space.

Record TV Shows to a Network Location

Medium

When you record TV in Windows Media Center, the program stores the resulting files—which use the Microsoft Recorded TV Show file type with the `.dvr-ms` extension—in the following folder:

- **Windows Vista**—`%SystemDrive%\Users\Public\Recorded TV`

- **Windows XP Media Center Edition**—`%SystemDrive%\Documents and Settings\Shared Documents\Recorded TV`

If you want to give other people access to your recorded shows, you must share the `Recorded TV` folder. That's not a big problem if you're dealing with one folder, but what if you want to share recorded TV from several machines? Even if you go to the trouble of sharing all those other folders, you're still left with the problem of trying to figure out which folder holds the TV shows you want.

> **CAUTION** Recording a TV show is incredibly bandwidth intensive, so the modification in this section stretches your home network to its limit. Even though it's possible to record shows to a remote location on a 100Mbps wired or 54Mbps (802.11g) wireless connection, for best results, you really should do this only on a network that uses either 1Gbps wired connections or an 802.11n wireless connection.

A much better idea is to set up a Recorded TV folder on a single network share and record all TV shows to that share. Unfortunately, this is not as simple as tweaking a folder value, because Media Center has no such setting. However, by modifying some Media Center services and Registry settings, you can get it done.

Here are the steps to follow:

1. On the Media Center computer, log on with a user who uses the Administrator account type.
2. Make sure this same user has Full access to the network share you're going to use.
3. On the Media Center computer, select Start, right-click Computer, and click Manage. In Vista, enter your User Account Control credentials to continue. The Computer Management snap-in appears.
4. Select Services and Applications, Services.
5. Double-click the Windows Media Center Extender Service to open the service's property sheet.
6. Display the Log On tab.

7. In the This Account text box, type the name of the user account from step 1.

8. Type the user's password into the Password and Confirm Password text boxes.

9. Click OK. (If you see a dialog box confirming that the user has been granted Log On as Service rights, click OK.)

10. Repeat steps 5–9 for the Windows Media Center Receiver Service and the Windows Media Center Scheduler Service.

11. Because these two services in step 10 are started, in each case Windows warns you that you must stop and restart the service to put the new user into effect. To do that, for each of those services, select it in the Services list, click the Stop link, and then click the Start link.

12. On the network computer, create a subfolder to hold your recorded TV shows. For best results, use a folder name without spaces, such as `RecordedTV`.

13. Return to the Media Center computer, press Windows Logo+R to open the Run dialog box, type `regedit`, and click OK to start the Registry Editor. (You'll need to enter your UAC credentials in Vista to continue.)

14. Navigate to the following key:

    `HKLM\SOFTWARE\Microsoft\Windows\CurrentVersion\Media Center\`
    `Service\Recording`

15. Double-click the RecordPath setting and change its value to the UNC path to the Windows Home Server folder you created in step 12.

16. If you don't see a WatchedFolders setting, select Edit, New, String Value, type `WatchedFolders`, and press Enter.

17. Double-click the WatchedFolders setting and change its value to the UNC path to the Windows Home Server folder you created in step 12. Figure 22.1 shows the resulting Registry values.

18. Reboot the Media Center computer.

When you return to Windows, all future TV recordings will go straight to the network share.

NOTE Windows Media Center is a large topic that can't possibly be covered in its entirety here. If you want to learn more about Windows Media Center, see *Unleashing Windows Vista Media Center*, by Mark Edward Soper, published by Que.

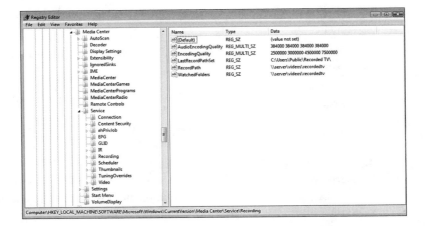

FIGURE 22.1
To get Media Center to record to a network share, you need to make a couple of Registry tweaks.

Edit Ads from a Recorded TV Show

Medium

If you have a TV tuner in your PC, you can connect a cable or other signal to the tuner and then use Media Center to record TV shows to your hard drive. You can then play back the TV shows at your leisure. If you have a Media Center remote control, you can skip through the commercials lickety-split. That's a reasonable option for shows that you're only going to watch once and then trash, but what about shows you plan to watch multiple times? Or what about a longer recording such as a movie that has lots of commercial breaks?

In these cases, you can improve your viewing experience immeasurably by editing the commercial from the recording. That sounds like a lot of work, but with the version of Windows Movie Maker that comes with Vista, all it takes is a few mouse clicks.

Here are the steps to follow:

1. Select Start, All Programs, Windows Movie Maker to open the Movie Maker program.

2. Click Import Media.

3. Open the %SystemDrive%\Users\Public\Recorded TV folder, click the TV show you want to edit, and then click Import. Movie Maker adds the TV show to the Imported Media list.

4. Select View, Timeline (or Press Ctrl+T).

5. Click and drag the TV show icon and drop it in the Video section of the timeline.

6. Locate the next commercial break.

7. Click in the time portion of the timeline at the beginning of the commercial break. Movie Maker adds a green box at the location.

8. Select Clip, Split. (You can also just press **M** or click the Split button.) Movie Maker splits the video into two clips: one that ends at the beginning of the commercial break and a second that starts at the beginning of the commercial break.

9. Click in the time portion of the timeline at the end of the commercial break. Movie Maker adds a green box at the location.

10. Select Clip, Split (or press **M** or click the Split button). Movie Maker splits the video into three clips, where the middle clip consists of the commercial break, as shown in Figure 22.2.

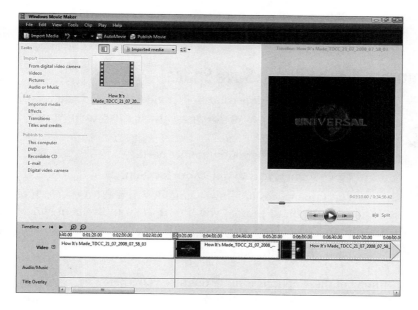

FIGURE 22.2

Split the TV show in three clips, where the middle clip consists of the commercial break you want to remove.

11. Right-click the clip that contains the commercials, and then click Remove. (You can also click the clip and then press Delete.) Movie Maker deletes the commercials.

12. Repeat steps 6–11 to remove all the commercial breaks in the TV show.

13. Click Publish Movie. Movie Maker launches the Publish Movie wizard.

> **NOTE** Because the edited show is no longer in the recorded TV file format, it won't show up in the Media Center's Recorded TV section. Instead, you need to access Media Center's Video Library and play the edited show from there.

14. Click This Computer and then click Next.

15. Enter a File Name for the movie, use the Browse button to select a folder (such as `%userProfile%\Videos` or `%SystemDrive%\Users\Public\Public Videos`), and then click Next.

16. Choose the Best Quality for Playback on My Computer option. (See the next section for a closer look at the options on this page.)

17. Click Publish. Movie Maker publishes the movie.

18. Click Finish.

Compress Video Files to Save Space

Easy

If you're managing a large collection of video files and you're worried about them usurping all your hard disk space, there are a number of solutions you can try:

- Delete any videos you no longer need.
- Move some videos to a network location.
- Edit large videos to remove content you don't need (such as the commercials that I showed you how to edit out in the previous tweak).
- Burn some videos to DVD and then delete them from your hard disk.
- Give up and just add more hard disk space.

If none of these options is quite right for you, there's yet another you can try: Compress the videos. I'm not talking about using NTFS file compression, because that won't have much effect on most videos (which are already compressed a certain amount). Instead, I'm talking about changing the videos to a format that uses more compression, or that uses lower-quality settings.

With an image, you can load the file into Paint or some other graphics program, run the Save As command, and then choose a different file format. Videos are a bit different because they must be encoded, and that takes quite a bit of effort. However, it's still possible to choose a different format if you use Movie Maker to publish the video.

Here are the steps to follow:

1. Select Start, All Programs, Windows Movie Maker to open the Movie Maker program.

2. Click Import Media.

3. Open the folder that contains the video you want to compress, and then click Import. Movie Maker adds the video to the Imported Media list.

4. Select View, Timeline (or Press Ctrl+T).

5. Click and drag the TV show icon and drop it in the Video section of the timeline.

6. Click Publish Movie. Movie Maker launches the Publish Movie wizard.

7. Click This Computer and then click Next.

8. Enter a File Name for the movie, use the Browse button to select a folder, and then click Next.

9. You have two ways to go from here:

   ■ **Compress To**—Choose this option and then use the text box to type the number of megabytes you want the final video file to be. (If you want to *really* compress the file, choose KB in the list.) Whatever number you enter, Movie Maker reduces the bit rate and possibly also the frames per second to achieve the desired size. Skip to step 11.

   ■ **More Settings**—Choose this option if you want to use a predefined format, which I describe in step 10.

10. If you selected the More Settings option, choose one of the formats in the associated drop-down list. To help you choose, Table 22.1 summarizes the formats and compares the bit rates, frame rates, and frame sizes. The formats are sorted by how much disk space each one takes up per minute of video.

Table 22.1 Comparing the Video Formats Available with Movie Maker's Publish Movie Wizard

Format	Bit Rate	Frame Rate	Frame Size	Size Per Minute of Video
DV-AVI (NTSC)	28.6Mbps	30fps	720×480	220MB
Windows Media HD 1080p	7.8Mbps	30fps	1440×1080	60MB
Windows Media HD for Xbox 360	6.9Mbps	30fps	1280×720	53MB
Windows Media HD 720p	5.9Mbps	30fps	1280×720	45MB
Windows Media DVD Quality	3.0Mbps	30fps	720×480	23MB
Windows Media DVD Widescreen Quality	3.0Mbps	30fps	720×480	23MB
Windows Media Portable Device	1.0Mbps	30fps	640×480	8MB
Windows Media VHS Quality	1.0Mbps	30fps	640×480	8MB
Windows Media Low Bandwidth	117Kbps	15fps	320×240	900KB

11. Click Publish. Movie Maker publishes the movie.

12. Click Finish.

Handy File and Folder Tweaks

ile and folder chores are among the most common day-to-day activities in Windows, but they rarely pay the bills. To free up time for more productive pursuits, it helps to know your way around the file system. This chapter will help by showing a few tweaks that should speed up some file and folder chores and solve some file system problems. Don't forget to also check out the next few chapters, too, which supply you with handy tweaks related to disk drives, searching, backups, and customizing the Windows file system.

Delete the Oldest Files in a Folder

Medium

Files have a way of sneakily adding up to significant chunks of disk real estate over time. For example, I use QuickBooks to manage my business and personal finances, and every time I make changes to my accounts, I make a backup copy of the company files. I save these backups in a separate folder, and I give each backup file a unique name so that I always have multiple backups should anything go wrong. A while back I happened to open that folder and was shocked to find that all those backup files had carved out well over 1GB of disk space!

The normal solution in such cases is to delete the oldest files because they are the least likely to be useful. However, that means sorting the folder on the Date Modified property, selecting the oldest files, deleting them, and then perhaps repeating the procedure if the remaining files still take up too much disk space.

This isn't an onerous task, but it seems like much more work than it needs to be. In other words, this calls for a script! Listing 23.1 presents a script I wrote that examines a folder to see if it's over a certain size. If it is, the script deletes the oldest files until the size is below the threshold.

> **NOTE** The file containing the script in Listing 23.1—DeleteOldestFiles.vbs—is available from my website at http://mcfedries.com/cs/content/TweakItFreakIt.aspx. See Chapter 32, "Running Programs," to learn how to run the script on your PC.

Listing 23.1   A Script That Deletes the Oldest Files from a Folder Until That Folder Is Below a Specified Size

```
Option Explicit
Dim objFSO, objFolder, objFiles, objFile
Dim intMaxFolderSize, intFolderSize, intFileSize
Dim intDeletedFiles, intDeletedFilesSize
Dim strFolder, strFileName, strOldestFileName
Dim dtFileDate, dtOldestFileDate
'
' Initialize some variables
'
' Set maximum folder size to 100MB (104,857,600 bytes)
'
intMaxFolderSize = 104857600
'
' Change the following value to path of the folder you want to work with
'
strFolder = "C:\SomeFolder"
strOldestFileName = ""
dtOldestFileDate = Now
intDeletedFiles = 0
intDeletedFilesSize = 0
'
' Initialize the file system object and get the folder
'
```

Listing 23.1   Continued

```
Set objFSO = CreateObject("Scripting.FileSystemObject")
Set objFolder = objFSO.GetFolder(strFolder)
'
' Get the size of the folder
'
intFolderSize = objFolder.Size
'
' Is it larger than our maximum size?
'
Do While intFolderSize > intMaxFolderSize
    '
    ' If so, return the files in the folder
    '
    Set objFiles = objFolder.Files
    '
    ' Run through the files
    '
    For Each objFile in objFiles
        '
        ' Get the file name, date, and size
        '
        strFileName = objFile.Path
        dtFileDate = objFile.DateCreated
        intFileSize = objFile.Size
        '
        ' Is it the oldest file in the folder so far?
        '
        If dtFileDate < dtOldestFileDate Then
            '
            ' If so, store its date as the oldest and save the file path
            '
            dtOldestFileDate = dtFileDate
            strOldestFileName = strFileName
        End If
    Next
    '
    ' Delete the oldest file
```

continues

Listing 23.1   Continued

```
        '
        objFSO.DeleteFile(strOldestFileName)
        '
        ' Update the number of files and total size deleted
        '
        intDeletedFiles = intDeletedFiles + 1
        intDeletedFilesSize = intDeletedFilesSize + intFileSize
        '
        ' Reset some variables for the next loop
        '
        strOldestFileName = ""
        dtOldestFileDate = Now
        intFolderSize = objFolder.Size
Loop
'
' Display the number of files deleted
' and the approximate size of the deleted files
'
MsgBox "Deleted " & intDeletedFiles & " file(s) (approximately " & _
        Int(intDeletedFilesSize / 1024 / 1024) & "MB)"
```

The script begins by initializing a few variables. In particular, it sets the
intMaxFolderSize variable to 104857600, which is the number of bytes in
100MB. The VBScript file system works in bytes, so we need to convert
megabytes to bytes. The script also initializes the strFolder variable to the full
path of the folder you want to work with. Remember to change both variables
to suit your needs.

The script initializes the VBScript FileSystemObject, stores the folder in the
objFolder variable, and then uses the Size property to get the total size of the
folder. The script then runs a Do While loop, which loops as long as the size of
the folder (intFolderSize) is larger than the maximum folder size we want.

Inside the loop, the script gets the collection of files using the Files property,
and then runs through the collection. Each time a file's date is older than the
currently oldest date, the script makes note of the file's path, date, and size.
When the For Each…Next loop is done, we have the oldest file in the folder, so
the script uses the DeleteFile method to delete it.

Rename Multiple Files in One Fell Swoop

Medium

In a Command Prompt session, you use the REN (or RENAME) command to change the name of one or more files and folders. Here's the syntax:

```
REN old_filename1 new_filename
```

old_filename	The original filename
new_filename	The new filename

For example, the following command renames Budget 2008.xlsx to Budget 2009.xlsx:

```
ren "Budget 2008.xlsx" "Budget 2009.xlsx"
```

A simple file or folder rename such as this probably isn't something you'll ever fire up a command-line session to do because renaming a single object is faster and easier in Windows Explorer. However, the real power of the REN command is that it accepts wildcards in the file specifications. This enables you to rename several files at once, something you can't do in Windows Explorer.

For example, suppose you have a folder full of files, many of which contain 2008 somewhere in the filename. To rename all those files by changing 2008 to 2009, you'd use the following command:

```
ren *2008* *2009*
```

Similarly, if you have a folder full of files that use the .htm extension and you want to change each extension to .asp, you'd use the following command:

```
ren *.htm *.asp
```

Note that for these multiple-file renames to work, in most cases the original filename text and the new filename text must be the same length. For example, digital cameras often supply photos with names such as img_1234.jpg and img_5678.jpg. If you have a number of related photos in a folder, you might want to give them more meaningful names. If the photos are from a vacation in Rome, you might prefer names such as Rome_Vacation_1234.jpg and Rome_Vacation_5678.jpg. Unfortunately, the

> **NOTE** In this section I assume you've already changed to the folder that contains the files you want to rename. To do that at the command prompt, type **cd**, a space, and then the full path to the folder, surrounded by quotation marks (just in case there's a space in the path).

REN command can't handle this. However, it can rename the files to
Rome1234.jpg and Rome5678.jpg:

```
ren img_* Rome*
```

The exception to the same length rule is if the replacement occurs at the end
of the filenames. For example, the following command renames all files with
the .jpeg extension to .jpg:

```
ren *.jpeg *.jpg
```

Open a Folder at the Command Prompt

Medium

When you're working in Windows Explorer, you might find occasionally that
you need to do some work at the command prompt. For example, the current
folder might contain multiple files that need to be renamed—a task that, as
you saw in the previous tweak, is most easily done within a command-line
session. Selecting Start, All Programs, Accessories, Command Prompt starts the
session in the %UserProfile% folder, so you have to use one or more CD (change
directory) commands to get to the folder you want to work in.

This is, of course, way too much work, but we can tweak Windows to make
life easier. The secret behind this is that Windows keeps tracks of hundreds of
different file types, from text documents to bitmap images to Excel workbooks.
Each of these file types comes with one or more defined *actions*, which are
tasks that you can perform with a file of that type. For example, most file
types have actions named Open (to open the file in its associated application)
and Print (to print the file using its associated application).

Windows has a Folder file type that, naturally, deals with folders. So our tweak
here is to create a new action for the Folder file type that launches the command prompt and automatically displays the current Windows Explorer
folder. This is one of the rare tweaks that's actually quite a bit easier in XP
than in Vista, so I'll handle them separately.

Tweaking XP to Open a Folder at the Command Prompt

Here are the steps to follow in Windows XP:

1. In Windows Explorer, select Tools,
   Folder Options to display the Folder
   Options dialog box.

2. Select the File Types tab.

> **NOTE** You can also get to
> the Folder Options
> dialog box by launching the Con-
> trol Panel's Folder Options icon.

3. In the Registered File Types list, select Folder.

4. Click Advanced to display the Edit File Type dialog box.

5. Click New to display the New Action dialog box.

6. Type Open &With Command Prompt in the Action text box (note that the letter W is the accelerator key).

7. In the Application Used to Perform Action text box, type the following:

   cmd.exe /k cd "%L"

8. Figure 23.1 shows a completed dialog box. Click OK when you're done. Windows XP adds your new action to the Folder type's Actions list.

NOTE The cmd.exe file is the command prompt executable file. The /k switch tells Windows XP to keep the command prompt window open after the CD (change directory) command completes. The %L placeholder represents the full pathname of the current folder.

TIP You can't edit or delete this new action in the Edit File Type dialog box. If you need to make changes to this action, use the following Registry key:

HKEY_CLASSES_ROOT\Folder\ shell

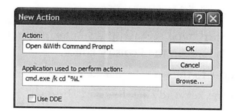

FIGURE 23.1

Use the New Action dialog box to define a new action for the file type.

9. Click Close.

In Figure 23.2, I right-clicked a folder. Notice how the new action appears in the shortcut menu.

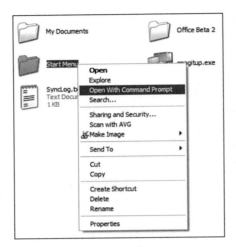

FIGURE 23.2
The new action appears in the file type's shortcut menu.

Tweaking Vista to Open a Folder at the Command Prompt

Here are the steps to follow in Windows Vista:

1. Select Start, type **regedit**, press Enter, and then provide your UAC credentials to open the Registry Editor.

2. Navigate to the HKCR\Folder key.

3. Open the key and click the shell branch.

4. Select Edit, New, Key, type **Open with Command Prompt**, and press Enter.

5. Select Edit, New, Key, type **command**, and press Enter.

6. In the command branch, double-click the Default value to open the Edit String dialog box.

7. Type the following:

    ```
    cmd.exe /k cd "%L"
    ```

8. Click OK. Figure 23.3 shows the Registry Editor with the new Open with Command Prompt action added to the HKCR\Folder\shell key.

In Figure 23.4, I right-clicked a folder, and you can see that the new action appears in the shortcut menu.

NOTE The cmd.exe file is the Command Prompt executable file. The /k switch tells Windows Vista to keep the command prompt window open after the CD (change directory) command completes. The %L placeholder represents the full pathname of the current folder.

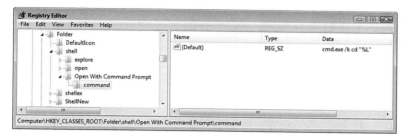

FIGURE 23.3

In Vista, modify the HKCR\Folder\shell key to define a new action for the Folder file type.

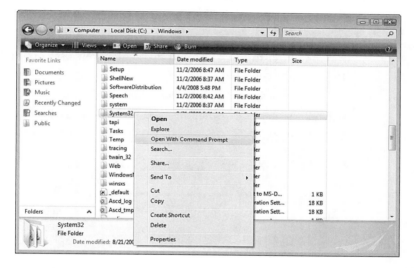

FIGURE 23.4

After you add the new action to the Folder file type's shell key, the action appears in the Folder file type's shortcut menu.

Fix Permission Problems by Taking Ownership of Your Files

Medium

When you're working in Vista or XP, you may have trouble with a folder (or a file) because Windows tells you that you don't have permission to edit (add to, delete, whatever) the folder. In XP the result is often a simple Access Denied error, whereas in Vista you get a series of annoying User Account Control dialog boxes.

You might think the solution is to give your user account Full Control permissions on the folder, but it's not as easy as that. Why not? Because you're not the owner of the folder. (If you were, you'd have the permissions you need automatically.) So the solution is to first take ownership of the folder, and then assign your user account full control permissions over the folder.

Here are the steps to follow:

1. Use Windows Explorer to locate the folder you want to take ownership of.
2. Right-click the folder and then click Properties to open the folder's property sheet.
3. Display the Security tab.
4. Click Advanced to open the Advanced Security Settings dialog box.
5. Display the Owner tab.
6. In Windows Vista, click Edit and then enter your User Account Control credentials to continue.
7. In the Change Owner To list, click your user account.
8. Activate the Replace Owner on Subcontainers and Objects check box, as shown in Figure 23.5.

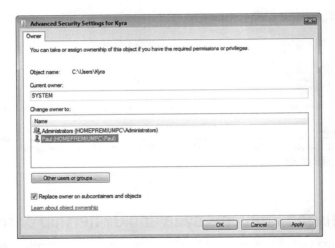

FIGURE 23.5
Use the Owner tab to take ownership of a folder.

9. Click OK. Windows Vista warns you that you need to reopen the property sheet to change the folder's permissions.

10. Click OK in the open dialog boxes.

11. Right-click the folder and then click Properties to open the folder's property sheet.

12. Display the Security tab.

NOTE   You can find the Registry Editor file (TakeOwnership.reg) on my website at www.mcfedries.com/cs/TweakItFreakIt.aspx.

13. If you do not see your user account in the Group or User Names list, click Edit (Vista only), click Add, type your username, and click OK.

14. Click your username.

15. Click the Full Control check box in the Allow column.

16. Click OK in the open dialog boxes.

Note that, obviously, this is quite a bit of work. If you only have to do it every once in a while, it's not a big thing, but if you find you have to take ownership regularly, you'll probably want an easier way to go about it. You've got it! Listing 23.2 shows a Registry Editor file that modifies the Registry in such a way that you end up with a Take Ownership command in the shortcut menu that appears if you right-click any folder and any file.

Listing 23.2   A Registry Editor File That Creates a Take Ownership Command

```
Windows Registry Editor Version 5.00

[HKEY_CLASSES_ROOT\*\shell\runas]
@="Take Ownership"
"NoWorkingDirectory"=""

[HKEY_CLASSES_ROOT\*\shell\runas\command]
@="cmd.exe /c takeown /f \"%1\" && icacls \"%1\" /grant administrators:F"
"IsolatedCommand"="cmd.exe /c takeown /f \"%1\" && icacls \"%1\" /grant
administrators:F"

[HKEY_CLASSES_ROOT\Directory\shell\runas]
@="Take Ownership"
"NoWorkingDirectory"=""

[HKEY_CLASSES_ROOT\Directory\shell\runas\command]
@="cmd.exe /c takeown /f \"%1\" /r /d y && icacls \"%1\" /grant
➥administrators:F /t"
"IsolatedCommand"="cmd.exe /c takeown /f \"%1\" /r /d y && icacls \"%1\"
➥/grant administrators:F /t"
```

To use the file, double-click it and then, in Vista, enter your UAC credentials when prompted. As you can see in Figure 23.6, right-clicking (in this case) a folder displays a shortcut menu with a new Take Ownership command. Click that command, enter your UAC credentials in Vista, and sit back as Windows does all the hard work for you!

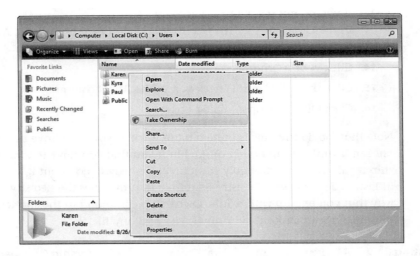

FIGURE 23.6

When you install the Registry mod, you see the Take Ownership command when you right-click a file.

Dealing with Disk Drives

Despite the timely demise of the floppy disk drive, these days we deal with disk drives more than ever. We still have internal hard drives to work with, of course, but with USB, IEEE 1394, and even eSATA (external SATA) ports commonplace on newer systems, external hard drives are all the rage. All systems have at least one optical (CD, DVD, or Blu-ray) drive, USB Flash drives are ubiquitous, and if your system has a memory card reader you probably have a half dozen or more extra drives to handle memory card formats such as CompactFlash, Memory Stick, and SD Card.

To help you handle this drive onslaught, and to help you keep the most important drive—your system's internal hard drive—in top shape, this chapter offers several disk drive-related tweaks for your enjoyment.

Schedule Automatic Defrags in XP

 One of the unheralded innovations in Windows Vista is automatic disk defragmentation. That is, right out of the box Vista is configured to run Disk Defragmenter automatically—the default schedule is weekly: every Sunday at 4:00 a.m. This is great because it means that you should never need to defragment your Vista system manually.

Medium

No such luck in Windows XP, which expects you to remember to defragment your system regularly. Most of us forget, of course, and the result is usually an XP system that does the whole molasses-in-January thing.

CAUTION The DEFRAG switches are case sensitive. So, for example, the following command will work properly:

```
defrag c: -a
```

However, this command will not:

```
defrag c: -A
```

What's a poor XP user to do? Why, tweak XP to work around the problem, of course! First, you need to know how to run a defrag using a command rather than the Disk Defragmenter GUI. To do this, you have to use the DEFRAG command-line tool. Here's the syntax:

```
DEFRAG volume [-a] [-f] [-v]
```

`volume`	Specifies the drive letter (followed by a colon) of the disk or the folder path of the mount point that you want to defragment.
`-a`	Tells DEFRAG only to analyze the disk.
`-f`	Forces DEFRAG to defragment the disk, even if it doesn't need defragmenting or if the disk has less than 15% free space. (DEFRAG normally requires at least that much free space because it needs an area in which to sort the files.)
`-v`	Runs DEFRAG in verbose mode, which displays both the analysis report and the defragmentation report.

For example, to get an analysis report of the fragmentation of the C: drive, enter the following command:

`defrag c: -a`

If the volume isn't too fragmented, you see a report similar to this:

```
Windows Disk Defragmenter
Copyright (c) 2001 Microsoft Corp. and Executive Software International,
Inc.


Analysis Report
    20.00 GB Total, 6.23 GB (31%) Free, 4% Fragmented (9% file
fragmentation)


You do not need to defragment this volume.
```

However, if the drive is quite fragmented, you see a report similar to the following:

```
Windows Disk Defragmenter
Copyright (c) 2001 Microsoft Corp. and Executive Software International,
Inc.


Analysis Report
    190 GB Total, 17.84 GB (9%) Free, 32% Fragmented (65% file
fragmentation)


You should defragment this volume.
```

In the latter example, notice that the volume only has 9 percent free disk space. If you try to defragment this volume, DEFRAG displays the following message:

```
Volume DATA has only 9% free space available for use by Disk
Defragmenter.
To run effectively, Disk Defragmenter requires at least 15% usable free
space.
There is not enough disk space to properly complete the operation.
Delete some unneeded files on your hard disk, and then try again.
```

If you can't delete files from the volume, you can try running DEFRAG with the -f switch to force the operation:

```
defrag d: -f
```

With all that in mind, your next step is to set up a task to run the DEFRAG command automatically on a regular schedule. Here's how it's done:

1. Select Start, Accessories, System Tools, Scheduled Tasks. The Scheduled Tasks folder appears.

2. Double-click the Add Scheduled Task icon. The Scheduled Task Wizard appears.

3. Click Next. The wizard prompts you to choose the program you want to run.

NOTE Forcing the defrag operation shouldn't cause problems in most cases. With less free space in which to work, DEFRAG just takes quite a bit longer to defragment the volume, and there may be parts of the volume that it simply can't defragment.

TIP You can also run Scheduled Tasks by selecting Start, Control Panel, and then double-clicking the Scheduled Tasks icon.

4. Click Browse to open the Select a Program to Schedule dialog box.

5. Open the %SystemRoot%\System32 folder (where %SystemRoot% is usually C:\Windows), select defrag.exe, and click Open.

6. Type a name for the task (such as **Weekly Disk Defrag**), click the Weekly option (see Figure 24.1), and then click Next.

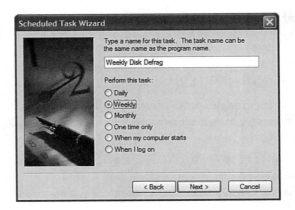

FIGURE 24.1

Name your task and choose the Weekly option.

7. Use the Start Time control to select a time to run the weekly defrag. I suggest a time when you won't be using your computer, such as 3:00 a.m. (or, if you're a dedicated night owl, 3:00 p.m.).

8. Activate the check box beside the day of the week you want the defrag to run (again, pick a day when you're less likely to need your machine, such as Sunday), and then click Next.

9. Type your username and password (twice) and click Next.

10. Activate the Open Advanced Properties for This Task When I Click Finish check box and then click Finish. The task's property sheet appears.

11. In the Task tab, use the Run text box to add the DEFRAG parameters and switches you want to use. For example, to force a defrag of the C: drive, you need to add **c: -f** to the Run text, as shown in Figure 24.2.

12. Click OK. Task Scheduler prompts you for your account data.

13. Type your username and password (twice) and click OK.

FIGURE 24.2

Use the Run text box to add your DEFRAG parameters and switches.

Divide Your Hard Drive into Two Partitions

Medium

In hard drive circles, a *partition*—it's also called a *volume*—is a subset of a hard drive that you can access and work with as a separate entity. Most hard drives consist of just a single partition that takes up the entire disk, and that partition is almost always drive C. However, it's possible to divide a single hard drive into two (or more) partitions and assign a drive letter to each—say, C and D.

Why would you want to do such a thing? Lots of reasons, but two are by far the most common:

  ■ You want to install a second operating system on your computer and dual-boot between them. In this case, you need to create a second partition and install the other operating system to that partition.

➜ **See** Chapter W6, "Dual-Booting Windows with Other Operating Systems," which is available at my website: www.mcfedries.com/cs/content/TweakItFreakIt.aspx.

  ■ You want to separate your data from Windows. In this case, you need to create a second partition and move your data to that partition. This is a good idea because if you ever have to reinstall Windows from scratch, you can wipe drive C: without having to worry about your data.

In Windows versions prior to Vista, partitioning a hard drive required third-party software such as Partition Magic (www.symantec.com) or Partition Manager (www.acronis.com). Windows Vista changes that by offering the welcome ability to manage partitions without extra software. You can reduce the size of a partition, enlarge a partition, create a new partition, and delete an existing partition.

> **TIP** To go directly to the Disk Management snap-in, display the Run dialog box, type **diskmgmt.msc**, and click OK.

In this tweak, you learn how to divide a hard drive into two partitions. You do that by first shrinking the existing partition, and then creating the new partition in the freed-up disk space. Here are the steps to follow:

1. Select Start, right-click Computer, and then click Manage. The User Account Control dialog box appears.

2. Enter your UAC credentials to continue. The Computer Management snap-in appears.

3. Click Disk Management. The Disk Management snap-in appears, as shown in Figure 24.3.

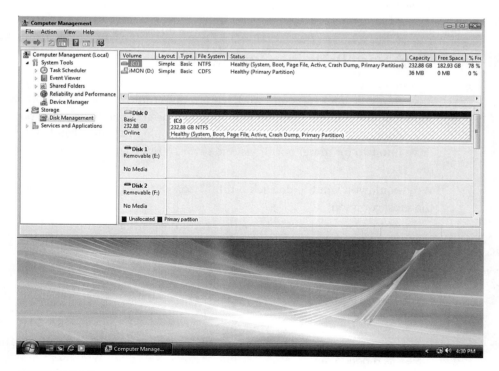

FIGURE 24.3

Use the Disk Management snap-in to work with your hard drive partitions.

4. Right-click the drive you want to partition and then click Shrink Volume. Disk Management displays the Shrink *D:* dialog box (where *D* is the drive letter of the partition).

5. Use the Enter the Amount of Space to Shrink in MB text box to type the amount by which you want the partition size reduced, as shown in Figure 24.4. Keep in mind that this will be the approximate size of the new partition that you create a bit later.

NOTE You can't enter a shrink size that's larger than the shrink space you have at your disposal, which is given by the Size of Available Shrink Space value. If you're shrinking drive C:, the available shrink space will be quite a bit less than the available free space because Windows reserves quite a bit of space on drive C: for the paging file and other system files that may grow over time.

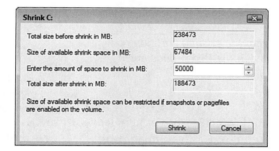

FIGURE 24.4

Enter the amount by which you want the existing partition reduced.

6. Click Shrink. Windows Vista shrinks the partition and displays the freed space as Unallocated, as you can see in Figure 24.5.

7. Right-click the Unallocated space and then click New Simple Volume. The New Simple Volume Wizard appears.

8. Click Next. The Specify Volume Size wizard appears.

9. Make sure that the Simple Volume Size in MB text box is set to the maximum value, and then click Next. The Assign Drive Letter or Path dialog box appears.

10. Select the Assign the Following Drive Letter option, use the list to select the drive letter you want to assign to the new partition, and then click Next.

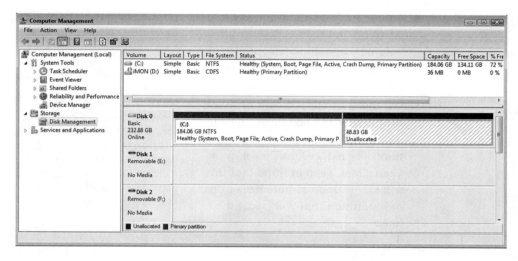

FIGURE 24.5
The space removed from the existing partition now appears as Unallocated in the Disk Management snap-in.

11. Select the Format This Volume with the Following Settings option, leave the settings as is (you might want to change the Volume Label, however), and click Next.

12. Click Finish. Windows Vista formats the partition and assigns the drive letter.

TIP If you have an optical disk and a card reader, you might end up with your new partition using a high drive letter such as J or M. What can you do if you'd prefer to use drive letter D for the new partition? Fortunately, Vista also enables you to assign new drive letters. Right-click the drive that is currently assigned the letter D, click Change Drive Letter and Paths, click Change, assign a new drive letter, click OK, and then click Yes to confirm. Now right-click the partition you just created, click Change Drive Letter and Paths, click Change, assign the letter D, click OK, and then click Yes to confirm.

Determine a Remote Computer's Disk Drive Free Space

Medium

You know it's important to keep an eye on the free disk space on your disks to avoid running low on space, which can cause all kinds of problems, particularly on the system drive. That's easy enough on your local computer (open the

Computer or My Computer window), but what about computers on your network? Assuming you don't want to (or can't) sit down in front of each computer, you need a remote way of checking free disk space. Sounds like a challenge, but you can do it using a Windows Management Instrumentation (WMI) script.

In the WMI examples you've seen so far, I've used `localhost` as the value of the `strComputer` variable, which connects to the local computer's WMI service:

```
strComputer = "localhost"
Set objWMI = GetObject("winmgmts:{impersonationLevel=impersonate}!\\" & _
          strComputer & "\root\cimv2")
```

You could also use the name of your computer, like this:

```
strComputer = "MyPC"
Set objWMI = GetObject("winmgmts:{impersonationLevel=impersonate}!\\" & _
          strComputer & "\root\cimv2")
```

In this case, I used the name of the local computer—`MyPC`—instead of `localhost`. However, WMI scripting doesn't restrict you to working only with the local machine. In fact, WMI was created so that IT types and network admins could manage remote computers on the network. This means that it's almost trivial to configure a script to run on a network client:

- You change the value of the `strComputer` variable to the name of the remote computer you want to manage.

- You configure the network client's firewall to accept remote administration traffic.

➜ For the details on configuring the remote administration firewall exception, **see** "Configure a Network Computer for Remote Administration," **p. 358**.

Listing 24.1 shows a script that returns disk drive information from a remote computer.

NOTE To get the file with the Listing 24.1 code—it's called `RemoteFreeSpace.vbs`—see my website: www.mcfedries.com/cs/content/TweakItFreakIt.aspx.

```
Option Explicit
Dim strComputer, strDriveData
Dim objWMI, objDrives, objDrive
'
' Get the WMI service
'
strComputer = "homepremiumpc"
Set objWMI = GetObject("winmgmts:" & _
                       "{impersonationLevel=impersonate}!\\" & _
                       strComputer & "\root\cimv2")
'
' Get the instances of hard disk drives (MediaType = 12)
'
Set objDrives = objWMI.ExecQuery("SELECT * FROM Win32_LogicalDisk " & _
                                 WHERE MediaType = 12")
'
' Initialize the display string
'
strDriveData = "Disk Drive Data for " & _
               UCase(strComputer) & ":" & vbCrLf & vbCrLf
    strDriveData = strDriveData & _
        "Letter:" & vbTab & _
        "Name:" & vbTab & _
        "System:" & vbTab & _
        "Size:" & vbTab & _
        "Free:" & vbTab & _
        "% Free:" & vbTab &  vbCrLf & _
        "=====" & vbTab & _
        "=====" & vbTab & _
        "=====" & vbTab & _
        "=====" & vbTab & _
        "=====" & vbTab & _
        "=====" & vbTab & vbCrLf
'
' Collect the drive data
'
For Each objDrive In objDrives
```

Listing 24.1   Continued

```
        strDriveData = strDriveData & _
            objDrive.Name & vbTab & _
            objDrive.VolumeName & vbTab & _
            objDrive.FileSystem & vbTab & _
            FormatNumber(objDrive.Size / 1073741824, 1) & " GB" & vbTab & _
            FormatNumber(objDrive.FreeSpace / 1073741824, 1) & " GB" & _
            vbTab & _
            FormatPercent(objDrive.FreeSpace / objDrive.Size, 1) & _
            vbTab & vbCrLf

Next
'
' Display the string
'
WScript.Echo strDriveData
'
' Release the objects
'
Set objWMI = Nothing
Set objDrives = Nothing
Set objDrive = Nothing
```

The script begins by setting the strComputer variable to homepremiumpc, which is the name of the client computer on my network. The script then gets the remote computer's WMI service and uses it to return the instances of the remote computer's Win32LogicalDisk class, which represents a computer's logical disk drives. In this case, I'm interested only in the hard drives, so I use the WHERE clause to return only those disks where the MediaType property equals 12.

The script initializes the strDriveData display variable, and then it uses For Each...Next to loop through the hard drive instances. In each case, six values are added to the strDriveData string: the Name (drive letter), VolumeName, FileSystem, Size, and FreeSpace properties, and a calculation of the percentage of free space available.

NOTE If you want to examine a computer's removable media drives (except its floppy drives), use WHERE MediaType = 11. Floppy drives use various values for the MediaType property, depending on the floppy format (3.5-inch versus 5.25-inch), the size (for example, 1.2MB or 1.44MB), and the number of bytes per sector (for example, 512 or 1024).

The strDriveData string is then displayed using the Echo method. Figure 24.6 shows an example.

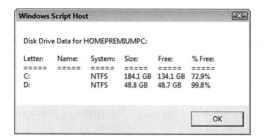

FIGURE 24.6

A remote computer's disk drive data displayed by the script in Listing 24.1.

Create an Instant Restore Point

Medium

The System Restore feature in Vista and XP has a simple job: to take periodic snapshots — called *restore points* (or sometimes *protection points*)—of your system, each of which includes the currently installed program files, Registry settings, and other crucial system data. The idea is that if a program or device installation causes problems on your system, you use System Restore to revert your system to the most recent restore point before the installation.

System Restore automatically creates restore points under the following conditions:

- Every 24 hours
- Before installing certain applications
- Before installing a Windows Update patch
- Before installing an unsigned device driver
- Before restoring backed-up files
- Before reverting to a previous configuration using System Restore

It's also possible to create a restore point manually using System Protection (in Vista) or System Restore (in XP). This is a good idea anytime you're about

to perform any relatively significant modification to your system, such as installing
a program or updating a device driver.

However, if you do these kinds of things a
lot, it can be a pain to load the programs
and go through all the steps. A much
faster way to go about this is to use a script
that creates a restore point instantly. Listing 24.2 shows just such a script.

NOTE   To get the file with
the Listing 24.2
code—it's called
InstantRestorePoint.vbs—see
my website: www.mcfedries.com/
cs/content/TweakItFreakIt.aspx.

Listing 24.2   A Script That Creates a Restore Point

```
Option Explicit
Dim strComputer, objWMI, objSR, strDesc, intResult
'
' Get the SystemRestore object
'
strComputer = "."
Set objWMI = GetObject("winmgmts:\\" & strComputer & "\root\default")
Set objSR = objWMI.Get("SystemRestore")
'
' Ask for a restore point description
'
strDesc = InputBox ("Enter a description for the restore point:", , _
                    "Instant Restore Point")
'
' Create the restore point
'
intResult = objSR.CreateRestorePoint (strDesc, 0, 100)
'
' Check the result
'
If intResult = 0 Then
    '
    ' Success!
    '
    WScript.Echo "Instant restore point '" & strDesc & "' created!"
Else
    '
    ' Failure!
```

continued

Listing 24.2 Continued

```
        WScript.Echo "Instant restore point '" & strDesc & "' failed!" & _
                vbCrLf & "Error code: " & intResult
End If
'
' Release the objects
'
Set objWMI = Nothing
Set objSR = Nothing
```

Note that you must run this script under the Administrator account, as described in Chapter 12.

➔ **See** "Run a Script as the Administrator," **p. 141**.

This script uses Windows Management Instrumentation (WMI) to return the `SystemRestore` class. The script displays a dialog box so that you can type a description of the restore point, and it then uses that description when it runs the `CreateRestorePoint` method. The script checks the result and displays a dialog box letting you know whether the restore point was created successfully.

Move the Paging File to a Faster Hard Drive

Medium

Your computer can address memory beyond the amount physically installed on the system. This nonphysical memory is called *virtual memory* and Windows implements it by setting up a piece of your hard disk to emulate physical memory. This hard disk storage is actually a single file called a *paging file* (or sometimes a *swap file*). When physical memory is full, Windows makes room for new data by taking some data that's currently in memory and swapping it out to the paging file.

No matter how much main memory your system boasts, Windows still creates and uses a paging file for virtual memory. To maximize paging file performance, you should make sure that Windows is working optimally with the paging file. In particular, the location of the paging file can have a major impact on its performance. There are three things you should consider:

- **If you have multiple physical hard disks, store the paging file on the hard disk that has the fastest access time**—The faster the access time, the better the performance of virtual memory because Windows can move data to and from the paging file faster.

- **Store the paging file on an uncompressed partition**—Windows is happy to store the paging file on a compressed NTFS partition. However, as with all file operations on a compressed partition, the performance of paging file operations suffers because of the compression and decompression required. Therefore, you should store the paging file on an uncompressed partition.

- **If you have multiple hard disks, store the paging file on the hard disk that has the most free space**—Windows expands and contracts the paging file dynamically depending on the system's needs. Storing the paging file on the disk with the most space gives Windows the most flexibility.

> **NOTE** The Pagefile.sys file is a hidden system file. To see it, open any folder window and select Organize, Folder and Search Options (in Vista) or Tools, Folder Options (in XP). In the Folder Options dialog box, click the View tab, activate the Show Hidden Files and Folders option, and deactivate the Hide Protected Operating System Files check box. When Windows asks you to confirm the display of protected operating system files, click Yes, and then click OK.

The paging file is named Pagefile.sys and it's stored in the root folder of the %SystemDrive%. Here's how to change the hard disk that Windows uses to store the paging file as well as the paging file sizes:

1. If necessary, defragment the hard disk that you'll be using for the paging file.

2. Display the advanced system properties:

   - **Windows Vista**—Select Start, right-click Computer, and then click Properties to display the System window. Click Advanced System Settings and then enter your User Account Control credentials.

   - **Windows XP**—Select Start, right-click My Computer, click Properties, and click the Advanced tab.

3. In the Performance group, click Settings to display the Performance Options dialog box.

4. Display the Advanced tab.

5. In the Virtual Memory group, click Change. Windows displays the Virtual Memory dialog box.

> **TIP** In both Vista and XP, you can also display the Advanced tab of the System Properties dialog box by opening the Run dialog box, typing **control sysdm.cpl,,3**, and clicking OK.

6. (Vista only) Deactivate the Automatically Manage Paging File Size for All Drives check box. Vista enables the rest of the dialog box controls, as shown in Figure 24.7.

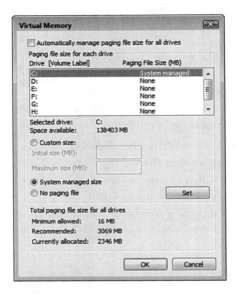

FIGURE 24.7
Use the Virtual Memory dialog box to select a different hard disk to store the paging file.

7. Use the Drive list to select the drive that currently has the paging file.

8. Select the No Paging File option.

9. Click Set and when Windows asks you to confirm, click Yes.

10. Use the Drive list to select the hard drive you want to use for the paging file.

11. Select a paging file size option:

    ■ **Custom Size**—Activate this option to set your own paging file sizes using the Initial Size (MB) and Maximum Size (MB) text boxes. Ensure that Windows is able to resize the paging file dynamically, as needed, by entering a maximum size that's larger than the initial size.

    ■ **System Managed Size**—Activate this option to let Windows manage the paging file sizes for you.

12. Click Set.

13. Click OK in all the open dialog boxes.

14. Restart your computer to put the changes into effect.

Super Searching

Thanks to Google's amazing search engine (which, as of mid-2008, passed the *trillion* page mark, a jaw-dropping number if there ever was one), we've become a nation of searchers. Remembering site addresses or even facts? How quaint! These days, the modern web surfer Googles the site or info tidbit he or she wants.

Getting the same level of search service on our PCs has been inexplicably problematic, despite the obvious fact that even the most stuffed computer contains only the teeniest fraction of the data that encompasses the web.

Searching your computer in Windows XP is a good example. It wasn't a terrible experience by any means, but no one raved about it, either. First, there was Microsoft's inexplicable decision to ship XP with the Indexing service turned off by default. Without the Indexing service, the search function was next-to-useless in XP, but turning it on required several relatively obscure clicks in the Search Companion. Even with the Indexing service running, searches that included entire partitions could take a frustratingly long time to complete.

Microsoft's goal in Vista was to make search a truly useful tool that provides complete results quickly. Did it succeed? For the most part, yes. The Windows Search Engine (WSE) service starts by default, which all by itself is a big improvement over XP. And indexed searches are reasonably quick, but not Google-quick. The Windows Search Engine also boasts lots of options and features, but they're pretty well hidden, and even if you stumble upon them, they can be downright inscrutable.

> **NOTE** To use advanced desktop searching in Windows XP, you need to download and install the latest version of Windows Search (version 4.0 as I write this). See the following Microsoft page: www.microsoft.com/windows/products/winfamily/desktopsearch/.

This chapter provides a bunch of tweaks that should help to demystify and improve desktop searching in Vista.

Add Folders to the Search Index

Medium

One of the major problems with desktop searches is that it can take Vista an absurdly long time to search, for example, all of the C: drive. That's because the Windows Search Engine does *not* index the entire drive. Instead, it just indexes the contents of your user profile, your offline files (local copies of network files), the items on your Start menu, and your email messages. If you're searching for one of these types of files, Vista searches are lightning quick.

Note that you can control what WSE indexes and force a rebuild of the index by following these steps:

1. Select Start, type **index**, and press Enter. The Indexing Options dialog box appears.

2. Click Modify to open the Indexed Locations dialog box.

3. Click Show All Locations and then enter your User Account Control credentials to continue.

4. In the Change Selected Locations list, open the branches to display the folder you want to add to the index, and then activate that folder's check box. Vista adds the folder to the Summary of Selected Locations list, as shown in Figure 25.1.

> **NOTE** To display the Indexing Options dialog box using Windows Search in XP, select Start, Search, click the View icon (second from the right in the Windows Search toolbar), and then click Search Options.

> **CAUTION** The Windows Search Engine takes a *long* time to index even a relatively small amount of data. If you're asking WSE to index dozens of gigabytes of data, wait until you're done working for the day and let the indexer run all night.

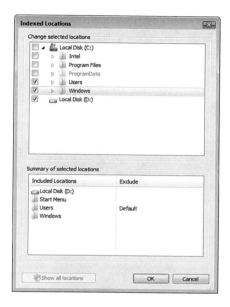

FIGURE 25.1

Activate the check box beside each drive or folder that you want to include in the index.

5. Click OK.

6. Click Advanced and then enter your User Account Control credentials to continue. The Advanced Options dialog box appears.

7. Click Rebuild and, if Vista asks you to confirm the rebuild, click OK.

8. Click Close.

Create Powerful Searches Using Properties and Filters

Medium

In an early beta version of Windows Vista, Microsoft introduced some amazingly powerful search capabilities called *advanced filters*. Using a series of lists and text boxes, you could build complex searches that used file properties (name, file type, bit rate,

> **TIP** If you find that a certain type of file isn't showing up in your search results, it could be that Vista either isn't indexing files of that type, or it's indexing only the properties of those files, and not their contents. To fix this, open the Indexing Options dialog box, click Advanced, and then enter your User Account Control credentials. Display the File Types tab, activate the check box beside the file extension you want to index, and select the Index Properties and File Contents option. (If you don't see your extension, type it into the text box and then click Add New Extension.)

you name it), operators (such as Starts With for text and Is Greater Than for numbers), and Boolean logic (such as AND and OR). It was, in short, a power user's dream, and that's probably what doomed it. Microsoft removed or dumbed down lots of power-user features in Vista, and advanced filters was just one of the casualties. (The interface was terrible, so that also played a part in its demise.) Microsoft ended up with the Advanced Search interface, shown in Figure 25.2.

FIGURE 25.2

The so-called Advanced Search pane.

To call this pane "advanced" is a stretch, to say the least. You can search on only a few properties, you get only a few operators with the Date and Size filters, and there's no way to perform Boolean searches. It is, in a word, pathetic.

If there's any good news to be gleaned from Microsoft's decimation of search, it's that Microsoft did *not* remove the underlying search engine. That is, you can still perform searches using any file property, you still have a bunch of operators you can use, and you can still add Boolean operators for even more powerful searches. In essence, Microsoft ditched the advanced filters interface, but still kept the advanced filters code. This means that you can run these advanced searches by using a special syntax—called Advanced Query Syntax (AQS)—in your search queries.

For file properties, use the following syntax:

property:*value*

Here, *property* is the name of the file property you want to search on, and *value* is the criteria you want to use. The property can be any of the metadata categories used by Windows. For example, as you can see in Figure 25.3, the categories in a music folder include Name, Artists, Album, # (track number), Genre, and Rating. Right-click any column header to see more properties such as Title and Bit Rate, and you can click More to see the complete list.

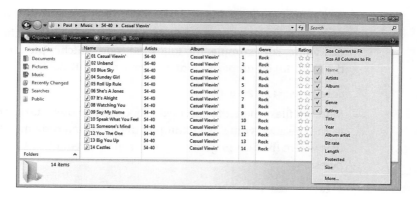

FIGURE 25.3

With AQS, you can search on any of the properties associated with a file type.

Here are a few things to bear in mind:

■ If the property name is a single word, use that word in your query. For example, the following code matches music where the Artists property is Coldplay:

```
artists:coldplay
```

■ If the property name uses two or more words, remove the spaces between the words and use the resulting text in your query. For example, the following code matches music where the Bit Rate property is 192:

```
bitrate:192
```

■ If the value uses two or more words and you want to match the exact phrase, surround the phrase with quotation marks. For example, the following code matches music where the Genre property is Alternative & Punk:

```
genre:"alternative & punk"
```

■ If the value uses two or more words and you want to match both words in any order, surround the parentheses. For example, the following code matches music where the Album property contains the words Head and Goats in any order:

```
album:(head goats)
```

■ If you want to match files where a particular property has no value, use empty braces —[]— as the value. For example, the following code matches files where the Tags property is empty: .

```
tags:[]
```

You can also refine your searches with the following operators and wildcards:

> \> Matches files where the specified property is greater than the specified value. For example, the following code matches pictures where the Date Taken property is later than January 1, 2008:

```
datetaken:>1/1/2008
```

> \>= Matches files where the specified property is greater than or equal to the specified value. For example, the following code matches files where the Size property is greater than or equal to 10000 bytes:

```
size:>=10000
```

> \< Matches files where the specified property is less than the specified value. For example, the following code matches pictures where the Date Taken property is earlier than December 31, 1999:

```
datetaken:<12/31/1999
```

> \<= Matches files where the specified property is less than or equal to the specified value. For example, the following code matches files where the Size property is less than or equal to 1024 bytes:

```
size:<=1024
```

> .. Matches files where the specified property is between (and including) two values. For example, the following code matches files where the Date Modified property is between and including August 1, 2008 and August 31, 2008:

```
datemodified:8/1/2008..8/31/2008
```

> * Substitutes for multiple characters. For example, the following code matches music where the Album property includes the word Hits:

```
album:*hits
```

> ? Substitutes for a single character. For example, the following code matches music where the Artists property begin with Blu and includes any character in the fourth position:

```
artists:blu?
```

For even more sophisticated searches, you can combine multiple criteria using Boolean operators:

> **NOTE** The Boolean operators AND, OR, and NOT must appear with all-upper-case letters in your query.

AND (or +)   Use this operator to match files that meet *all* of your criteria. For example, the following code matches pictures where the Date Taken property is later than January 1, 2008 and the Size property is greater than 1000000 bytes:

```
datetaken:>1/1/2008 AND size:>1000000
```

OR   Choose this option to match files that meet *at least one* of your criteria. For example, the following code matches music where the Genre property is either Rock or Blue:

```
genre:rock OR genre:blues
```

NOT (or –)   Choose this option to match files that do not meet the criteria. For example, the following code matches pictures where the Type property is not JPEG:

```
type:NOT jpeg
```

Search for Files Using Natural Language Queries

Medium

In the previous tweak, I showed you how to use Advanced Query Syntax to create powerful search queries. The only problem is that it's a chore having to memorize all those operators and what they're used for. If you're not up for all that, Microsoft offers an alternative if you're using Vista. It's called *natural language search*, and it enables you to perform complex searches without using *any* operators. Sweet!

First, follow these steps to turn on natural language search:

1. Open the Folder Options dialog box using either of the following techniques:

   - **From the Start menu**—Select Start, type **fold**, press Enter, and then display the Search tab.

   - **From a Search Results window**—Select Search Tools, Search Options.

2. Activate the Use Natural Language Search check box, as shown in Figure 25.4.

3. Click OK to put the new setting into effect.

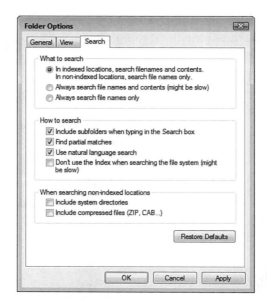

FIGURE 25.4

Activate the Use Natural Language Search check box.

Crafting natural language queries is a bit of a black art because Microsoft has no documentation available. Feel free to experiment to get the feel of these queries.

A basic natural language query looks like this:

```
adjective kind verb value
```

Here, `adjective` is an optional value that narrows down the search, usually by using a value from a property (such as a genre for music or a file type for images); `kind` is the type of file, such as `music` or `images`; `verb` is a verb that more or less corresponds to the property you want to match, such as *modified* (the Date Modified property), `created` (the Date Created Property), `from` (the From property in an email), and `by` (the Artist property in a music file); and `value` is the specific value you want to match.

For example, if you want to return all the pop music done by the band Sloan, you'd enter the following query:

```
pop music by sloan
```

Similarly, if you want all the JPEG images that were created today, you'd use the following query:

```
jpeg images created today
```

You can keep adding more properties and values to target your searches. For example, if we want our Sloan search to return only those songs rated with five stars, we'd modify the search as follows:

NOTE Unlike with AQS, the Boolean operators OR and NOT can appear in lowercase letters. (The Boolean operator AND is implied in all multiterm natural language queries, so you never have to use it.)

```
pop music by sloan rating *****
```

You can still perform Boolean searches in natural language queries. For example, if you want documents where the Author property includes *Paul* or *Karen*, you'd use the following query:

```
documents by paul or karen
```

Similarly, if you want to return all your videos except those in the QuickTime format, you'd use the following:

```
videos not quicktime
```

Finally, note that when you're working with dates, there are several keywords you can use in your natural language queries, including the following: `yesterday`, `today`, `tomorrow`, `week`, `month`, `year`, `last`, `this`, and `next`. For example, if you want to see all the TIFF images created this week, you'd use the following:

```
jpeg images created this week
```

Make Searches More Targeted by Finding Only Exact Matches

Easy

When you search for files in Windows Vista, Windows Search assumes you want to find partial matches. For example, if you search for *fire*, Windows Search not only matches files that contain the word *fire*, but also those that contain *afire*, *firewall*, and *wildfire* (to name just a few). That's often what you want because it saves you from having to also search for other forms of the word (for example, *fires* and *fired*). However, it often means that you end up with too many results because Windows Search is returning all kinds of documents that contain irrelevant matches.

To prevent this from happening, you can configure Windows Search to return only exact matches. Here are the steps to follow:

1. Open the Folder Options dialog box using either of the following techniques:

   - **From the Start menu**—Select Start, type **fold**, press Enter, and then display the Search tab.

   - **From a Search Results window**—Select Search Tools, Search Options.

2. Deactivate the Find Partial Matches check box, as shown in Figure 25.5.

3. Click OK to put the new setting into effect.

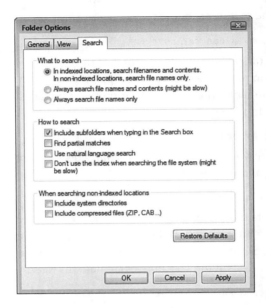

FIGURE 25.5
Deactivate the Find Partial Matches check box to match only documents that contain your exact search text.

Save Searches to Save Time

Medium

You've seen that you can use Advanced Query Syntax or natural language for your searches. These are powerful tools for finding files on your system, but setting up a search—particularly one that uses multiple search filters—can be time-consuming. The time it takes to set up an advanced search is not a big problem if you'll be running the search only once. However, there may be some searches that you plan to run regularly. After taking all that time to get a search just right, it would be a real pain if you had to repeat the entire procedure to run the same search later.

Fortunately, Windows Vista takes pity on searchers by enabling you to save your searches and rerun them anytime you like. That is, you can save your search as one of Windows Vista's *search folders*. A search folder is a collection of files and folders from your system that match a specified set of search criteria. After you set up and run a search, you can save it as a search folder and then reuse it anytime you need it.

Here are the steps to follow:

1. Set up and run a search using the criteria you want to use.
2. Click Save Search. The Save As dialog box appears (see Figure 25.6).
3. Type a filename for the search folder.
4. Click Save. Windows Vista saves the search as a search folder.

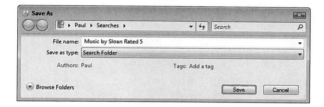

FIGURE 25.6

After you run your search, click Save Search to save the query as a search folder.

To reuse your saved search, open a folder window and click Searches. Vista displays the Searches folder, and you see an icon for your shared folder (as well as several predefined searches), as shown in Figure 25.7. Double-click the search folder, and Vista runs the search and displays the results.

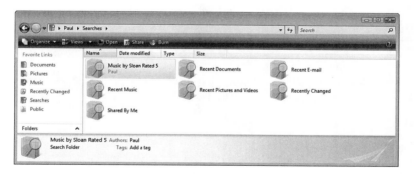

FIGURE 25.7

In any folder window, click Searches to see your saved search, as well as Vista's predefined search folders.

Building Better Backups

Most technical writers would open a backup-related chapter with an appeal to the reader to please, *please* make regular backups because you never know when disaster could strike, it's happened to me, the sky is falling, yadda yadda yadda. However, even though I've written a few of those rants myself, I'll spare you the spiel this time around because this chapter is about building *better* backups. That is, I'm assuming right up front that you're *already* doing backups and what you *really* want are some pointers to make backups easier and faster.

I hear you! So you won't find any backup-your-computer-now-or-else lectures from me in this chapter. Instead, you just get a few of my favorite backup-related tweaks and techniques that I hope will help you build better backups.

Back Up to a Network Location

Medium

The biggest hurdle facing would-be backer-uppers is the sheer size of the data we all carry around these days. With all our MP3 files, photos, video files, email stores, and other documents, we're talking tens or even *hundreds* of gigabytes of data. Nobody with a lick of sense wants to back up all that data to multiple media (such as writable optical discs or USB flash drives), so the backup destination-of-choice these days is a second hard drive that has enough storage capacity to handle a full backup. With 500GB external hard drives available for about 20 cents a gigabyte, and 750GB hard drives only slightly more expensive (and with affordable terabyte drives just around the corner), you can add an easy-to-use backup medium to your computer.

NOTE Yes, it's still possible that a thief could make off with *all* your computer equipment, or a large house fire could destroy everything. If you're still worried, buy two network hard drives and swap them once a week or so. When you're using one, keep the other in an offsite location, such as a safety deposit box or storage locker.

Backing up to an attached hard drive is a useful solution, but it's by no means a perfect one. For example, if your computer is stolen, the second hard drive might get stolen along with it, and then you're in big trouble. Similarly, a fire in your office or den could torch both the computer and the second hard drive.

A solution that avoids both of these problems is to use the network as your backup location:

- You can back up to a folder on a network share that has lots of free space.
- You can add a large hard drive to a network computer, share that drive, and then back up to the drive.
- You can add a *network-attached storage* (NAS) device to the network and back up to that device.

Even better, the backup features in Windows Vista and Windows XP support backing up to a network share. In Vista, after you configure the backup program, backing up is completely automated, particularly if you back up to a resource that has plenty of room to hold your files (such as a roomy network share).

Back Up to a Network in Windows Vista

In Windows Vista, you use the Back Up Files Wizard to set up your backups. Follow these steps to configure a network share as the backup location and activate Vista's Automatic File Backup feature:

1. Select Start, type **backup**, and then click Backup Status and Configuration.

2. You have two choices (you need to enter your User Account Control credentials after either one):

- If you've never configured backups in Vista, click Set Up Automatic File Backup.

- If you've previously configured backups in Vista, click Change Backup Settings.

3. In the first Back Up Files Wizard dialog box, select the On a Network option.

4. Use the On a Network text box to type the network address of the share you want to use as the backup destination. Figure 26.1 shows an example. (Alternatively, click Browse to use the Browse for Folder dialog box to select the shared network folder.)

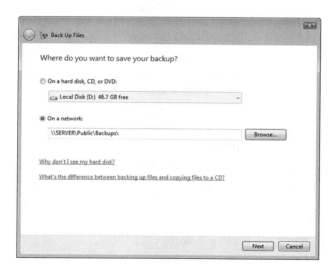

FIGURE 26.1

Activate the On a Network option, and then type the network address of the shared folder you want to use as the backup location.

5. Click Next. If your user account doesn't have access to the network folder, the Connect to *Share* dialog box appears (where *Share* is the network address you typed in step 4).

6. Use the User Name and Password text boxes to type the credentials you need to access the shared folder, and then click OK.

7. If your system has multiple hard drives, the wizard asks you to select which of them you want to include in the backup. Deactivate the check box beside any drive you don't want to include in the backup (you can't exclude the system drive, however), and then click Next.

8. The next dialog box provides you with a long list of file types to back up, including documents, pictures, videos, and email. You probably want to leave all of these check boxes activated. Click Next when you're ready to continue.

9. The next wizard dialog box asks you to set up a backup schedule:

How Often	Select Daily, Weekly, or Monthly.
What Day	If you chose Weekly, select the day of the week you want the backups to occur; if you chose Monthly, select the day of the month you want the backups to occur.
What Time	Select the time of day you want the backup to run. (Choose a time when you won't be using your computer.)

> **TIP** The one exception in the list of file types to back up might be TV shows. Because most recorded TV shows produce multigigabyte files, you might have dozens or even hundreds of gigabytes of TV content. If most of these shows are ones you'll be deleting soon after you watch them, excluding them makes the backup perform faster and take up much less room on the network share. If you have important shows that you're saving, however, then by all means include them in the backup.

10. Click Save Settings and Start Backup to save your configuration and launch the backup. Windows Backup lets you know that it will perform a full backup of your system now.

11. Click Yes.

12. When the backup is done, click Close.

Back Up to a Network in Windows XP

In the Backup program that comes with Windows XP, a *backup job* is a file that defines your backup. It includes three things:

- A list of the files you want to include in your backup.
- The Backup options you selected, including the type of backup you want to use.
- The destination for the backed-up files. In our case, we want the destination to be a shared folder on the network.

Here are the steps to follow to define and run a backup job:

1. Select Start, All Programs, Accessories, System Tools, Backup. The Backup or Restore Wizard appears.

2. Click the Advanced Mode link to display the Backup Utility window.

3. Select the Backup tab.

4. Select Tools, Options to display the Options dialog box, and then set the following options, as desired (click OK when you're done):

   - To specify the backup type, display the Backup Type tab and then use the Default Backup Type list to select the backup type you want to use.

   - To verify that the backed-up data contains no errors, display the General tab and activate the Verify Data After the Backup Operation check box. Note, however, that this roughly doubles the length of the backup operation.

   - To exclude files based on the file type, display the Exclude Files tab and click Add New (the one under the Files Excluded for All Users list) to display the Add Excluded Files dialog box. In the Registered File Type list, select the file type you want to exclude and click OK.

5. Use the folder and file lists to activate the check boxes for the drives, folders, and files you want to include in the backup job.

6. In the Backup Destination list, choose File. (This list will be disabled if you don't have any backup drives attached to your system, but that's okay because File is the default choice.)

7. Use the Backup Media or File Name text box to enter the path of the shared network folder you want to use, as well as a filename for the backup file, as shown in Figure 26.2.

8. Select Job, Save Selections. If you're creating a new backup job, enter a name in the Save As dialog box and then click Save.

9. Click Start Backup to perform the backup.

NOTE To back up the Registry, your system's boot files, and its COM+ Class Registration Database, activate the System State check box.

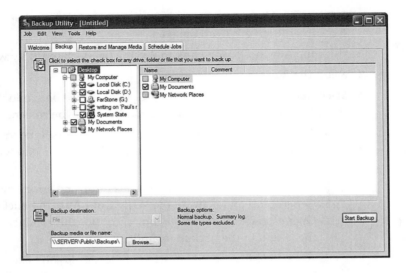

FIGURE 26.2
Specify a shared network folder for your backup file.

Create a Backup of Your Entire Computer

Medium

The worst-case scenario for PC problems is a system crash that renders your hard disk or system files unusable. Your only recourse in such a case is to start from scratch with either a reformatted hard disk or a new hard disk. This usually means that you have to reinstall Windows and then reinstall and reconfigure all your applications. In other words, you're looking at the better part of a day or, more likely, a few days, to recover your system. However, Windows Vista and Windows XP have features that take most of the pain out of recovering your system. In Vista it's called Complete PC Backup, and in XP it's called Automated System Recovery. I show you how to use both tools a bit later in this chapter (see "Recover from Disaster Using Your Complete PC Backup"). For now, the next couple of sections show you how to prepare for disaster.

Back Up Your Entire Computer in Windows Vista

The safety net used by Vista's Complete PC Backup is actually a complete backup of your Windows Vista installation; this is called a *system image*. It takes a long time to create a system image (at least several

> **NOTE** The Complete PC Backup feature is available only in Vista Business, Enterprise, and Ultimate.

hours, depending on how much stuff you have), but it's worth it for the peace of mind. Here are the steps to follow to create the system image:

1. Select Start, type **backup**, and then click Backup Status and Configuration.

2. Select Complete PC Backup.

3. Click Create a Backup Now and enter your UAC credentials to launch the Windows Complete PC Backup Wizard.

4. The wizard asks you to specify a backup destination. You have two choices (click Next when you're ready to continue):

   ■ **On a Hard Disk**—Select this option if you want to use a disk drive on your computer. If you have multiple drives, use the list to select the one you want to use.

   ■ **On One or More DVDs**—Select this option if you want to use DVDs to hold the backup.

5. Windows Complete PC Backup automatically includes your internal hard disk in the system image, and you can't change that. However, if you also have external hard drives, you can add them to the backup by activating their check boxes. Click Next. Windows Complete PC Backup asks you to confirm your backup settings.

6. Click Start Backup. Windows Complete PC Backup creates the system image.

7. When the backup is complete, click Close.

Back Up Your Entire Computer in Windows XP

XP's Automated System Recovery utility requires a little advance planning on your part, but it's worth it because it can help you recover from a crash in just a few steps. What kind of advance planning is required? Just two things:

■ You must run the Automated System Recovery Preparation Wizard. This wizard backs up your system files and creates a floppy disk that enables you to restore your system.

■ You must run a full backup of all your data and application files.

> **NOTE** Yes, you read that right: a *floppy* disk. Because very few systems come with floppy disks these days, the Automated System Recovery utility is a bit useless on almost any modern system. If you really want the security of Automated System Recovery, get yourself a USB floppy drive and at least one floppy disk.

Because your system, application, and data files change regularly, to ensure a smooth recovery, you must do both of these things regularly.

Here are the steps to following to run the Automated System Recovery Preparation Wizard:

> **NOTE** If you're not replacing your hard disk and if you have your application files and data files on a separate partition, you don't have to back up that partition because you won't be formatting it.

1. Select Start, All Programs, Accessories, System Tools, Backup. The Backup or Restore Wizard appears.

2. Click the Advanced Mode link to display the Backup Utility window.

3. In the Welcome tab, click the Automated System Recovery Wizard button. Alternatively, select Tools, ASR Wizard. The Automated System Recovery Preparation Wizard appears.

> **CAUTION** Don't back up the system files to the `%SystemDrive%` partition because it is the partition you'll be formatting as part of your recovery effort.

4. Click Next. The wizard prompts you for a backup destination for your system files.

5. Choose the Backup Media Type and then enter the backup media name or filename. Click Next.

6. Click Finish. The wizard backs up your system files. When it's done, it prompts you to insert a floppy disk in drive A.

7. Insert a blank, formatted disk and click OK. The wizard copies the files `Asr.sif`, `Asrpnp.sif`, and `Setup.log` to the disk and lets you know when it has finished.

8. Click OK.

Recover from Disaster Using Your Complete PC Backup

Medium

If nothing can get Windows up and running again, you have no choice but to start with a clean slate. This means either formatting the `%SystemDrive%` partition or, if hard disk errors are the culprit, replacing your hard disk. Ouch! Wait until the initial panic subsides, recall that you've got your entire PC backed up (from reading the previous tweak), breathe a sigh of relief, and then follow the steps in the next two sections (depending on your Windows version) to get your system back on its feet.

Recover from Disaster in Windows Vista

Here's how to restore your Windows Vista computer from a Complete PC backup:

1. Insert the Windows Vista DVD.

2. Restart your computer. If your system prompts you to boot from the DVD, press the required key or key combination.

3. In the initial Install Windows screen, click Next.

4. Click Repair Your Computer.

5. In the Operating System list, click your Windows Vista operating system and then click Next. The System Recovery Options window appears, as shown in Figure 26.3.

> **TIP** If your system won't boot from the Windows Vista DVD, you need to adjust the system's BIOS settings to allow this. Restart the computer and watch the monitor for a startup message that prompts you to press a key or key combination to modify the BIOS settings (which might be called *Setup* or something similar). Find the boot options and either enable a DVD drive-based boot or make sure that the option to boot from the DVD drive comes before the option to boot from the hard disk. If you use a USB keyboard, you may also need to enable an option that lets the BIOS recognize keystrokes after the POST but before the OS starts.

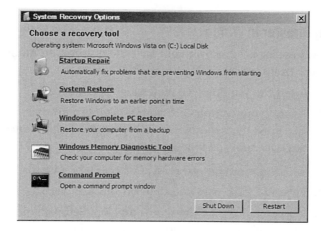

FIGURE 26.3
Use the System Recovery Options window to restore your Complete PC backup.

6. If you backed up your computer to an external hard drive, make sure that drive is connected and turned on; if you backed up to DVDs, remote the Vista Install disc and insert the first backup disc.

7. Click Windows Complete PC Restore. Setup scans your system for backup disks and then displays the Restore Your Entire Computer from a Backup dialog box with the most likely backup displayed.

> **NOTE** If after completing the restore your system still won't boot, try running the Complete PC Restore again, but this time format and repartition the hard drive.

8. You have two choices:

   - If the displayed backup is the one you want to use, click the Restore the Following Backup option and then click Next.

   - Otherwise, click the Restore a Different Backup option, click Next, select the backup you want to use, and then click Next.

9. If you've installed a new hard drive, activate the Format and Repartition Disks check box; if you're restoring to the original hard drive, you can leave this check box deactivated to speed up the restore.

10. Click Finish. Windows Complete PC Restore asks you to confirm.

11. Activate the I Confirm That I Want to Erase All Existing Data and Restore the Backup check box, and then click OK. Windows Complete PC Restore begins the restore process.

Recover from Disaster in Windows XP

Follow these steps to recover your XP system using the Automated System Recovery (ASR) utility:

1. Insert the Windows XP Professional CD-ROM.

2. Restart your computer. If your system prompts you to boot from the CD, press the required key or key combination. Watch the bottom of the screen for the following prompt:

```
Press F2 to run Automated System Recovery (ASR)...
```

3. Press F2. Setup asks you to insert the ASR disk.

4. Insert the disk and then press any key. Setup continues the Windows XP installation. Note that, along the way, Setup automatically formats the %SystemDrive% partition.

From here, the Setup program proceeds normally, except that it uses the information on the ASR disk to restore your system files and settings from the backup you made using the ASR Preparation Wizard. If you also backed up your application and data files, use the Backup utility to restore them now.

Restore an XP Backup to Vista

Medium

Here's a conundrum faced by many a former XP user who has recently switched to Vista: You're missing a file or two that you know are sitting in an XP backup file, but you can't get at them because Vista's backup utility doesn't recognize XP backups. You need those files, but they seem to be stuck in backup limbo. What to do?

You *could* install XP's Backup utility in Vista as described in the next tweak, but that might be overkill if you just need a file or two. Fortunately, Microsoft offers a useful alternative: the Windows NT Backup-Restore Utility. This simple program installs on a Vista system and enables you to view and work with XP backup files.

Before installing the program, note that it requires a Vista feature called Removable Storage Management, which is likely not installed on your system. Follow these steps to install it:

1. Select Start, type **features** into the Search box, and then click Programs and Features.

2. Click the Turn Windows Features On or Off link. The User Account Control dialog box appears.

3. Enter your UAC credentials to continue. The Windows Features dialog box appears.

4. Activate the Removable Storage Management check box, as shown in Figure 26.4.

FIGURE 26.4

To use the Windows NT Backup-Restore utility, you need to install the Removable Storage Management feature.

5. Click OK. Vista installs Removable Storage Management.

Now open your web browser and head for the following address to download and then install the program:

www.microsoft.com/downloads/
details.aspx?familyid=7DA725E2-8B69-
4C65-AFA3-2A53107D54A7

After the program is installed, run it by selecting Start, All Programs, Windows NT Backup-Restore Utility, NtBackup-Restore Utility. If you see the User Account Control dialog box, click Allow.

You can either click Restore Wizard in the Welcome tab to use a wizard to restore your files, or you can follow these steps:

TIP If you don't feel like typing that long-winded URL, go to www.microsoft.com/downloads/, type **nt backup restore** into the Search box, and press Enter. Click the Download Details: Windows NT Backup-Restore Utility link.

NOTE If you're running a 32-bit version of Vista, be sure to download the NtBackupRestore_x86.msi file; 64-bit Vista users need to download the NtBackupRestore_Win64.msi file, instead.

1. Display the Restore and Manage Media tab.

2. Select Tools, Catalog a Backup File. The Open Backup File dialog box appears.

3. Click Browse, use the Select File to Catalog dialog box to select your XP backup file, click Open, and then click OK.

4. Open the folder branches until you find the folder that contains the file you want to restore to Vista.

5. Activate the check box beside the file, as shown in Figure 26.5.

6. Repeat steps 4 and 5 to select the other files you want to restore.

7. Click Start Restore.

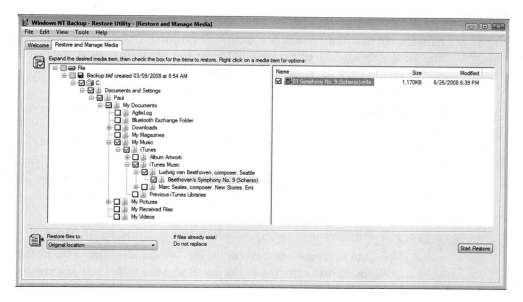

FIGURE 26.5
Activate the check box beside the file you want to restore to Vista.

Use XP's Backup Utility in Vista

Medium

You can argue the merits of Windows Vista versus Windows XP until you're blue in the face (a distressingly common occurrence on the Web these days, unfortunately), but there's one thing almost everyone agrees on: The Vista backup feature is utterly lame compared to XP's. Why? The main reason is that Vista's backup doesn't let you select specific folders and files to back up. Instead, you have to back up "Pictures" or "Music," which means *all* your pictures and *all* your music. That's fine for novices who don't want to sweat the details, but for everyone else it's a real pain to have to back up everything all the time.

If you want more control over your backups, and you still have either an XP Professional installation disc or a computer running XP Pro, you can grab the files for the XP Backup Utility and add them to your Vista system. This will enable you to back up your Vista computer using the XP Backup Utility.

Your first chore is to create a folder to hold the Backup Utility files. Use Windows Explorer to open the Program Files folder in your system drive (usually drive C:). Select Organize, New Folder, enter your User Account Control credentials, type a name for the new folder (such as **XPBackup**), and press Enter.

How you proceed from here depends on whether you have an XP Professional installation disc or a computer running XP Pro. The latter is the easier method, so let's start with that.

On your XP Pro computer, launch Windows Explorer and do two things:

■ Open the %SystemRoot%\System32 folder (where %SystemRoot% is usually C:\Windows) and copy the following files to the folder you just created on your Vista PC:

```
ntbackup.exe
ntmsapi.dll
vssapi.dll
```

■ Open the %SystemRoot%\Help folder and copy the following files to the folder you created on your Vista PC:

```
ntbackup.chm
ntbackup.hlp
```

If you just have the XP Pro installation disc, you need to use Vista's EXPAND tool to extract the compressed Backup Utility files from the disc. Insert the disc and then launch Command Prompt under the Administrator account as described in Chapter 36, "Running the Command Prompt."

➜ **See** "Running Command Prompt as the Administrator," **p. 427.**

At the command line, run the following command to switch to the folder you created earlier to store the XP Backup Utility files (where *folder* is the name of the folder):

```
cd %programfiles%\folder
```

Now you need to run the following five commands (where *D* is the letter of the drive that contains the XP installation disc):

NOTE In the second-to-last command, note that the disc file is named ntbckupw.ch_ and not ntbackup.ch_ as you might expect.

```
expand D:\i386\ntbackup.ex_ ntbackup.exe
expand D:\i386\ntmsapi.dl_ ntmsapi.dll
expand D:\i386\vssapi.dl_ vssapi.dll
expand D:\i386\ntbckupw.ch_ ntbackup.chm
expand D:\i386\ntbackup.hl_ ntbackup.hlp
```

To use the XP Backup Utility in Vista, open the folder you created earlier to store the program's files, and then double-click the

> **NOTE** If you see the Removable Storage Not Running dialog box, you can safely ignore this warning. Activate the Do Not Show This Message Again check box, and then click OK.

ntbackup.exe file. Figure 26.6 shows the Backup Utility running on a Vista system.

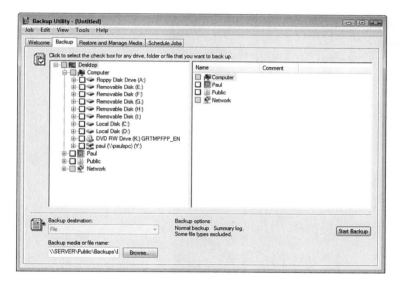

FIGURE 26.6

Windows XP's Backup Utility running on a Windows Vista PC.

CHAPTER 27

Customizing the File System

ile maintenance is a big part of the necessary grunt work that we all have to perform to keep our PCs and our files in reasonable condition. That's just part of being a responsible PC owner, but fiddling with files doesn't exactly pay the bills. This means that a savvy Windows user will try to minimize the amount of time he or she spends on file-related chores, which frees up time for more productive (and better paying) pursuits.

This short chapter presents you with three tweaks that should help cut time off your file maintenance tasks. Specifically, I show you three ways to customize the file system to suit the way you work. Two of the tweaks are built right in to Windows itself: customizing the New menu and the Open With menu. The third tweak is a nifty utility that brings Internet Explorer's tabbed browsing concept to Windows Explorer.

Customize the New Menu

Medium

One of the handiest features in Windows is the New menu, which enables you to create a new file without working within an application. In Windows Explorer (or on the desktop), right-click an empty part of the folder and then select New. In the submenu that appears, you see items that create new documents of various file types, including a folder, shortcut, bitmap image, contact, rich text document, text document, compressed folder, and possibly many others, depending on your system configuration and the applications you have installed. Figure 27.1 shows the standard New menu from a Vista system, whereas Figure 27.2 shows a modified New menu from an XP system.

FIGURE 27.1

Vista's default New menu.

FIGURE 27.2

XP's New menu with some extra commands added by Microsoft Office.

Because applications can customize the New menu, you might think that you can, too, and you'd be right. You can do this via the Registry. To see how this works, start the Registry Editor and open the HKEY_CLASSES_ROOT key. The first part of this key consists of a large collection of extension subkeys (such as .bmp and .txt), and these represents all the extensions (both registered and unregistered) on your Windows PC. Most of the extension subkeys have only a Default setting that's either blank (if the extension isn't associated with a registered file type) or a string that points to the extension's associated file type.

→ To learn how to start and navigate the Registry Editor, **see** Chapter 34, "Tweaking Windows with the Registry Editor," **p. 401**.

However, many of these extension keys also have subkeys and a few of them have a subkey named ShellNew, in particular. For example, open the .bmp key and you see that it has a subkey named ShellNew (see Figure 27.3). This subkey is what determines whether a file type appears on the New menu.

Specifically, if the extension is registered with Windows and it has a `ShellNew` subkey, the New menu sprouts a command for the associated file type.

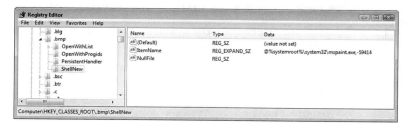

FIGURE 27.3

Some extension subkeys come with a `ShellNew` subkey.

The `ShellNew` subkey always contains a setting that determines how Windows Vista creates the new file. Five settings are possible:

`NullFile` This setting, the value of which is always set to a null string (""), tells Vista to create an empty file of the associated type. Of the file types that appear on the default New menu, three use the `NullFile` setting: Text Document (`.txt`), Bitmap Image (`.bmp`), and Shortcut (`.lnk`).

`Directory` (Windows Vista only) This setting tells Windows Vista to create a folder. The New menu's Briefcase (see the `Briefcase\ShellNew` key in the Registry) command uses this setting.

`FileName` (Windows XP only) This setting tells Windows XP to create the new file by making a copy of another file. Windows XP has special hidden folders to hold these template files. These folders are user specific, so you'll find them in `%UserProfile%\Templates`. On the default New menu, only the Wave Sound (`.wav`) file type uses the `FileName` setting, and its value is `sndrec.wav`. To see this value, you need to open the following key:

`HKEY_CLASSES_ROOT\.wav\ShellNew`

`Command` This setting tells Windows to create the new file by executing a specific command. This command usually invokes an executable file with a few parameters. In Vista, two of the New menu's commands use this setting:

- **Contact**—The .contact\ShellNew key contains the following value for the Command setting:

  "%ProgramFiles%\Windows Mail\Wab.exe" /CreateContact "%1"

- **Journal Document**—In the .jnt\jntfile\ShellNew key, you'll see the following value for the Command setting:

  "%ProgramFiles%\Windows Journal\Journal.exe" /n 0

In XP, the following New menu commands use this setting:

- **Shortcut**—The .lnk\ShellNew key contains the following value for the Command setting:

  rundll32.exe appwiz.cpl,NewLinkHere %1

- **Briefcase**—In the .bfc\ShellNew key, you'll see the following value for the Command setting:

  %SystemRoot%\system32\rundll32.exe
  ➥%SystemRoot%\system32\syncui.dll,
  ➥Briefcase_Create %2!d! %1

Data   This setting contains a value, and when Windows creates the new file, it copies this value into the file. In Vista, the New menu's Rich Text Document (.rtf) uses this setting. In Vista and XP, the Compressed (Zipped) Folder (.zip) command uses this setting.

To make the New menu even more convenient, you can add new file types for documents you work with regularly. For any file type that's registered with Windows, you follow a simple three-step process:

1. Add a ShellNew subkey to the appropriate extension key in HKEY_CLASSES_ROOT.

2. Add one of the settings discussed previously: NullFile, Directory (Vista only), FileName (XP Only), Command, or Data.

3. Type a value for the setting.

In most cases, the easiest way to go is to use NullFile to create an empty file. For example, in Figure 27.4 you can see that I added ShellNew to the .html extension subkey, and then added the NullFile setting. In the folder below, I right-clicked and then clicked New. As you can see, an HTML Document type now appears in the New menu.

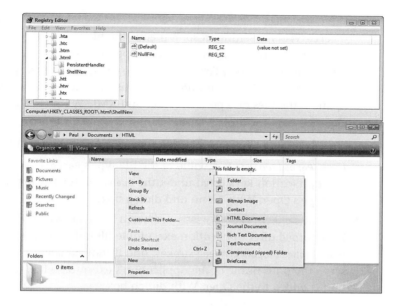

FIGURE 27.4

Add a `ShellNew` subkey to the `.html` key to add the HTML Document file type to the New menu.

Customize the Open With List

Medium

Back in Chapter 6, "Fundamental File Tweaks," you learned how to open a document with a different application by using the Open With dialog box. This is a truly useful dialog box, but you can make it even more useful by customizing it. In this tweak, you learn various Open With customizations.

➔ **See** "Open a Document Using a Different Application," **p. 62**.

Before you learn about the more advanced Open With customizations, you need to know how Windows compiles the list of applications that appear on the Open With list:

- Windows checks `HKEY_CLASSES_ROOT\.ext` (where `.ext` is the extension that defines the file type). If it finds an `OpenWith` subkey, the applications listed under that subkey are added to the Open With menu, and they appear in the Open With dialog box in the Recommended Programs section.

- Windows checks `HKEY_CLASSES_ROOT\`.*ext* to see whether the file type has a `PerceivedType` setting. If so, it means the file type also has an associated *perceived type*. This is a broader type that groups related file types into a single category. For example, the Image perceived type includes files of type BMP, GIF, and JPEG, whereas the Text perceived type includes the files of type TXT, HTM, and XML. Windows Vista then checks the following:

  `HKEY_CLASSES_ROOT\SystemFileAssociations\`*PerceivedType*`\OpenWithList`

  Here, *PerceivedType* is a value of the file type's `PerceivedType` setting. The application keys listed under the `OpenWithList` key are added to the file type's Open With menu and dialog box.

- Windows checks `HKEY_CLASSES_ROOT\Applications`, which contains subkeys named after application executable files. If an application subkey has a `\shell\open\command` subkey, and if that subkey's `Default` value is set to the path name of the application's executable file, the application is added to the Open With dialog box.

- Windows checks the following key:

  `HKEY_CURRENT_USER\Software\Microsoft\Windows\CurrentVersion\Explorer\`
  ↪`FileExts\`.*ext*`\OpenWithList`

  Here, *ext* is the file type's extension. This key contains settings for each application that the current user has used to open the file type via Open With. These settings are named a, b, c, and so on, and there's an `MRUList` setting that lists these letters in the order in which the applications have been used. These applications are added to the file type's Open With menu.

Removing an Application from a File Type's Open With Menu

When you use the Open With dialog box to choose an alternative application to open a particular file type, that application appears on the file type's Open With menu (that is, the menu that appears when you select the File, Open With command). To remove the application from this menu, open the following Registry key (where *ext* is the file type's extension):

`HKEY_CURRENT_USER\Software\Microsoft\Windows\CurrentVersion\Explorer\`
↪`FileExts\`.*ext*`\OpenWithList`

Delete the setting for the application you want removed from the menu. Also, edit the `MRUList` setting to remove the letter of the application you just deleted.

For example, if the application setting you deleted was named b, delete the letter b from the MRUList setting.

Removing a Program from the Open With List

Rather than customizing only a single file type's Open With menu, you might need to customize the Open With dialog box for all file types. To prevent a program from appearing in the Open With list, open the Registry Editor and navigate to the following key:

NOTE The NoOpenWith setting works only for applications that are not the default for opening a particular file type. For example, if you add NoOpenWith to the notepad.exe subkey, Notepad will still appear in the Open With list for text documents, but it won't appear for other file types, such as HTML files.

```
HKEY_CLASSES_ROOT/Applications
```

Here you'll find a number of subkeys, each of which represents an application installed on your system. The names of these subkeys are the names of each application's executable file (such as notepad.exe for Notepad). To prevent Windows from displaying an application in the Open With list, highlight the application's subkey, and create a new string value named NoOpenWith. (You don't have to supply a value for this setting.) To restore the application to the Open With list, delete the NoOpenWith setting.

Adding a Program to the Open With List

You can also add an application to the Open With dialog box for all file types. Again, you head for the following Registry key:

```
HKEY_CLASSES_ROOT/Applications
```

Display the subkey named after the application's executable file. (If the subkey doesn't exist, create it.) Now add the \shell\open\command subkey and set the Default value to the pathname of the application's executable file.

Disabling the Open With Check Box

The Open With dialog box enables you to change the application associated with a file type's Open action by activating the Always Use the Selected Program to Open This Kind of File check box. If you share your computer with other people, you might not want them changing this association, either accidentally or purposefully. In that case, you can disable the check box by adjusting the following Registry key:

```
HKEY_CLASSES_ROOT\Unknown\shell\opendlg\command
```

The `Default` value of this key is the following:

```
%SystemRoot%\system32\rundll32.exe %SystemRoot%\system32\shell32.dll,
➥OpenAs_RunDLL %1
```

To disable the check box in the Open With dialog box, append `%2` to the end of the `Default` value:

```
%SystemRoot%\system32\rundll32.exe %SystemRoot%\system32\shell32.dll,
➥OpenAs_RunDLL %1 %2
```

Add Tabs to Windows Explorer

Easy

When I'm working, I routinely have at least four or five Windows Explorer windows open, and it's not unusual for me to have eight or nine Explorers on the go. That's just the way I roll, and I suspect it's how lots of other people manage their files. If you do this, too, then you know it's often a real hassle: it's a hassle to switch from one Explorer to another; it's a hassle to move or copy files between the windows; and it's a hassle having all those open windows cluttering the screen.

Internet Explorer used to be the same way, and Microsoft fixed that problem by adding tabs to Internet Explorer 7. This meant that instead of multiple Internet Explorer windows on the go, you could use just a single window and load multiple sites into separate tabs.

Unfortunately, the Microsoft programmers haven't yet added this feature to Windows Explorer, so we're stuck with having Explorer windows multiplying like digital rabbits.

Or are we?

I've come across a nifty little utility called QT TabBar that adds tabs to Windows Explorer. Now you can load multiple drives and folders into a single Explorer window, navigate from one to another with a single click, and even move and copy files from one tab to another. See the following site to download QT TabBar:

http://qttabbar.wikidot.com/

Extract the files from the compressed folder (`.zip` file) that you downloaded, save them in a folder, and then navigate to that folder. If you're using Vista, right-click `QTTabBar.exe`, click Run As Administrator,

NOTE To use QT TabBar in XP, you need to have Microsoft .NET Framework 2.0 installed. To check, select Start, Control Panel, Add or Remove Programs, and in the list of installed programs look for Microsoft .NET Framework 2.0. If you don't see it, you can download it here:

```
http://www.microsoft.com/
downloads/details.aspx?
familyid=0856eacb-4362-
4b0d-8edd-aab15c5e04f5
```

and then enter your User Account Control credentials. If you're using XP and you're logged on with an administrator account, just double-click QTTabBar.exe. Follow the onscreen instructions for installing the plug-in, and then restart your computer.

Now follow these steps to enable the QT TabBar and the separate toolbar that enables you to add and remove tabs:

1. Open Windows Explorer in any folder.

2. (Windows Vista only) Press Alt to display the menu bar.

3. Select View, Toolbars, QT TabBar.

4. Select View, Toolbars, QT Tab Standard Buttons.

5. Select View, Lock the Toolbars to deactivate this command.

6. Click and drag the QT TabBar and the QT Tab Standard Buttons toolbar so that they're visible.

Figure 27.5 shows the QT Tab Standard Buttons toolbar on the right and the QT TabBar on the left, with three tabs open. To create a new tab, click the Clone This button (pointed out in Figure 27.5).

FIGURE 27.5

The QT TabBar plug-in lets you open multiple tabs with Windows Explorer.

28

Working with Network Computers

When people talk about living in a "wired world," they're most often musing about life in a time when most folks (at least in developed countries) are connected to the Internet at home, at work, or even on the road via Wi-Fi hookups and cellular connections. But that "wired" adjective also applies to another trend that has happened over the same time frame, although with far less fanfare: Almost all of us are connected to local networks, certainly at work, but increasingly at home, as well.

This means that many of us have become de facto network administrators charged with installing network hardware, setting up routers and wireless access points, running network cables, connecting PCs, and fixing network problems. In this chapter and the next three, my goal is to provide you with a few useful tweaks that I trust will help you with these networking chores and will help you get more out of your networked computers.

- Give a Computer a Static IP Address
- Make XP Computers Appear in Vista's Network Map
- Access Mac Shares via Windows

Give a Computer a Static IP Address

Medium

Your network's router also acts as a Dynamic Host Control Protocol (DHCP) server, which means that it provides a unique IP address to each device that connects to the router. In most cases that IP address expires after 24 hours, and when the expiration time approaches the client asks for a new IP address. In small networks, the DHCP server often assigns each client the same IP address each time, but that's not guaranteed. In your day-to-day Windows work you rarely need to know a connection's IP address, so a changing IP address is no big deal the vast majority of the time.

However, there are times when a constantly changing IP address can be a big problem. For example, when you learn how to access your desktop over the Internet in Chapter 30, "Making Remote Connections," you see that a dynamic IP address makes it much harder to make the connection. You can fix this problem by assigning a static IP address to your computer.

➜ **See** "Connect to Your Desktop via the Internet," **p. 354**.

When you use a dynamic IP address, in most cases you also use dynamic DNS (*domain name system*) addresses, which are supplied by your Internet service provider. (The DNS enables computers and servers connected to the Internet to find resources using domain names rather than IP addresses.) When you switch your computer to a static IP address (as described later), Windows also disables the feature that allows it to obtain DNS addresses automatically. In other words, when you specify a static IP address, you must also specify static DNS addresses.

Therefore, before performing the procedure for converting Windows to a static IP

> **TIP** Instead of assigning a static IP address to the Vista computer, you might be able to get your router to handle this for you. Log on to your router's configuration pages and look for an option that enables you to map a static IP address to the computer MAC (see "Finding a Connection's MAC Address," later in this chapter) address. This means that whenever the computer requests a new DHCP lease, the router supplies the computer the same IP address each time. Note that not all routers offer this option.

> **NOTE** The instructions in this section work for both wired and wireless connections.

> **NOTE** Remember that when using MORE, you control the output of the results by either pressing Enter (to scroll through the results one line at a time) or press the spacebar (to see the results one screen at a time).

address, you need to determine your ISP's current DNS addresses. To find out
the current DNS addresses for a network connection, open Command Prompt,
type **ipconfig /all | more** and press Enter. Windows displays information
about each network connection, including the IP addresses of your ISP's DNS
servers, as shown in the following (partial) example output:

```
Windows IP Configuration

    Host Name . . . . . . . . . . . : OfficePC
    Primary Dns Suffix  . . . . . . :
    Node Type . . . . . . . . . . . : Hybrid
    IP Routing Enabled. . . . . . . : No
    WINS Proxy Enabled. . . . . . . : No

Ethernet adapter Local Area Connection 2:

    Connection-specific DNS Suffix  . :
    Description . . . . . . . . . . : D-Link DGE-530T Gigabit
Ethernet Adapter
    Physical Address. . . . . . . . : 00-13-46-95-84-28
    DHCP Enabled. . . . . . . . . . : Yes
    Autoconfiguration Enabled . . . . : Yes
    Link-local IPv6 Address . . . . . :
fe80::94ba:8241:988d:c199%12(Preferred)
    IPv4 Address. . . . . . . . . . : 192.168.1.101(Preferred)
    Subnet Mask . . . . . . . . . . : 255.255.255.0
    Lease Obtained. . . . . . . . . : Tuesday, August 28, 2008
10:01:41 AM
    Lease Expires . . . . . . . . . : Wednesday, August 29, 2008
10:01:40 AM
    Default Gateway . . . . . . . . : 192.168.1.1
    DHCP Server . . . . . . . . . . : 192.168.1.1
    DHCPv6 IAID . . . . . . . . . . : 301994822
    DNS Servers . . . . . . . . . . : 207.164.234.193
                                      67.69.184.223
    NetBIOS over Tcpip. . . . . . . : Enabled
```

You're now just about ready to assign a static IP address to your computer.
The last bit of information you need to know is the IP address to use. This is
important because you don't want to use an address that your router has
already assigned to another computer. The easiest way to do this is to choose

an address outside of the DHCP server's range. For example, if your DHCP server is configured to assign addresses from the range 192.168.1.100 to 192.168.1.150, an address such as 192.168.1.50 or 192.168.1.200 will work. (Remember, too, not to use the address assigned to your router.)

With an IP address in hand, follow these steps to assign it to a network connection in Windows Vista:

NOTE To find out the range of addresses that your router's DHCP uses, you need to access the router's setup pages. The easiest way to do this is to plug the router's IP address into a web browser. The router address is usually either 192.168.0.1 or 192.168.1.1.

TIP It's probably a good idea to also check your router's DHCP table to see which addresses it has assigned.

1. Open the Network Connections window:

   - **Windows Vista**—Select Start, type **network**, click Network and Sharing Center, and then click Manage Network Connections.

   - **Windows XP**—Select Start, All Programs, Accessories, Communications, Network Connections.

2. Right-click the connection you want to work with and then click Properties. In Vista, the User Account Control dialog box appears.

3. (Windows Vista only) Enter your UAC credentials to continue.

4. In the connection's Properties dialog box, display the Networking tab.

5. In the list of items, select Internet Protocol Version 4 (TCP/IPv4).

6. Click Properties to display the Properties dialog box for Internet Protocol Version 4.

7. Click to activate the Use the Following IP Address option.

8. Use the IP Address box to type the IP address you want to use.

9. Use the Subnet Mask box to type the IP addresses for the subnet mask. (Windows Vista should fill this in for you automatically; the most common value is 255.255.255.0.)

10. Use the Default Gateway box to type the IP address of your network's router.

11. Use the Preferred DNS Server and Alternate DNS Server boxes to type the IP addresses of your ISP's DNS servers. Figure 28.1 shows a completed version of the dialog box.

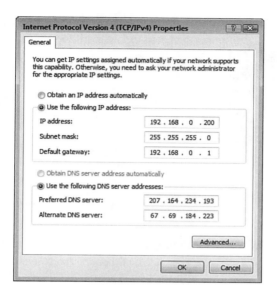

FIGURE 28.1

You can assign a static IP address to a network connection on a Windows computer.

    12. Click OK to return to the connection's Properties dialog box.

    13. Click Close.

Make XP Computers Appear in Vista's Network Map

Medium

Windows Vista comes with a new Network Map feature that gives you a bird's-eye view of everything your computer is connected to: network connections (wired and wireless), ad hoc (computer-to-computer) connections, Internet connections, and the devices associated with these connections (such as a router and/or a switch). Network Map also gives you a visual display of the connection status so that you can easily spot problems.

Select Start, type **network**, and then click Network and Sharing Center. In the Network and Sharing Center window that shows up, the top part of the window displays your local portion of the network map, and the layout depends on your current connections. You always see an icon for your computer on the left. If your computer is connected to a network, a green line joins the computer icon and the network icon. If the network is connected to the Internet, another green line joins the network icon and the Internet icon on the right (see Figure 28.2). If there is no connection, you see a red X through the connection line.

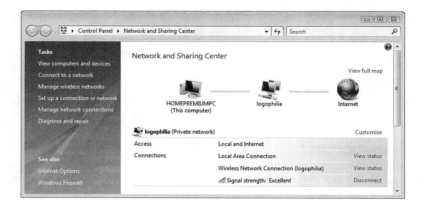

FIGURE 28.2

The top part of the Network and Sharing Center window displays your local portion of the net-work map.

The Network and Sharing Center also comes with a more detailed version of Network Map. To view it, click the View Full Map link. Figure 28.3 shows an example of the full network map. If you have multiple network connections, use the Network Map Of list to select a different connection and see its map.

> **TIP** To see the IP address of any device in the Network Map, hover your mouse pointer over the device. A balloon appears and displays the device name, its IPv4 address, its IPv6 address, and its MAC (Media Access Control) address (a unique address assigned to every networking device).

Notice in Figure 28.3 that there's a problem with the Network Map: There are two icons at the bottom—TABLETPC and SERVER—that Network Map claims "can not [sic] be placed in the map." Here the TABLETPC icon represents a Windows XP computer, and the SERVER icon represents a Windows Home Server machine. These machines don't get along with Network Map, because this feature requires a protocol called Link Layer Topology Discovery (LLTD). LLTD is baked into every version of Windows Vista, but it's not part of Windows XP (or Windows Home Server). This means that XP PCs either don't show up at all in the Network Map, or they get relegated to the limbo at the bottom of the map.

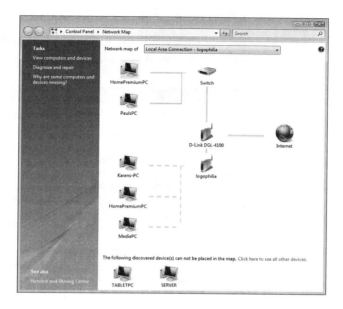

FIGURE 28.3

The full version of the Network Map.

To fix this in XP, you have two choices:

- If you're running XP with Service Pack 2 or earlier, download and install the Link Layer Topology Discovery (LLTD) Responder package, which is available from Microsoft:

  www.microsoft.com/downloads/details.aspx?FamilyId=4F01A31D-EE46-481E-BA11-37F485FA34EA

- If you're running XP with Service Pack 3, Microsoft has not yet released a hotfix for this problem. Check the following Knowledge Base article to see if the hotfix is ready:

  http://support.microsoft.com/kb/922120

If there's no hotfix in sight, all is not lost. You can load the LLTD Responder package, but it takes quite a bit of extra work, unfortunately. Here are the steps:

1. Download the LLTD Responder package and save it to your hard drive.

2. Open the folder containing the LLTD Responder package, right-drag the file (that is, hold down the right mouse button and drag the file), drop it inside the same folder, and then click Create Shortcuts Here.

3. Right-click the new shortcut and then click Properties.

4. In the Shortcut tab, click inside the Target text box and add a space followed by **-x**, as shown in Figure 28.4. Click OK.

FIGURE 28.4

In the Target text box, you need to add a space and -x to the existing command.

5. Double-click the shortcut. XP prompts you for a folder location to extract the files (the default is the current folder).

6. Type a folder path (or leave the current path as is), and click OK. XP extracts the files in the package.

7. Locate the extracted files and open the SP2GDR folder.

8. Copy the rspndr.exe file and paste it in %SystemRoot%\System32 (where $SystemRoot% is usually C:\Windows).

9. Copy the rspndr.sys file and paste it in %SystemRoot%\System32\ drivers.

10. Open the ic subfolder.

11. Copy the rspndr.inf file and paste it in %SystemRoot%\inf.

NOTE If you don't see %SystemRoot%\inf, you need to display hidden files. Select Tools, Folder Options, display the View tab, activate the Show Hidden Files and Folders option, and then click OK.

12. Start a Command Prompt session and enter the following command:

`%SystemRoot%\System32\rspndr.sys -i`

Windows XP installs the LLTD Responder package. Your XP SP 3 computer will now appear properly in the Windows Vista Network Map, as shown in Figure 28.5. (If you still have problems, reboot the XP machine.)

> **TIP** Notice in Figure 28.5 that the Server machine also appears correctly in the Network Map. This is a Windows Home Server computer; the steps in this section also work with Windows Home Server.

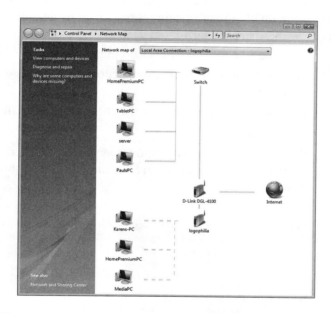

FIGURE 28.5

With the LLTD Responder package installed, the XP computer (TabletPC) appears properly in the Network Map.

Access Mac Shares via Windows

One of the important networking layers used by all Microsoft networks—including, of course, your Windows Home Server network—is called Server Message Block (SMB). It is via SMB that Windows PCs can share folders on the network and access folders that other Windows PCs have shared. In a very real sense, SMB *is* the network.

Medium

SMB's central role in Windows networking is good news if you have a Mac in your household. That's because all versions of OS X support SMB natively, so you can use your Mac not only to view the Windows shares, but also to open and work with files on those shares (provided, of course, that you have permission to access the share and that OS X has an application that's compatible with whatever file you want to work with).

NOTE These steps assume your Mac is running at least Mac OS X 10.5 (Leopard).

SMB not only lets your Mac see shares on the Windows Home Server network, it also can let Windows PCs see folders shared by the Mac, and that's what this tweak is all about. This feature is turned off by default in OS X, but you can follow these steps to turn it on:

1. Click the System Preferences icon in the Dock.

2. In the Internet & Network group, click Sharing to open the Sharing preferences.

3. In the list of services, activate the check box beside File Sharing.

4. Click Options.

5. Deactivate the Share Files and Folders Using AFP and activate the Share Files and Folders Using SMB check boxes, as shown in Figure 28.6.

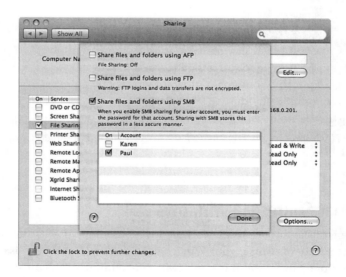

FIGURE 28.6

Deactivate AFP sharing and activate SMB sharing.

6. Activate the check box for each user account you want to give access, and then click Done.

7. To share a folder, click the + icon under Shared Folders, select the folder, and then click Add.

8. Click the folder in the Shared Folders list, click + under Users, select a user, and then click Add.

9. Click a user in the Users list and then click the permission level you want to assign: Read & Write, Read Only, or Write Only.

10. Repeat steps 7–9 to share other folders and set other user permissions. Figure 28.7 shows the Sharing preferences with several folders and users.

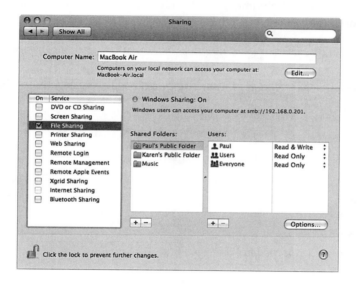

FIGURE 28.7

The Sharing preferences with Windows Sharing activated.

11. Select System Preferences, Quit System Preferences.

One way to access the Mac shares from a Windows PC is to enter the share address directly, using either the Run dialog box or Windows Explorer's Address bar. You have two choices:

`\\IP\user`

`\\Computer\user`

Here *IP* is the IP address shown in the OS X Sharing window (see Figure 28.7), *Computer* is the Mac's computer name (also shown in the OS X Sharing window), and in both cases *user* is the username of the account enabled for

Windows Sharing. For example, I can use either of the following addresses to access my Mac:

```
\\192.168.1.119\paul
\\MacBook-Air\paul
```

Alternatively, open your workgroup and look for the icon that has the same name as the Mac's computer name. Double-click that icon.

Unless you're logged on to Windows with the same username and password as the Mac, you're prompted for the username and password of the Mac account that you enabled for Windows Sharing. For the username, use the form *Computer\UserName*, where *Computer* is the name of your Mac and *UserName* is the name of the Windows Sharing account. Figure 28.8 shows a Mac share opened in Windows Vista.

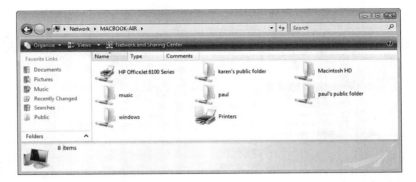

FIGURE 28.8
A shared Mac folder opened in Windows Vista.

TIP If you have trouble logging on to your Mac from Windows Vista, the problem is likely caused by Vista's use of NT LAN Manager version 2 (NTLMv2) authentication, which doesn't work properly when negotiated between some versions of Vista and some versions of OS X. To fix this, on the Vista PC, press Windows Logo+R (or select Start, All Programs, Accessories, Run), type `secpol.msc`, and click OK to open the Local Security Policy snap-in. Open the Security Settings, Local Policies, Security Options branch. Double-click the Network Security: LAN Manager Authentication Level policy, change the authentication level to Send LM & NTLM-Use NTLMv2 Session Security If Negotiated, and then click OK.

If your version of Vista doesn't come with the Local Security snap-in (it's not available in Home and Home Premium), open the Registry Editor (press Windows Logo+R, type `regedit`, and click OK), and navigate to the following key:

```
HLM\SYSTEM\CurrentControlSet\Control\Lsa\
```

Change the value of the `LMCompatibilityLevel` setting to 1.

Tightening Network Security

When you join your computer to a network that contains multiple users, your setup is no longer secure. Assuming you're sharing at least a folder or two, the nature of a network means that other people have access to that information. If you want to control not only who has access to your data, but also what those users can do with the data, you need to implement a few network security precautions. Of course, other users inadvertently seeing data they shouldn't is one problem, but an outsider gaining unauthorized access to the network is quite another. Fortunately, you can take steps to minimize this sort of intrusion. This chapter takes you through a few useful techniques for securing your network.

Lock Down Network Shares with Advanced Security Permissions

Medium

If your Windows PC is on a network, chances are you want to share at least some of your data with at least some of the users on the network. The big question, however, is how do you do this in a way that's easy, flexible, and secure? Hah! Pick two, as they say:

- **Easy and flexible**—Use the `Public` folder (in Vista) or the `SharedDocs` folder (in XP) for all your shared data, and allow anyone to access that folder.

- **Easy and secure**—Use the `Public` folder (in Vista) or the `SharedDocs` folder (in XP) for all your shared data, and protect it with a password.

- **Flexible and secure**—Share your other folders directly, as needed, protect those folders with passwords, and set security permissions on those folders.

Before getting into the details, your first network security chore on any Windows PC should be to enable advanced sharing permissions. By default, Vista and XP use a simplified form of network sharing—it's called the Sharing Wizard in Vista, and Simple File Sharing in XP—that's aimed at novice users. If you want secure access to the data you share, you need to disable these brain-dead sharing schemes and use the much more powerful advanced sharing permissions. Here's how to disable the default sharing schemes:

- **Windows Vista**—In any folder window, select Organize, Folder and Search Options. In the Folder Options dialog box, click the View tab, deactivate the Use Sharing Wizard check box, and then click OK.

- **Windows XP**—In any folder window, select Tools, Folder Options. In the Folder Options dialog box, click the View tab, deactivate the Use Simple File Sharing check box, and then click OK.

Easy and Flexible Network Sharing

If the data you want to share doesn't need to be secure, and you want to share it with anyone on the network without a lot of fuss, you need to implement the easy and flexible sharing solution:

- **Windows Vista**—You need to store all your shared data in the Public folder, which is located at `%SystemDrive%\Users\Public` (where `%SystemDrive%` is the drive where Vista is installed, usually `C:`). To enable access to this folder, click Start, type **network**, and then click Network and Sharing Center in the search results. (You can also click the Network icon and then click Network and Sharing Center.) In the Sharing and Discovery section, configure the following options:

  Network Discovery—This setting should be On.

  File Sharing—This setting should be On.

  Public Folder Sharing—This setting should be On. If you don't want people to make changes to anything in the Public folder, choose the Turn On Sharing So Anyone with Network Access Can Open Files option; otherwise, if you want people to make changes within the Public folder,

NOTE If you don't see the Everyone group, click Add, type **everyone**, and click OK.

choose the Turn On Sharing So Anyone with Network Access Can Open, Change, and Create Files option.

Password Protected Sharing—This setting should be Off.

- **Windows XP**—You need to store all your shared data in the `SharedDocs` folder, which is located at `%SystemDrive%\Documents and Settings\All Users\Documents` (where `%SystemDrive%` is the drive where Vista is installed, usually `C:`). To enable access to this folder, select Start, My Computer, right-click Shared Documents, and then click Properties. Click the Sharing tab, click Permissions, and then click Everyone. Click Full Control and then click OK in the open dialog boxes.

Easy and Secure Network Sharing

If the data you want to share needs to be secure, but you don't want to spend tons of time or effort securing it, you need to implement the easy and secure sharing solution. Note that this solution requires setting up one or more user accounts on your computer for the network users; see "Creating User Accounts for Sharing," later in this chapter.

Here's what you do:

- **Windows Vista**—You need to store all your shared data in the Public folder, which is located at `%SystemDrive%\Users\Public` (where `%SystemDrive%` is the drive where Vista is installed, usually `C:`). To enable secure access to this folder, click Start, type **network**, and then click Network and Sharing Center in the search results. (You can also click the Network icon and then click Network and Sharing Center.) In the Sharing and Discovery section, configure the following options:

  Network Discovery—This setting should be On.

  File Sharing—This setting should be On.

  Public Folder Sharing—This setting should be On. If you don't want people to make changes to anything in the Public folder, choose the Turn On Sharing So Anyone with Network Access Can Open Files option; otherwise, if you want people to make changes within the Public folder, choose the Turn On Sharing So Anyone with Network Access Can Open, Change, and Create Files option.

  Password Protected Sharing — This setting should be On.

■ **Windows XP**—You need to store all your shared data in the SharedDocs folder, which is located at %SystemDrive%\Documents and Settings\All Users\Documents (where %SystemDrive% is the drive where Vista is installed, usually C:). To enable secure access to this folder, select Start, My Computer, right-click Shared Documents, and then click Properties. Click the Sharing tab, click Permissions, click Everyone, and then click Remove. For each user you want to access the folder, click Add, type the username, click OK, and then click the permission level: Full Control, Change, or Read.

Flexible and Secure Network Sharing

If the data you want to share needs to be secure, and you want the flexibility of controlling who gets access to it, you need to implement the flexible and secure sharing solution. Note that this solution requires setting up one or more user accounts on your computer for the network users; see "Creating User Accounts for Sharing," later in this chapter.

Here's what you do:

■ **Windows Vista**—Open the Network and Sharing Center and set up the Sharing and Discovery settings as described in the previous section. For each folder you want to share, right-click the folder and then click Share. In the Sharing tab, click Advanced Sharing and enter your UAC credentials. Activate the Share This Folder check box and then click Permissions. Click Everyone, and then click Remove. For each user you want to access the folder, click Add, type the username, click OK, and then click the permission level: Full Control, Change, or Read.

■ **Windows XP**—For each folder you want to share, right-click the folder and then click Properties. Click the Sharing tab, click Permissions, click Everyone, and then click Remove. For each user you want to access the folder, click Add, type the username, click OK, and then click the permission level: Full Control, Change, or Read.

Creating User Accounts for Sharing

If you want to use either of the secure sharing solutions, you have to do one of the following:

■ **Set up separate accounts for each user that you want to access a shared resource**—Do this if you want to assign each user a different set of permissions, or if you want the usernames and passwords to match each user's local username and password.

- **Set up a single account for all remote users to use**—Do this if you want to assign the same set of permissions for all users.

Here are some notes to bear in mind for creating users who will access your computer over a network:

- Windows does *not* allow users without passwords to access network resources. Therefore, you must set up your network user accounts with passwords.

- The usernames you create do not have to correspond with the names that users have on their local machines. You're free to set up your own usernames, if you like.

- If you create a user account that has the same name and password as an account of a user on his or her local machine, that user will be able to access your shared resources directly. Otherwise, a Connect To dialog box appears so that the user can enter the username and password that you established when setting up the account on your computer.

NTFS SECURITY PERMISSIONS

If you want even more control over the use of your shared resources across the network, you should also set NTFS security permissions on the folder. (Ideally, you should do this before sharing the resource.) To do this, right-click the folder, click Sharing and Security, and then display the Security tab. This tab is similar to the Permissions dialog box, except that you get a longer list of permissions for each group or user:

- **Full Control**—Users can perform any of the actions listed. Users can also change permissions.

- **Modify**—Users can view the folder contents, open files, edit files, create new files and subfolders, delete files, and run programs.

- **Read and Execute**—Users can view the folder contents, open files, and run programs.

- **List Folder Contents**—Users can view the folder contents.

- **Read**—Users can open files, but cannot edit them.

- **Write**—Users can create new files and subfolders, and open and edit existing files.

- **Special Permissions**—Advanced settings for permissions, auditing, ownership, and effective permissions.

Hide Your Shared Folders

Medium

Setting up user accounts with strong passwords and then applying shared-folder permissions on those accounts are the necessary network security tasks, and in most small networks they're also sufficient for achieving a decent level of security. However, when it comes to securing your network, a healthy dose of paranoia is another good "tool" to have at hand. For example, the properly paranoid network administrator doesn't assume that no one will ever infiltrate the network, just the opposite: The admin assumes that someday someone *will* get access, and then he or she wonders what can be done in that case to minimize the damage.

NOTE The techniques that follow assume that you've turned off the default sharing features in Vista or XP, as described in the previous tweak.

TIP You can also right-click the folder and then click Share.

One of the first things these paranoid administrators do (or should do) is hide what's valuable, private, or sensitive. For example, if you have a shared folder named, for instance, Confidential Documents, you're simply *begging* a would-be thief to access that share. Yes, you could rename the share to something less inviting, but the thief may chance upon it anyway. To prevent this, it's possible to share a resource *and* hide it at the same time.

Even better, hiding a shared folder is also extremely easy to do, as you will see in the following sections.

Hide a Shared Folder in Windows Vista

Here are the steps to follow to hide an existing shared folder in Windows Vista:

1. In Windows Explorer, select the shared folder you want to hide.
2. Click the Share button in Vista's task pane.
3. Click Advanced Sharing. The User Account Control dialog box appears.
4. Enter your UAC credentials to continue. The Advanced Sharing dialog box appears.
5. Click Add to open the New Share dialog box.
6. Use the Share Name text box to type the name you want to use, followed by **$**, and then click OK.
7. In the Share Name list, select the old share name.
8. Click Remove.
9. Click OK.

Hide a Shared Folder in Windows XP

To hide an existing shared folder in Windows XP, follow these steps:

1. In Windows Explorer, select the shared folder you want to hide.

2. Click the Share This Folder link. Windows Vista displays the object's Properties sheet with the Sharing tab selected.

3. Add a dollar sign ($) to the end of the share name.

4. Click OK.

TIP You can also right-click the folder and then click Sharing and Security.

CAUTION Hiding shares will work for the average user, but a savvy snoop will probably know about the $ trick. Therefore, you should set up your hidden shares with nonobvious names.

Viewing a Hidden Share

Adding $ to the end of the share name prevents the resource from appearing in the list of resources when you open a remote computer from the Network windows (Vista) or the My Network Places window (XP). The shared resource also doesn't show up when you type **net view \\computer** at the command prompt, where *computer* is the name of the remote PC.

How do you connect to a hidden share? You need to know the name of the shared resource, of course, which enables you to use any of the following techniques:

- In the Run dialog box, type the network path for the hidden resource, and click OK. For example, to display the hidden share F$ on OfficePC, you'd enter this:

```
\\officepc\f$
```

- In a command prompt session, type **start**, a space, the network path, and then press the Enter key. For example, to launch the hidden share F$ on OfficePC, you would enter this:

```
start \\officepc\f$
```

- Select Start, right-click Computer (in Vista) or My Computer (in XP), and then click Map Network Drive. In the Map Network Drive dialog box, type the UNC path for the hidden share in the Folder text box.

Disable the Hidden Administrative Shares

Medium

I mentioned in the previous tweak that you can add $ to a share name to hide the share, and that it was a good idea to also modify the share name to something not easily guessable by some snoop. Note, however, that Windows sets up certain hidden shares for administrative purposes, including one for drive C: (C$) and any other hard disk partitions you have on your system. Windows Vista also sets up the following hidden shares:

Share	Shared Path	Purpose
ADMIN$	%SystemRoot%	Remote administration
IPC$	N/A	Remote interprocess communication
print$	%SystemRoot%\System32\spool\drivers	Access to printer drivers

To see these shares, open a command prompt session, type **net share**, and press Enter. In Vista you see a listing like this (the XP listing is similar):

```
Share name   Resource                   Remark
-------------------------------------------------------------------
C$           C:\                        Default share
D$           D:\                        Default share
ADMIN$       C:\WINDOWS                 Remote Admin
IPC$                                    Remote IPC
print$       C:\System32\spool\drivers  Printer Drivers
Public       C:\Users\Public
```

So although the C$, D$, and ADMIN$ shares are otherwise hidden, they're well known, and they represent a small security risk should an intruder get access to your network.

To close this hole, you can force Windows to disable these shares. Here are the steps to follow:

1. Run the Registry Editor.

➤   To learn how to use the Registry Editor, **see** Chapter 34, "Tweaking Windows with the Registry Editor," **p. 401**.

2. Open the HKEY_LOCAL_MACHINE branch.

3. Open the SYSTEM branch.

4. Open the CurrentControlSet branch.

5. Open the Services branch.

6. Open the LanmanServer branch.

7. Select the Parameters branch.

8. Select Edit, New, DWORD (32-bit) Value. Windows adds a new value to the `Parameters` key.

9. Type **AutoShareWks** and press Enter. (You can leave this setting with its default value of 0.)

10. Restart Windows to put the new setting into effect.

CAUTION Some programs expect the administrative shares to be present, so disabling those shares may cause those programs to fail or generate error messages. If that happens, enable the shares by opening the Registry Editor and either deleting the `AutoShareWks` setting or changing its value to 1.

Again, select Start, All Programs, Accessories, Command Prompt to open a command prompt session, type **net share**, and press Enter. The output now looks like this:

```
Share name     Resource                      Remark
-----------------------------------------------------------------------

IPC$                                         Remote IPC
print$         C:\System32\spool\drivers     Printer Drivers
Public         C:\Users\Public
```

Remove Stored Remote Desktop Credentials

Medium

When you log on to a network computer using Remote Desktop Connection as described in see Chapter 30, "Making Remote Connections"), you have the option of saving your credentials:

- **Windows Vista**—The Vista logon dialog box includes a check box named Remember My Credentials.

- **Windows XP**—The General tab of the Remote Desktop Connection dialog box (select Start, All Programs, Accessories, Remote Desktop Connection) has a check box named Allow Me to Save Credentials. (You may need to click the Options button to see it.) If you activate this check box, the logon dialog box includes a check box named Remember My Password.

If you activate either the Remember My Credentials or Remember My Password check box, Windows won't prompt you to enter a password when you connect to the computer in the future.

→   To learn how to log on with Remote Desktop Connection, **see** "Connect to a Remote Desktop," **p. 350.**

That's certainly convenient, but it's a gaping security hole because it enables anyone who can access your computer to also access the remote computer's desktop. Therefore, it's never a good idea to activate the Remember My Credentials (or Remember My Password) check box.

However, what if you activated that option earlier? Fortunately, you're not stuck because Windows gives you a way to "unremember" those credentials. Here are the steps to follow:

1. Open the Run dialog box, type `control userpasswords2`, and select OK.
2. (Windows Vista only) Enter your User Account Control credentials to continue.
3. In the User Accounts dialog box, select the Advanced tab.
4. Click Manage Password. Windows displays the Stored User Names and Passwords dialog box, shown in Figure 29.1.

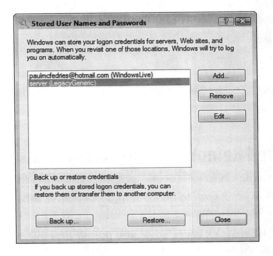

FIGURE 29.1

If you save your Remote Desktop Connection logon credentials, they appear in the Stored User Names and Passwords dialog box.

5. Select the Remote Desktop Connection credentials you want to delete.
6. Click Remove. Windows tells you that the logon information will be deleted.
7. Click OK.
8. Repeat steps 6–8 to remove other saved credentials.
9. Click Close.

> **TIP** Another way to remove saved Remote Desktop Connection credentials is to select Start, All Programs, Accessories, Remote Desktop Connection. In the Remote Desktop Connection dialog box, click Options to expand the dialog box, select the General tab, and then click the Delete link in the Logon Settings group. Click Yes when Remote Desktop Connection asks you to confirm.

30

Making Remote Connections

ou probably share a folder or three on your computer, and it's likely that other folks on your network are similarly generous with their stuff. Sharing folders is an easy way to give and get access to other users' files, but it doesn't solve all the sharing problems you might come across. For example, you can't share programs, and you can't share data such as email messages.

To solve these and similar problems, you need to go beyond shared folders and establish a more powerful connection to the remote computer. That is, you need to connect to the remote machine's desktop, which enables you to open folders, run programs, edit documents, and tweak settings. In short, anything you can do while physically sitting in front of the other computer you can do remotely from your own computer. As you see in this chapter, the Windows Remote Desktop feature enables you to connect to a computer's desktop over the network. It's also possible to configure your network to allow you to make a Remote Desktop connection over the Internet. This is a great way to give yourself access to your home computer while you're traveling with a laptop, or you can provide tech support to far-flung family and friends.

- Configure Windows as a Remote Desktop Host
- Connect to a Remote Desktop
- Connect to Your Desktop via the Internet
- Configure a Network Computer for Remote Administration
- Connect to a Remote Computer with a Script

You also learn some tweaks for setting up PCs for remote administration tasks, and for connecting to remote computers via scripts.

Configure Windows as a Remote Desktop Host

Medium

Remote Desktop is easy to configure and use, but it does require a small amount of prep work to ensure trouble-free operation. Let's begin with the remote computer, also called the *host* computer. The next few sections tell you how to set up a machine to act as a Remote Desktop host.

The first thing you need to know is that not all versions of Windows can act as Remote Desktop hosts:

- With Vista, the only versions that support Remote Desktop hosting are Vista Business, Vista Enterprise, and Vista Ultimate.
- If you want to use a Windows XP computer as the host, you can use any version except XP Home.

Also, for security reasons, not just anyone can connect to a remote computer's desktop. By default, Windows gives permission to connect remotely to the host to the following:

- The user who is currently logged on to the host machine
- Members of the host's Administrators and Remote Desktop Users groups

Note, however, that all these users must have password-protected accounts to use Remote Desktop.

For anyone else, if you want to give a person permission to connect to the host remotely, you first need to set up an account for the username with which you want that person to connect from the client, and you must assign a password to this account.

Configuring Vista to Act as a Remote Desktop Host

If the host machine is running Vista Business, Enterprise, or Ultimate, you have to do three things to prepare the computer for its Remote Desktop hosting duties:

- Disable automatic sleep mode.
- Allow Remote Desktop through the Windows Firewall.
- Activate the Remote Desktop service.

Disabling Automatic Sleep Mode

Most Vista machines are configured to go into sleep mode after one hour of inactivity. Sleep is a low-power mode that turns everything off except power to the memory chips, which store the current desktop configuration. When you turn the machine back on, the desktop and your open programs and documents appear within a few seconds. However, remote clients won't be able to connect to the host if it's in sleep mode, so you have to disable this feature.

NOTE All we're doing here is disabling the feature that puts your computer into sleep mode automatically after a period of inactivity. If need be, you can still put the computer into sleep mode manually by selecting Start and clicking the Sleep button.

Here are the steps to follow:

1. Select Start, type **power** in the Search box, and then click Power Options in the search results. The Power Options window appears.

2. Click the Change When the Computer Sleeps link. Vista opens the Edit Plan Settings window.

3. In the Put the Computer to Sleep list, select Never.

4. Click Save Changes.

Configuring a Windows Firewall Exception for Remote Desktop

By default, Windows Firewall doesn't allow Remote Desktop connections. This is a sensible security precaution because connecting to someone's desktop gives you nearly complete control over that PC. To enable remote connections, you must configure a Windows Firewall exception for Remote Desktop.

Here are the steps you need to follow:

1. Select Start, type **firewall** in the Search box, and then click Windows Firewall in the search results. The Windows Firewall window appears.

2. Click the Allow a Program Through Windows Firewall link. The User Account Control dialog box appears.

3. Enter your User Account Control (UAC) credentials to continue. Vista opens the Windows Firewall Settings dialog box with the Exceptions tab displayed.

4. Activate the check box beside Remote Desktop, as shown in Figure 30.1.

5. Click OK. Vista enables the firewall exception for Remote Desktop.

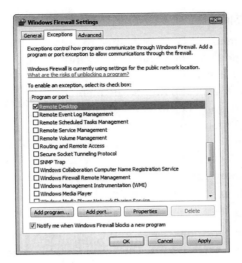

FIGURE 30.1

On the host, activate the Remote Desktop firewall exception.

Activating the Remote Desktop Service

Now follow these steps to activate the Remote Desktop service:

1. Select Start, type `systempropertiesremote`, and press Enter. The User Account Control dialog box appears.

2. Enter your UAC credentials to continue. Vista opens the System Properties dialog box with the Remote tab displayed, as shown in Figure 30.2.

3. In the Remote Desktop group, you need to choose one of the following options:

   - **Allow Connections from Computers Running Any Version of Remote Desktop**—Select this option if you want people running previous versions of Remote Desktop to be able to access the host.

   - **Allow Connections Only from Computers Running Remote Desktop with Network Level Authentication**—Select this option if you only want the most secure form of Remote Desktop access. In this case, Vista checks the client computer to see whether its version of Remote Desktop supports Network Level Authentication (NLA). NLA is an authentication protocol that authenticates the user before making the Remote Desktop connection. NLA is built in to every version of Windows Vista, but is not supported on older Windows systems.

FIGURE 30.2
On the remote host, select an option in the Remote Desktop group to enable remote connections to the computer's desktop.

4. If you didn't add more users earlier, skip to step 7. Otherwise, click Select Users to display the Remote Desktop Users dialog box.

5. Click Add to display the Select Users dialog box, type the username, and click OK. (Repeat this step to add other users.)

6. Click OK to return to the System Properties dialog box.

7. Click OK.

Configuring XP to Act as a Remote Desktop Host

If the would-be host machine is running any version of XP except XP Home, here are the steps to follow to set it up to host Remote Desktop sessions:

1. Select Start, Run (or press Windows Logo+R) to open the Run dialog box, type **control sysdm.cpl,,6**, and click OK. The System Properties dialog box appears with the Remote tab displayed.

2. In the Remote Desktop group, activate the Allow Users to Connect Remotely to This Computer check box.

3. If you didn't add more users earlier, skip to step 6. Otherwise, click Select Remote Users to display the Remote Desktop Users dialog box.

4. Click Add to display the Select Users dialog box, type the username, and click OK. (Repeat this step to add other users.)

5. Click OK to return to the System Properties dialog box.

6. Click OK.

Installing Remote Desktop on an XP Client Computer

A computer that connects to a remote computer's desktop is said to be a Remote Desktop *client*. To act as a client, the computer must have the Remote Desktop Connection software installed. Remote Desktop Connection is installed by default in all versions of Windows Vista, but some versions of XP don't come with the program installed. However, you can install the Remote Desktop Connection software from the Windows XP CD (if you have one):

> **NOTE** You can also download the latest client software from Microsoft:
>
> `www.microsoft.com/windowsxp/downloads/tools/rdclientdl.mspx`
>
> You can also use this client if you're running Windows XP and don't have access to the XP installation disc.

1. Insert the Windows XP CD and wait for the Welcome to Microsoft Windows XP screen to appear.

2. Click Perform Additional Tasks.

3. Click Set Up Remote Desktop Connection.

Connect to a Remote Desktop

Medium

Remote Desktop Connection comes with a large number of advanced connection options and settings. If you don't want to bother with those advanced features right now, you can connect to the host in just a few steps. On the client computer, you make a basic connection to the host computer's desktop by following these steps:

1. Select Start, type `remote`, and click Remote Desktop Connection in the search results. (In XP, select Start, Run, type `mstsc`, and click OK.) The Remote Desktop Connection dialog box appears.

2. In the Computer text box, type the name or the IP address of the host computer.

3. Click Connect.

4. Log on to the remote desktop host:

   ■ **Windows Vista**—In the Windows Security dialog box, type the username and password of the host account you want to use for the logon, and then click OK. (Note that in subsequent logons, you need to type only the password.)

■ **Windows XP**—In the logon screen, click the icon of the user account with which you want to connect, type the account's password, and press Enter to complete the connection.

The basic remote connection may be all you need to use for your remote sessions. However, Remote Desktop Connection comes with many settings that enable you to configure options such as the size of the remote desktop screen, whether your Windows keyboard shortcuts (such as Alt+Tab) apply to the remote computer or your computer, and much more.

In the Remote Desktop Connection dialog box, click Options to expand the dialog box to the version shown in Figure 30.3.

FIGURE 30.3

Click the Options button to expand the dialog box so that you can customize Remote Desktop.

The General tab offers the following options:

■ **Computer**—The name or IP address of the remote computer.

■ **User Name** (Windows XP only)—The username you want to use to log in to the host computer.

■ **Password** (Windows XP Service Pack 2 or earlier only)—The password to use to log on to the host computer.

■ **Domain** (Windows XP Service Pack 2 or earlier only)—Leave this text box blank.

- **Allow Me to Save Credentials** (Windows XP Service Pack 3 only)—Activate this check box to see a logon dialog box when you connect to the remote host. This dialog box includes a Remember My Password check box which, when activated, tells XP to remember your logon data.

- **Save My Password** (Windows XP Service Pack 2 or earlier only)—Activate this check box to have Windows XP Service Pack 2 or earlier save your logon password.

- **Always Ask for Credentials**—Activate this check box to force Windows Vista to always ask you for a username and password when you log on to the host. Note that you see this check box in XP only when you activate the Allow Me to Save Credentials check box and then save the host's logon credentials.

- **Save** (Windows Vista or Windows XP Service Pack 3 only)—Click this button to have Windows remember your current settings so that you don't have to type them again the next time you connect. This is useful if you connect to only one remote host.

- **Save As**—Click this button to save your connection settings to a Remote Desktop (.rdp) file for later use. This is convenient if you regularly connect to multiple hosts.

- **Open**—Click this button to open a saved .rdp file.

The Display tab offers three options for controlling the look of the Remote Desktop window:

- **Remote Desktop Size**—Drag this slider to set the resolution of Remote Desktop. Drag the slider all the way to the left for a 640×480 screen size; drag the slider all the way to the right to have Remote Desktop take up the entire client screen, no matter what resolution the host is currently using.

- **Colors**—Use this list to set the number of colors used for the Remote Desktop display. Note that if the number of colors on either the host or the client is fewer than the value you select in the Colors list, Windows uses the lesser value.

- **Display the Connection Bar When in Full Screen Mode**—When this check box is activated, the Remote Desktop Connection client displays a connection bar at the top of the Remote Desktop window, provided you selected Full Screen for the Remote Desktop Size setting. You use the connection bar to minimize, restore, and close the Remote Desktop window. If you find that the connection bar just gets in the way, deactivate this check box to prevent it from appearing.

The Local Resources tab offers four options for controlling certain interactions between the client and host:

- **Remote Computer Sound**—Use this list to determine where Windows plays the sounds generated by the host. You can play them on the client (if you want to hear what's happening on the host), on the host (if you want a user sitting at the host to hear the sounds), or not at all (if you have a slow connection).

- **Keyboard**—Use this list to determine which computer is sent special Windows key combinations—such as Alt+Tab and Ctrl+Esc—that you press on the client keyboard. You can have the key combos sent to the client, to the host, or to the host only when you're running the Remote Desktop window in full-screen mode. What happens if you're sending key combos to one computer and you need to use a particular key combo on the other computer? For such situations, Remote Desktop offers several keyboard equivalents, outlined in the following table:

Windows Key Combo	Remote Desktop Equivalent
Alt+Tab	Alt+Page Up
Alt+Shift+Tab	Alt+Page Down
Alt+Esc	Alt+Insert
Ctrl+Esc or Windows Logo	Alt+Home
Print Screen	Ctrl+Alt+- (numeric keypad)
Alt+Print Screen	Ctrl+Alt++ (numeric keypad)

- **Local Devices and Resources**—Leave the Printers check box activated to display the client's printers in the host's Printers and Faxes window. The client's printers appear with the syntax *Printer* (from *COMPUTER*),

> **TIP** Here are three other useful keyboard shortcuts that you can press on the client computer and have Windows send to the host:
>
> Ctrl+Alt+ End — Displays the Windows Security dialog box. This is equivalent to pressing Ctrl+Alt+ Delete, which Windows always applies to the client computer.
>
> Alt+Delete — Displays the active window's Control menu.
>
> Ctrl+Alt+ Break — Toggles the Remote Desktop window between full-screen mode and a regular window.

where *Printer* is the printer name and *COMPUTER* is the network name of the client computer. Leave the Clipboard check box activated to use the client's Clipboard during the remote session. In XP, you can also connect disk drives and serial ports, which I describe in the next step.

■ **More** (Windows Vista or Windows XP Service Pack 3 only)—Click this button to see the Local Devices and Resources dialog box. Use the check boxes to configure more client devices and resources on the host. For example, if you activate the Drives check box, the client's drives appear in the Computer (or My Computer) window's Other group with the syntax *D* on *Computer*, where *D* is the drive letter and *Computer* is the network name of the client computer. Click OK when you have finished.

Use the Programs tab to specify a program to run on connection. Activate the Start the Following Program on Connection check box, and then use the Program Path and File Name text box to specify the program to run. After connecting, the user can work with only this program, and when the user quits the program, the session also ends.

Use the Experience tab to set performance options for the connection. Use the Choose Your Connection Speed to Optimize Performance drop-down list to set the appropriate connection speed. Because you're connecting over a network, you should choose the LAN (10Mbps or higher) option.

Finally, you can safely ignore the options in the Advanced tab.

Connect to Your Desktop via the Internet

Medium

Connecting to a Remote Desktop host over your network is easy to set up and fast, but your local area network might not always be so local. If you're traveling, what do you do if you want to connect to your desktop or to the desktop of some computer on your network? This is possible, but it requires some care to ensure that you don't open up your computer or your network to Internet-based hackers.

➔ To learn more about what constitutes a strong password, **see** "Bulletproof Your Password," **p. 146**.

CAUTION Besides the security precautions I present in this section, you should also set up your accounts with robust passwords, as described in Chapter 13, "Crucial Password Hacks." Using Remote Desktop over the Internet means that you open up a small window on your network that is at least visible to others on the Net. To ensure that other Internet users cannot exploit this hole, a strong password is a must.

To configure your system to allow Remote Desktop connections via the Internet, you need to perform these general steps (I explain each step in more detail in the sections that follow):

1. Configure Remote Desktop to use a listening port other than the default.

2. Configure Windows Firewall to allow TCP connections through the port you specified in step 1.

3. Determine the IP address of the Remote Desktop host or your network's router.

4. Configure your network router (if you have one) to forward data sent to the port specified in step 1 to the Remote Desktop host computer.

5. Use the IP address from step 3 and the port number from step 1 to connect to the Remote Desktop host via the Internet.

Changing the Listening Port

Your first task is to modify the Remote Desktop software on the host computer to use a listening port other than 3389, which is the default port. This is a good idea because there are hackers on the Internet who use port scanners to examine Internet connections (particularly broadband connections) for open ports. If the hackers see that port 3389 is open, they could assume that it's for a Remote Desktop connection, so they try to make a Remote Desktop connection to the host. They still have to log on with an authorized username and password, but knowing the connection type means they've cleared a very large hurdle.

To change the Remote Desktop listening port on the host, follow these steps:

1. In Windows Vista, select Start, type **regedit**, press Enter, and then enter your User Account Control credentials. (In Windows XP, press Windows Logo+R or select Start, Run), type **regedit**, and then click OK.) Windows opens the Registry Editor.

CAUTION I would be remiss if I didn't remind you that the Vista Registry contains settings that are vitally important for both Vista and your installed programs. Therefore, when you're working with the Registry Editor, don't make changes to any keys or settings other than the ones I describe in this section. And it's always a good idea to make a backup of your Registry before you do any mucking around with it. See Chapter 34, "Tweaking Windows with the Registry Editor," for directions on backing up your Registry.

2. Open the following key:

   `HKLM\SYSTEM\CurrentControlSet\Control\TerminalServer\WinStations\`
   `RDP-Tcp`

3. Double-click the `PortNumber` setting to open the Edit DWORD (32-bit) Value dialog box.

4. Select the Decimal option.

5. Replace the existing value (`3389`) with some other number between 1024 and 65536.

6. Click OK.

7. Reboot the computer to put the new port setting into effect.

Configuring Windows Firewall

Now you have to configure Windows Firewall to allow data to pass through the port you specified in the previous section. Here are the steps to follow on the host:

1. In Vista, select Start, type **firewall** into the Search box, and then click Windows Firewall in the search results. (In XP, select Start, Run, type **firewall.cpl**, and then click OK.) The Windows Firewall window appears.

2. In Vista, click the Allow a Program Through Windows Firewall link and then enter your User Account Control (UAC) credentials to continue. (In XP, display the Exceptions tab.)

3. Click Add Port to display the Add a Port dialog box.

4. Use the Name text box to type a name for the unblocked port (such as *Remote Desktop Alternate*).

5. In the Port Number text box, type the port number you specified in the previous section.

6. Make sure that the TCP option is activated.

7. Click OK to return to the Windows Firewall Settings dialog box.

8. Click OK to put the firewall exception into effect.

Determining the Host IP Address

To connect to a remote desktop via the Internet, you need to specify an IP address rather than a computer name. Specifically, you need to use your router's Internet IP address, which is the IP address assigned to the router by your ISP. To see the router's external IP address, open the router's setup pages and look for the status page. (See your router's manual to learn how to do this.) When you set up your Remote Desktop connection, you connect to the router, which will then forward your connection (thanks to your efforts in the next section) to the Remote Desktop host.

> **TIP** Another way to determine your router's external IP address is to navigate to any of the free services for determining your current IP. Here are two:
> WhatIsMyIP
> (www.whatismyip.com)
> DynDNS
> (http://checkip.dyndns.org)

Setting Up Port Forwarding

Finally, you need to configure your network's router to forward data sent to the port specified in step 1 to the IP address of the Remote Desktop host computer. This is *port forwarding*, and the steps you follow depend on the device. See your manual. Figure 30.4 shows a D-Link router configured to forward port 12345 to the computer with the address 192.168.1.110.

➜   It helps to give the Remote Desktop host a static IP address; **see** "Give a Computer a Static IP Address," **p. 324**.

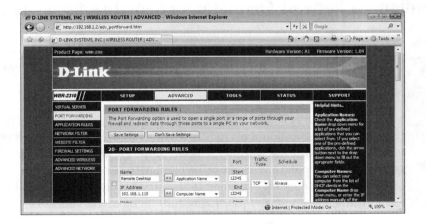

FIGURE 30.4
On your router, configure port forwarding to forward remote desktop data to the host PC.

Connecting Using the IP Address and New Port

You're now ready to make the connection to the Remote Desktop host via the Internet. Here are the steps to follow:

1. Connect to the Internet.

2. Select Start, type `remote`, and click Remote Desktop Connection in the search results. (In XP, select Start, Run, type `mstsc`, and click OK.) The Remote Desktop Connection dialog box appears.

3. In the Computer text box, type the external IP address of the router and the alternative port you specified in step 1, separated by a colon. For example, if the router's IP address is 123.45.67.89 and the alternate part is 12345, then you type the following address:

   `123.45.67.89:12345`

4. Set up your other Remote Desktop options as needed. For example, click Options, display the Experience tab, and then select the appropriate connection speed, such as Modem (28.8Kbps), Modem (56Kbps), or Broadband (128Kbps–1.5Mbps).

5. Click Connect.

Configure a Network Computer for Remote Administration

You can use Windows' remote administration tools to work with remote computers from the comfort of your own PC. For example, you saw in Chapter 24, "Dealing with Disk Drives," that you can use a script to find out how much free space exists on a remote PC's disk drive.

Medium

➤ **See** "Determine a Remote Computer's Disk Drive Free Space," **p. 276**.

Remote administration tools mostly use the Remote Procedure Call (RPC) protocol to communicate with the remote computer. RPC enables a local computer to run a program on a remote computer. For this to happen successfully, you must configure an exception in the remote computer's firewall that allows RPC traffic.

Here are the steps to follow:

1. In Windows Vista, select Start, type `firewallsettings`, press Enter, and then enter your User Account Control credentials. (In Windows XP, select Start, Run to open the Run dialog box, type `firewall.cpl`, and then click OK.)

2. Display the Exceptions tab.

3. Activate the Remote Administration check box, as shown in Figure 30.5.

FIGURE 30.5

Activate the Remote Administration exception to allow your computer to control the remote computer using the RPC protocol.

4. Click OK to put the exception into effect.

Connect to a Remote Computer with a Script

Most of the scripts you'll run will tweak settings or display data from your own computer. However, it's also possible to have a script reach out and interact with a remote computer on your network. This isn't a problem with XP machines, but Vista PCs are more problematic thanks to User Account Control and other Vista security settings. To configure a Vista computer to allow remote scripts to access the system, you need to do four things (each of which I discuss in more detail in the rest of this section):

> **TIP** You can also activate the Remote Administration exception in a command prompt session. (In Windows Vista, this must be an elevated session: Select Start, All Programs, Accessories, right-click Command Prompt, click Run as Administrator, and then enter your UAC credentials.) At the prompt, enter the following command:
>
> ```
> netsh firewall set service
> type=remoteadmin
> mode=enable
> ```

- Configure Windows Firewall exceptions to allow remote scripts.
- Make sure that whatever user account you use to run the scripts on your local computer is also a user account on the remote computer.
- Add your username to the remote computer's WMI namespace.
- Configure security in Component Services to allow your username to make remote connections.

Here are the steps to follow to set the up Windows Firewall exceptions on the remote Vista computer:

1. Click Start, type `firewall` in the Search box, and then click Windows Firewall in the search results. The Windows Firewall window appears.
2. Click Allow a Program Through Windows Firewall, and then enter your UAC credentials when prompted. The Windows Firewall Settings dialog box appears with the Exceptions tab displayed.
3. Click to activate the check box beside each of the following exceptions:
   - Remote Administration
   - Windows Management Instrumentation (WMI)
4. Click OK.

If your local user account doesn't have a corresponding account (same username and password) on the remote Vista computer, go ahead and add the account on the remote machine. After that's done, you need to configure WMI to accept remote connections for that account.

First you need to configure the WMI namespace. Follow these steps on the remote Vista computer:

1. Click Start, right-click Computer, click Manage, and then enter your UAC credentials. The Computer Management window appears.
2. Open the Services and Applications branch.
3. Right-click WMI Control and then click Properties. The WMI Control Properties dialog box appears.
4. Click the Security tab.
5. Open the Root branch and click CIMV2. (This is the default WMI namespace.)
6. Click Security.
7. Click Add, type your account username, and click OK.

8. In the Security tab, click your user account and click to activate the Remote Enable check box in the Allow column, as shown in Figure 30.6.

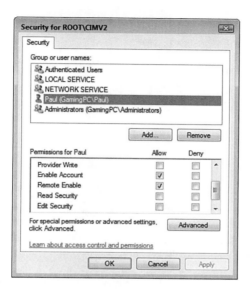

FIGURE 30.6

Allow the Remote Enable permission for your user account.

9. Click OK in the open dialog boxes.

Okay, almost there. Now you need to configure Com security on the remote Vista PC:

1. Select Start, type **dcomcnfg**, press Enter, and then enter your UAC credentials. The Component Services window appears.

2. Open the Component Services, Computers branch, right-click My Computer, and then click Properties.

3. Click the COM Security tab.

4. In the Access Permissions group, click Edit Limits.

5. Click Add, type your account username, and click OK.

6. In the Security Limits tab, click your user account and click to activate the Remote Access check box in the Allow column, as shown in Figure 30.7.

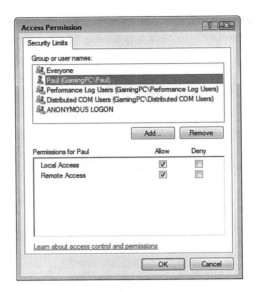

FIGURE 30.7
Allow the Remote Access permission for your user account.

7. In the Launch and Activation Permissions group, click Edit Limits.

8. Click Add, type your account username, and click OK.

9. In the Security Limits tab, click your user account and click to activate the Remote Launch and Remote Activation check boxes in the Allow column, as shown in Figure 30.8.

10. Click OK in the open dialog boxes.

The next two sections show you a couple of scripts that take advantage of this new configuration.

Determine a Remote Computer's Windows Version

You've seen throughout this book that it often matters a great deal what version of Windows a PC is running. For example, you know that if a PC is running Vista Home Basic or Home Premium, or XP Home, you don't have access to the Group Policy Editor. Listing 30.1 shows a script that uses Windows Management Instrumentation (WMI) to get the Windows version from a network PC that has been configured for remote administration.

> **NOTE** See Chapter 37, "Running Scripts," to learn how to run this script. The file containing the script in Listing 30.1—GetWindowsVersion. vbs—is available from my website at http://mcfedries.com/cs/ content/TweakItFreakIt.aspx.

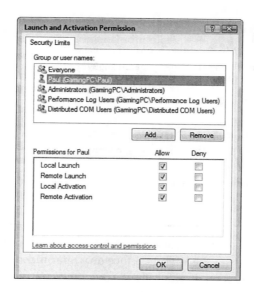

FIGURE 30.8

Allow the Remote Launch and Remote Activation permissions for your user account.

Listing 30.1   A Script That Returns the Windows Version of a Remote PC

```
Option Explicit
Dim compName, objWMI, colOperatingSystems, objOS
'
' This script uses WMI to connect to a remote computer
' and get the Windows version
'
' Be sure to change "REMOTEPC" to the name of the remote computer
' that you want to work with.
'
compName = "REMOTEPC"
'
' Get the WMI interface
'
Set objWMI = GetObject("winmgmts:{(Security)}!\\" & _
                     compName & "\root\cimv2")
'
' Return the computer's installed operating systems
'
```

Continues

Listing 30.1   Continued

```
Set colOperatingSystems = objWMI.ExecQuery _
    ("Select * from Win32_OperatingSystem")
'
' Display the OS name and version
'
For Each objOS In colOperatingSystems
    WScript.Echo "Windows Version on " & compName & ":" & _
        vbCrLf & vbCrLf & _
        objOS.Caption & vbCrLf & _
        "Version " & objOS.Version
Next
```

This script sets the compName variable to the name of the remote computer. It then connects to the WMI interface and returns the operating systems on that PC. The loop then displays the operating system name and version number. Figure 30.9 shows an example.

FIGURE 30.9
Sample output from the script in Listing 30.1.

Determine a Remote Computer's Service Pack Version

As the de facto administrator of your network, it's your responsibility to keep your PCs patched with the latest updates and, in particular, the most recent service pack. Rather than logging on to each PC to determine what service pack is installed, you can do it remotely. Listing 30.2 shows a script that uses WMI to get the service pack version number from a network PC that has been configured for remote administration.

NOTE See Chapter 37, "Running Scripts," to learn how to run this script. The file containing the script in Listing 30.2—GetServicePackVersion. vbs—is available from my website at http://mcfedries.com/cs/content/TweakItFreakIt.aspx.

**Listing 30.2   A Script That Returns the Windows Service Pack Version of a
Remote PC**

```
Option Explicit
Dim compName, objWMI, colOperatingSystems, objOS
'
' This script uses WMI to connect to a remote computer
' and get the service pack version number
'
' Be sure to change "REMOTEPC" to the name of the remote computer
' that you want to work with.
'
'compName = "REMOTEPC"
compName = "GAMINGPC"
'
' Get the WMI interface
'
Set objWMI = GetObject("winmgmts:{(Security)}!\\" & _
                    compName & "\root\cimv2")
'
' Return the computer's installed operating systems
'
Set colOperatingSystems = objWMI.ExecQuery _
    ("Select * from Win32_OperatingSystem")
'
' Display the OS name and service pack version number
'
For Each objOS In colOperatingSystems
    WScript.Echo "Windows Service Pack Version on " & compName & ":" & _
        vbCrLf & vbCrLf & _
        objOS.Caption & vbCrLf & _
        "Service Pack " & _
        objOS.ServicePackMajorVersion & _
        "." & objOS.ServicePackMinorVersion
Next
```

This script sets the compName variable to the name of the remote computer. It
then connects to the WMI interface and returns the operating systems on that
PC. The loop then displays the operating system name and the service pack
version numbers. Figure 30.10 shows an example.

FIGURE 30.10

Sample output from the script in Listing 30.2.

Tweaking Wireless Connections

These days it's becoming increasingly rare to find a small network that doesn't have a wireless component set up. Wired connections—particularly Gigabit Ethernet connections, which run at a theoretical speed of 1000Mbps— are the networking speed champs, but they're not always convenient. If you want to access your network or your router's Internet connection from another room, another floor, or even the back patio, the only practical solution is to cut the cables and go wireless.

This chapter assumes you have a wireless network up and running and that you'd like to make it more secure and more convenient, and the tweak here should help you do just that.

Ramp Up Wireless Network Security

Medium

Wireless networks are less secure than wired ones because the wireless connection that enables you to access the network from afar can also enable an intruder from outside your home or office to access the network. In particular, *wardriving* is an activity where a person drives through various neighborhoods with a portable computer or another device set up to look for available wireless networks. If the person finds a nonsecured network, he uses it for free Internet access or to cause mischief with shared network resources.

Here are a few tips and techniques you can easily implement to enhance the security of your wireless network:

- **Specify a new administrative password**—By far the most important configuration chore for any new router is to change the default logon password (and username, if your router requires one). Note that I'm talking here about the administrative password, which is the password you use to log on to the router's setup pages. This password has nothing to do with the password you use to log on to your Internet service provider (ISP) or to your wireless network. Changing the default administrative password is particularly crucial if your router also includes a wireless Access Point (AP) because a nearby malicious hacker can see your router. This means that the intruder can easily access the setup pages just by navigating to one of the common router addresses—usually http://192.168.1.1 or http://192.168.0.1—and then entering the default password, which for most routers is well known or easy to guess.

- **Position the access point for maximum security**—Almost all wireless network security problems stem from a single cause: wireless signals that extend outside of your home or office. This is called *signal leakage*, and if you can minimize the leakage, you're well on your way to having a secure wireless network. First, try to position the wireless AP away from a window. Glass doesn't obstruct radio frequency (RF) signals, so they're a prime source for wireless leakage. If your wireless AP must reside in a particular room, try to position it as far away as possible from any windows in that room. Also, try to position the wireless AP close to the center of your

> **NOTE** If you're using the wireless AP as your network router, remember that you need the device relatively close to your broadband modem so that you can run ethernet cable from the modem's ethernet or LAN port to the router's Internet or WAN port.

house or building. This will ensure that the bulk of the signal stays in the building.

- **Encrypt wireless signals with WPA**—Some wardriving hackers are interested more in your data than in your Internet connection. They come equipped with *packet sniffers* that can pick up and read your network packets. Typically, these crackers are looking for sensitive data such as passwords and credit card numbers. Therefore, it's absolutely crucial that you enable encryption for wireless data so that an outside user who picks up your network packets can't decipher them. Older wireless networks use a security protocol called Wired Equivalent Privacy, or WEP, that protects wireless communications with (usually) a 26-character security key. That sounds impregnable, but unfortunately there were serious weaknesses in the WEP encryption scheme, and now software exists that can crack any WEP key in minutes, if not seconds. In newer wireless networks, WEP has been superseded by Wi-Fi Protected Access, or WPA, which is vastly more secure than WEP. WPA uses most of the IEEE 802.11i wireless security standard, and WPA2 implements the full standard. WPA2 Personal requires a simple pass phrase for access (so it's suitable for homes and small offices). Be sure to use the strongest encryption that your equipment supports.

CAUTION Positioning the AP to minimize signal leakage assumes that a wardriver is using a standard antenna to look for wireless signals. That may be true in some cases, but many wardrivers use super-powerful antennas that offer many times the range of a regular antenna. There is, unfortunately, nothing you can do to hide your signal from such hackers. However, it's still worthwhile to reposition your access point to minimize signal leakage because this will help thwart those hackers using regular antennas. Also, many wireless APs come with an option to extend the range of the wireless signal. Unless you really need the range extended to ensure that some distant device can connect to the AP, you should disable this option.

CAUTION Unfortunately, encryption is a "lowest common denominator" game. That is, if you want to use a strong encryption standard such as WPA2, *all* your wireless devices must support WPA2. If you have a device that supports only WEP, you either need to drop your encryption standard down to WEP, or you need to replace that device with one that supports the stronger standard. (You might also be able to upgrade the existing device; check with the manufacturer.) Note that some APs come with a setting that enables you to support both WPA and WPA2 devices.

■ **Disable network SSID broadcasting**—Windows sees your wireless network because the AP broadcasts the network's *service set identifier* (SSID). However, Windows remembers the wireless networks that you have successfully connected to, so after all your computers have accessed the wireless network at least once, you no longer need to broadcast the network's SSID. Therefore, you should use your AP setup program to disable broadcasting and prevent others from seeing your network. However, you should know that when previously authorized devices attempt to connect to a nonbroadcasting network, they include the network's SSID as part of the probe requests they send out to see whether the network is within range. The SSID is sent in unencrypted text, so it would be easy for a snoop with the right software (easily obtained from the Internet) to learn the SSID. If the SSID is not broadcasting to try to hide a network that is unsecure or uses an easily breakable encryption protocol, such as WEP, hiding the SSID in this way actually makes the network *less* secure. Of course, *you* aren't trying to hide an unsecure network, right? From the previous point, you should now have WPA or WPA2 encryption enabled. So in your case, disabling SSID broadcasting either keeps your security the same or improves it. (If a cracker detects your nonbroadcasting SSID, you're no worse off; if the snoop doesn't have the necessary software to detect your nonbroadcasting SSID, he won't see your network, so you're more secure.)

■ **Change the default SSID**—Even if you disable broadcasting of your network's SSID, users can still attempt to connect to your network by guessing the SSID. All wireless APs come with a predefined name, such as linksys, dlink, or default, and a would-be intruder will attempt these standard names first. Therefore, you can increase the security of your network by changing the SSID to a new name that is difficult to guess. Even if you're broadcasting your wireless network's SSID, it's still a good idea to change the default SSID. Because in most cases the default SSID includes the name of the manufacturer, the SSID gives a would-be intruder valuable information on the type of AP you're using. In some cases, the default

NOTE Another good reason to change the default SSID is to prevent confusion with other wireless networks in your area. If the Windows list of available wireless network includes two (or more) networks named, for example, linksys, how will you know which one is yours?

SSID offers not only the name of the manufacturer, but also information about the specific model (for example, `belkin54g`), which is of course even more useful to a cracker.

Connect to a Hidden Wireless Network

Medium

Each wireless network has a network name: the service set identifier, or SSID. The SSID identifies the network to wireless devices and computers with wireless network cards. By default, most wireless networks broadcast the network name so that you can see the network and connect to it. However, some wireless networks disable network name broadcasting as a security precaution. As I described in the previous tweak, the idea is that if unauthorized users can't see the network, they can't attempt to connect to it.

However, you can still connect to a hidden wireless network by entering the connection settings by hand. You need to know the network name, the network's security type and encryption type, and the network's security key or passphrase.

Connect to a Hidden Wireless Network in Windows Vista

Here are the steps to follow to connect to a nonbroadcasting wireless network in Windows Vista:

1. Select Start, Connect To. Vista displays the Select a Network to Connect To dialog box.

2. Click the Set Up a Connection or Network link. The Choose a Connection Option dialog box appears.

3. Select Manually Connect to a Wireless Network, and then click Next. Vista prompts you for the network connection data, as shown in Figure 31.1 (which shows a completed version of the dialog box).

4. Provide the following connection data:

   - **Network Name**—The SSID of the hidden wireless network.
   - **Security Type**—The security protocol used by the wireless network. Select No Authentication (Open) if the network is unsecured.
   - **Encryption Type**—The method of encryption used by the wireless network's security protocol.
   - **Security Key/Passphrase**—The key or password required for authorized access to the network.

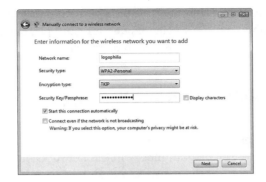

FIGURE 31.1
Use this dialog box to specify the connection settings for the hidden wireless network.

- **Start This Connection Automatically**—Leave this check box activated to have Vista connect to the network now (that is, when you click Next in step 5) and automatically the next time the network comes within range. If you always want to connect to the network manually, deactivate this option.

- **Connect Even If the Network Is Not Broadcasting**—If you activate this check box, Vista will send probe requests to see whether the network is in range even if the network isn't broadcasting its SSID. Note, however, that this lessens security (because the SSID is sent in plain text in the probe request, as described in the previous tweak), so you should leave this check box deactivated.

5. Click Next. Vista connects to the network and adds it to the list of wireless networks.

6. Click Close.

Connect to a Hidden Wireless Network in Windows XP

Follow these steps to connect to a nonbroadcasting wireless networking in Windows XP:

1. Select Start, All Programs, Accessories, Communications, Network Connections. XP opens the Network Connections folder.

2. Right-click the icon for your wireless adapter (it's usually called Wireless Network Connection), and then click Properties.

3. Display the Wireless Networks tab.

4. In the Preferred Networks section, click Add. XP prompts you for the network connection data, as shown in Figure 31.2 (which shows a completed version of the dialog box).

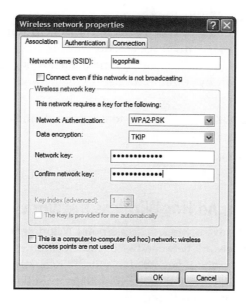

FIGURE 31.2

Specify the connection settings for the hidden wireless network.

5. Provide the following connection data:

- **Network Name (SSID)**—The SSID of the hidden wireless network.

- **Connect Even If the Network Is Not Broadcasting**—If you activate this check box, Vista will send probe requests to see whether the network is in range even if the network isn't broadcasting its SSID. Note, however, that this lessens security (because the SSID is sent in plain text in the probe request, as described in the previous tweak), so you should leave this check box deactivated.

- **Network Authentication**—The security protocol used by the wireless network. Select No Authentication (Open) if the network is unsecured.

- **Data Encryption**—The method of encryption used by the wireless network's security protocol.

- **Network Key**—The key or password required for authorized access to the network.

- **Confirm Network Key**—The key or password once again (not sure why!).

- **Connect When This Network Is In Range** (Connection tab)— Leave this check box activated to have XP connect to the network automatically each time the network comes within range. If you always want to connect to the network manually, deactivate this option.

6. Click OK. Vista connects to the network and adds it to the list of wireless networks.

7. Click OK.

Create Your Own Ad Hoc Wireless Network

Medium

If you don't have a wireless access point, Windows enables you to set up a temporary network between two or more computers. This is an *ad hoc connection*, and it's useful if you need to share folders, devices, or an Internet connection temporarily. Note that the computers must be within 30 feet of each other for this type of connection to work.

Create an Ad Hoc Wireless Network in Windows Vista

Here are the steps to follow to set up an ad hoc wireless network in Windows Vista:

1. Select Start, Connect To. Vista displays the Select a Network to Connect To dialog box.

2. Click the Set Up a Connection or Network link. The Choose a Connection Option dialog box appears.

3. Select Set Up a Wireless Ad Hoc (Computer-to-Computer) Network, and then click Next. Vista displays the Set Up a Wireless Ad Hoc Network dialog box.

4. Click Next.

5. Provide the following data to set up the network (see Figure 31.3):

- **Network Name**—The name of the ad hoc network.

- **Security Type**—The security protocol used by the ad hoc wireless network. Select Open or Shared.

- **Security Key/Passphrase**—Type the key or password required for authorized access to the ad hoc network.

- **Save This Network**—Activate this check box to save the network in the Manage Wireless Networks list.

FIGURE 31.3

Use this dialog box to configure your ad hoc network's name and security type.

6. Click Next. Vista sets up the ad hoc network.

7. If you want to share your computer's Internet connection, click Turn on Internet Connection Sharing.

8. Click Close. Windows Vista adds the ad hoc network to your list of networks in the Manage Wireless Networks window, as shown in Figure 31.4.

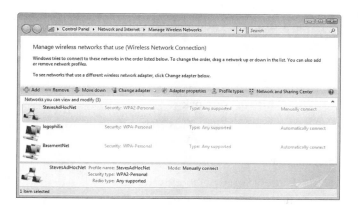

FIGURE 31.4

The new ad hoc network appears in the Manage Wireless Networks window.

Now, other people within 30 feet of your computer will see your ad hoc network in their list of available wireless networks. Note that the network remains available as long as at least one computer is connected to it, including the computer that created the network. The network is discarded when all computers (including the machine that created the network) have disconnected from it.

Create an Ad Hoc Wireless Network in Windows XP

Follow these steps to configure an ad hoc wireless network in Windows XP:

1. Select Start, All Programs, Accessories, Communications, Network Connections. XP opens the Network Connections folder.

2. Right-click the icon for your wireless adapter (it's usually called Wireless Network Connection), and then click Properties.

3. Display the Wireless Networks tab.

4. In the Preferred Networks section, select any existing network and click Remove.

5. Click Advanced to open the Advanced dialog box.

6. Select the Computer-to-Computer (Ad Hoc) Networks Only option, and then click Close.

7. Click Add. XP prompts you for the network connection data, as shown in Figure 31.5 (which shows a completed version of the dialog box).

8. Provide the following connection data:

   - **Network Name (SSID)**—The SSID of the ad hoc wireless network.
   - **Network Authentication**—Select Open.
   - **Data Encryption**—Your only choice here is WEP.
   - **The Key Is Provided For Me Automatically**—Deactivate this check box.
   - **Network Key**—Enter a 5- or 13-character password.
   - **Confirm Network Key**—Enter the key or password again.
   - **Connect When This Network Is In Range** (Connection tab)—Leave this check box activated.

9. Click OK.

10. Click OK. Windows XP adds the ad hoc network to your list of networks in the Choose a Wireless Network window, as shown in Figure 31.6.

> **TIP** If you have trouble connecting the host XP machine to the ad hoc network, first try connecting another computer to the network.

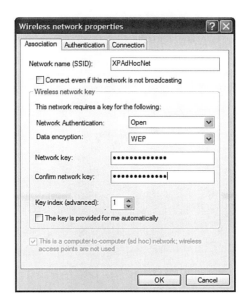

FIGURE 31.5

Specify the connection settings for the ad hoc wireless network.

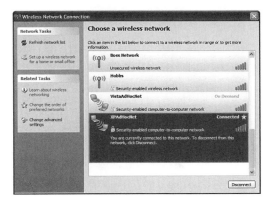

FIGURE 31.6

The new ad hoc network appears in the Choose a Wireless Network window.

Running Programs

One of the hats that Windows wears is labeled "Application Launcher." That is, unless you have Windows lurking
in the background, you can't do all that much with your
computer because you can't run any programs. (Notable
exceptions are the BIOS Setup program that you can launch
when your computer first boots and software that runs
directly from a CD or DVD at startup, such as the Ubuntu
Linux operating system.) Conversely, just because you have
Windows running, it doesn't mean your computer will do
anything interesting because Windows itself doesn't do anything interesting. To get your PC out of boat anchor mode,
you must run a program or three.

Now you might not think that there's much to say about
launching programs. After all, you click a Start menu icon or
perhaps type an executable file path into the Run dialog
box, and off the program goes. That's true, but even this
seemingly simple aspect of Windows is tweakable, as you
see in this chapter.

Use the Windows Key to Start Quick Launch Programs in Vista

Easy

The Quick Launch toolbar is the collection of icons that appears to the right of the Start button on the Vista taskbar. (If you don't see the Quick Launch toolbar, right-click an empty part of the taskbar and then select Toolbars, Quick Launch.) By default, Windows Vista adds icons for showing the desktop, activating Flip 3D, Internet Explorer, and Windows Media Player (this icon shows up after the first time you launch Media Player). Third-party programs will often toss an icon or two into Quick Launch, as well.

I'm a big fan of the Quick Launch toolbar because it offers the easiest way to launch a program: Just click the icon. However, even that easy-as-pie method is ever-so-slightly inconvenient when your hands are busy typing. It would be a tad more efficient if you could fire up Quick Launch icons from the comfort of your keyboard.

But wait, you can! In Windows Vista, you can use the Windows Logo key and the numbers across the top of your keyboard (*not* the ones on the numeric keypad) to press Quick Launch icons into service without having to reach all the way over to the mouse.

The trick here is that Vista numbers the Quick Launch icons starting at 1 for the leftmost icon, 2 for the icon to its right, and so on. The first nine icons are numbered from 1 to 9 (again, left to right), and if there's a tenth icon it's numbered as 0. To select a particular Quick Launch icon from the keyboard, hold down the Windows Logo key and press the corresponding icon number on the top row of the keyboard. For example, on most Vista systems, Internet Explorer is the third Quick Launch icon from the left, so you can start it by pressing Windows Logo+3.

What if you have multiple rows of icons, as shown in Figure 32.1? In this case, the icons are numbered from left to right along the top row (1 to 5) and then left to right along the bottom row (6 to 9 and then 0).

> **TIP** Here's a super-easy way to add an icon to the Quick Launch toolbar: Open the Start menu, right-click the icon you want to add, and then click Add to Quick Launch.

> **NOTE** If you can't see all your Quick Launch icons, right-click an empty section of the taskbar and then click the Lock the Taskbar command to deactivate it. Click and drag the sizing handle that appears to the right of the Quick Launch icons until you can see all the icons, and then release. Right-click an empty section of the taskbar and then click the Lock the Taskbar command to activate it. (I prefer to keep my taskbar locked because I rarely adjust it, and when it's unlocked it's too easy for an accidental click-and-drag to resize or move the taskbar.)

FIGURE 32.1

If you have multiple rows of Quick Launch icons, they're numbered from left to right and from top to bottom.

Make a Program Think It's Running Under an Earlier Version of Windows

Medium

Most new software programs are certified as Windows Vista–compatible, meaning that they can be installed and run without mishap on any Windows Vista system. But what about older programs that were coded before Windows Vista was released? They can be a bit more problematic. Because Windows Vista is based on the code for Windows NT, programs that are compatible with that operating system and Windows XP will probably (although not definitely) be compatible with Windows Vista. But the real problems lie with programs written for Windows 9x and Me. Windows Vista—even Windows Vista Home—uses a completely different code base than the old consumer versions of Windows, so it's inevitable that some of those legacy programs will either be unstable while running under Windows Vista or they won't run at all.

Why do such incompatibilities arise? One common reason is that the programmers of a legacy application hardwired certain data into the program's code. For example, installation programs often poll the operating system for its version number. If an application is designed for, say, Windows 98, the programmers might have set things up so that the application installs if and only if the operating system returns the Windows 98 version number. The program might run perfectly well under any later version of Windows, but this simplistic brain-dead version check prevents it from even installing on anything but Windows 98.

These types of problems might make it seem as though getting older programs to run under Windows Vista and Windows XP would be a nightmare. Fortunately, that's

> **NOTE** All this compatibility info applies just as well to Windows XP.

not usually true because the Windows programmers did something very smart: Because many of these application incompatibilities are predictable, they gave both Vista and XP the capability to make allowances for them and to enable many older programs to run under Vista or XP without modification. In Vista and XP, *application compatibility* refers to a set of concepts and technologies that enable the operating system to adjust its settings or behavior to compensate for the shortcomings of legacy programs. In this tweak, you learn how to work with the Windows application compatibility tools.

> **CAUTION** Although application compatibility can work wonders to give aging programs new life under Vista, it doesn't mean that *every* legacy program will benefit. Some programs simply will not run under Vista, no matter which compatibility rabbits you pull out of Vista's hat. In some of these cases you may be able to get a program to run by installing a patch from the manufacturer, so check the program's website to see if updates are available that make the program Vista friendly.

To help you run programs under Vista and XP, especially those programs that worked properly in an earlier version of Windows, Windows offers a new way to run applications using *compatibility layers*. This means that Windows Vista runs the program by doing one or both of the following:

- **Running the program in a *compatibility mode*—**This involves emulating the behavior of previous version of Windows:

  Windows Vista can emulate the behavior of Windows 95, Windows 98, Windows Me, Windows NT 4.0 with Service Pack 5, and Windows Millennium, as well as two more versions that are new to Windows Vista: Windows 2003 with Service Pack 1 and Windows XP with Service Pack 2.

  Windows XP can emulate the behavior of Windows 95, Windows 98, Windows Me, Windows NT 4.0 with Service Pack 5, and Windows Millennium.

- **Altering the display settings—**This involves temporarily changing the system's visual display so that it's compatible with the program:

  Windows Vista—There are five possibilities here: setting the color depth to 256 colors, changing the screen resolution to 640×480, disabling the Windows Vista visual themes, disabling desktop composition, and disabling displaying scaling on high-DPI settings.

  Windows XP—There are three choices in XP: setting the color depth to 256 colors, changing the screen resolution to 640×480, and disabling the Windows XP visual themes.

These are the broad compatibility layers that Windows Vista and XP support. To set up a compatibility layer, follow these steps:

1. Right-click the program's executable file or a shortcut to the file, and then click Properties. The program's property sheet appears.
2. Display the Compatibility tab.
3. Activate the Run This Program in Compatibility Mode For check box (see Figure 32.2).
4. Use the list to choose the Windows version the program requires.
5. Use the check boxes in the Display Settings group to adjust the video mode that Windows will switch to when you use the program.
6. Click OK.

FIGURE 32.2

In the property sheet for an executable file, use the Compatibility tab to set the compatibility layer for the program.

Set Up a Program to Launch Automatically at Startup

Medium

If you have one or more programs that you use each day, or that you use as soon as Windows starts, you can save yourself the hassle of launching these programs manually by getting Windows to do it for you automatically at startup. Similarly, you can also get Windows to automatically launch scripts or batch files at startup. You can set up a program or script for automatic startup launch using the Startup folder, the Registry, and the Group Policy snap-in.

> **TIP** You can also launch a program automatically at startup using the Task Scheduler. In Vista, select Start, type **schedule**, click Task Scheduler, and then enter your User Account Control credential; in XP, select Start, All Programs, Accessories, System Tools, Scheduled Tasks. Start a new task (click Create Basic Task in Vista; double-click Add Scheduled Task in XP), and when the wizard asks when you want the task to run, select either When the Computer Starts or When I Log On.

Using the Startup Folder

The Startup folder is a regular file folder, but it has a special place in Windows: You can get a program or script to run automatically at startup by adding a shortcut for that item to the Startup folder. Note that the Startup folder appears twice in the Windows interface:

- Via the Start menu (click Start, All Programs, Startup)
- Via Windows Explorer, as follows:

   Windows Vista—In Vista, the Startup folder appears in each user profile:

   d:\Users*user*\AppData\Roaming\ Microsoft\Windows\Start Menu\Programs\Startup

> **CAUTION** Although it's certainly handy to get Windows to load a program for you at startup, this is not a time to go overboard with the startup stuff. The more programs you ask Windows to load during the boot, the slower that boot will be, and the more resources Windows will consume right off the bat. A few small startup programs are fine, but avoid launching at startup either lots of small programs or one or two behemoth applications (such as Office apps).

Here, *d* is the system drive and *user* is the name of a user defined on the system. A shortcut placed in this folder will run automatically when this user logs on to the system.

Windows XP—In XP, the Startup folder appears in each user profile:

d:\Documents and Settings*user*\Start Menu\Programs\Startup

Here, *d* is the system drive and *user* is the name of a user defined on the system. A shortcut placed in this folder will run automatically when this user logs on to the system. XP also defines two other `Startup` folders within *d*:`\Documents and`

> **TIP** You can prevent the Startup items from running by holding down the Shift key while Windows loads (hold down the Shift key after logging on).

`Settings`. A shortcut placed in the `\All Users\Start Menu\Programs\Startup` folder will run automatically when any user logs on to the system, and a shortcut placed in the `\Default User\Start Menu\Programs\Startup` folder will be automatically copied to a user's Startup folder when you create a new user account. Note that only users with Administrator-level rights can access all three of these subfolders. Users with lesser privileges can work only with their own Startup folder. They can see the All Users version of the Startup folder, but Windows XP prevents them from adding files to it.

Using the Registry

The Startup folder method has two drawbacks: Users can easily delete shortcuts from their own Startup folders, and users can bypass Startup items by holding down the Shift key while Windows loads. To avoid both problems, you can use the Registry Editor to define your startup items. Assuming that you're logged in as the user you want to work with, the Registry offers two keys:

`HKCU\Software\Microsoft\Windows\CurrentVersion\Run`—The values in this key run automatically each time the user logs on.

`HKCU\Software\Microsoft\Windows\CurrentVersion\RunOnce`—The values in this key run only the next time the user logs on; they are then deleted from the key. (This key might not be present in your Registry. In that case, you need to add this key yourself.)

If you want an item to run at startup no matter who logs on, use the following keys:

`HKLM\Software\Microsoft\Windows\CurrentVersion\Run`—The values in this key run automatically each time any user logs on.

`HKLM\Software\Microsoft\Windows\CurrentVersion\RunOnce`—The values in this key run only the next time any user logs on; they are then deleted from the key. Don't confuse this key with the `RunOnceEx` key. `RunOnceEx` is an extended version of RunOnce that's used by developers to create more robust startup items that include features such as error handling and improved performance.

To create a startup item, add a string value to the appropriate key, give it whatever name you like, and then set its value to the full pathname of the executable file or script file that you want to launch at startup.

Using Group Policies

If you prefer not to edit the Registry directly, or if you want to place a GUI between you and the Registry, the Group Policy snap-in can help. (See Chapter 35, "Controlling Windows with the Group Policy Editor," for details on using this snap-in.) Note, however, that Group Policy doesn't work directly with the Run keys in the HKLM and HKCU hives. Instead, these are considered to be *legacy keys*, meaning that they're mostly used by older programs. The new keys (new as of Windows Millennium, that is) are the following:

```
HKLM\Software\Microsoft\Windows\
CurrentVersion\policies\Explorer\Run

HKCU\Software\Microsoft\Windows\
CurrentVersion\Policies\Explorer\Run
```

These keys do not appear in Windows by default. You see them only after you specify startup programs in the Group Policy Editor, as discussed later. Alternatively, you can add these keys yourself using the Registry Editor.

CAUTION Placing the same startup item in both the HKCU and the HKLM hives will result in that item being started twice: once during the initial boot and again at logon.

TIP If the program is in the %SystemRoot% folder, you can get away with entering only the name of the executable file. In addition, if the program you want to run at startup is capable of running in the background, you can load it in this mode by appending /background after the pathname.

NOTE The startup items run in the following order:

```
HKLM\Software\Microsoft\
Windows\CurrentVersion\
RunOnce
```

```
HKLM\Software\Microsoft\
Windows\CurrentVersion\
policies\Explorer\Run
```

```
HKLM\Software\Microsoft\
Windows\CurrentVersion\Run
```

```
HKCU\Software\Microsoft\
Windows\CurrentVersion\Run
```

```
HKCU\Software\Microsoft\
Windows\CurrentVersion\
Policies\Explorer\Run
```

```
HKCU\Software\Microsoft\
Windows\CurrentVersion\
RunOnce
```

Startup folder (all users)

Startup folder (current user)

As I mentioned, you can either add values to these keys via the Registry Editor or you can use the Group Policy snap-in. You have two choices:

- To work with startup programs for all users, select Computer Configuration, Administrative Templates, System, Logon. The items here will affect the Registry keys in the HKLM (all users) Registry hive.

- To work with startup programs for the current user, select User Configuration, Administrative Templates, System, Logon. The items here will affect the Registry keys in the HKCU (current user) hive.

Either way you'll see at least the following three items:

- **Run These Programs at User Logon**—Use this item to add or remove startup programs using the \Policies\Explorer\Run keys in the Registry. To add a program, double-click the item, select the Enabled option, and then click Show. In the Show Contents dialog box, click Add, enter the full pathname of the program or script you want to run at startup, and then click OK.

- **Do Not Process the Run Once List**—Use this item to toggle whether Windows Vista processes the RunOnce Registry keys (discussed in the previous section). Double-click this item and then activate the Enabled option to put this policy into effect; that is, programs listed in the RunOnce key are not launched at startup.

- **Do Not Process the Legacy Run List**—Use this item to toggle whether Windows Vista processes the legacy Run keys. Double-click this item and then activate the Enabled option to put this policy into effect; that is, programs listed in the legacy Run key are not launched at startup.

You also can use the Group Policy snap-in to specify script files to run at startup. You can specify script files at two places:

- **Computer Configuration, Windows Settings, Scripts (Startup/Shutdown)**—Use the Startup item to specify one or more script files to run each time the computer starts (and before the user logs on). Note that if you specify two or more scripts, Windows runs them synchronously. That is, Windows runs the first script, waits for it to finish, runs the second script, waits for it to finish, and so on.

- **User Configuration, Windows Settings, Scripts (Logon/Logoff)**—Use the Logon item to specify one or more script files to run each time any user logs on. Logon scripts are run asynchronously.

Finally, note that Windows has policies dictating how these scripts run. For example, you can see the startup script policies by selecting Computer Configuration, Administrative Templates, System, Scripts. Three items affect startup scripts:

- **Run Logon Scripts Synchronously**—If you enable this item, Windows Vista will run the logon scripts one at a time.

- **Run Startup Scripts Asynchronously**—If you enable this item, Windows Vista will run the startup scripts at the same time.

- **Run Startup Scripts Visible**—If you enable this item, Windows Vista will make the startup script commands visible to the user in a command window.

> **CAUTION** Logon scripts are supposed to execute before the Windows interface is displayed to the user. However, the improved logon of Windows Vista can interfere with that by displaying the interface before all the scripts are done. Windows Vista runs both the computer logon scripts and the user logon scripts asynchronously, which greatly speeds up the logon time because no script has to wait for another to finish.
>
> To prevent this, select Computer Configuration, Administrative Templates, System, Logon, and enable the Always Wait for the Network at Computer Startup and Logon setting.

For logon scripts, a similar set of policies appears in the User Configuration, Administrative Templates, System, Scripts section.

Prevent Programs from Starting Automatically

Medium

If you find that your Windows startups are a lot slower than they used to be, the most likely culprit is an overly long list of programs and services that Windows has to load during startup. Depending on the startup programs your system is running, you can shave anywhere from 5 to 25 seconds off your boot time by disabling any startup programs that you know you don't need.

I mentioned in the previous tweak that you can bypass *all* startup items by holding down Shift during the boot. That's an easy way to go, but you might not want to disable everything that runs at startup.

The most straightforward way to disable only some of the startup items is to essentially use the opposite techniques that I showed you in the previous tweak. That is, use the Startup folder, the Registry Editor, or the Group Policy Editor to remove the startup items you don't want to run at startup.

However, Windows also gives you two other methods:

- **System Configuration Utility**—In Windows Vista, select Start, type `msconfig`, press Enter, and then enter your UAC credentials. (In Windows XP, select Start, Run to open the Run dialog box, type `msconfig`, and then click OK.) In the System Configuration Utility window that appears, display the Startup tab (see Figure 32.3) and then deactivate the check box beside any program you're certain you don't need. Do the same in the Services tab. In each case, if you're not sure about disabling something leave it enabled.

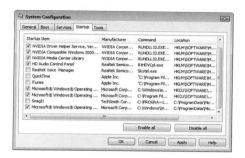

FIGURE 32.3

In the System Configuration Utility, display the Startup tab and deactivate the check box for each item you want to prevent from loading.

- **Windows Defender**—In Windows Vista, select Start, type `defender`, and then press Enter. (In Windows XP, select Start, All Programs, Windows Defender.) Click Tools, click Software Explorer, and then use the Category list to select Startup Programs. In Vista, click Show for All Users, and then enter your UAC credentials. Click the program you want to prevent from starting (see Figure 32.4), and then click Disable.

NOTE Windows Defender is installed by default in all Windows Vista systems. For XP, you need to download and install it from www.microsoft.com/defender/.

TIP See www.pacs-portal.co.uk/startup_index.htm for a list of which startup programs are required and which ones you can disable.

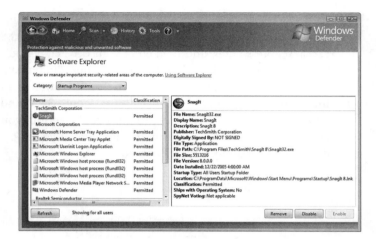

FIGURE 32.4

Using the Software Explorer in Windows Defender, you can disable those programs that you don't want to load at startup.

CHAPTER 33

More Program Tweaks

In this chapter I'll continue with the program-related tweaks and techniques. These tweaks are a bit more obscure, but you never know when this stuff will come in handy. You learn how to make an application run on a single processor or core; how to remove even hidden Windows components from your system; how to force Windows to shut down malfunctioning programs right away; how to write a list of all your installed applications to a text file; and how to get a broken service back on its feet.

Restrict a Program to a Single CPU

Medium

The processor *core* (short for *execution core*) refers to the actual processing unit that performs all the tasks a CPU is asked to handle. Until recently, the terms *core* and *processor* were equivalent because all CPUs contained just one core. In early 2005, however, Intel changed everything by introducing the Pentium D and the Pentium Extreme Edition, both of which somehow managed to shoehorn *two* cores into a single chip. Older CPUs were now described as *single core*, and these newfangled processors were described as *dual core*.

Does dual core mean twice the performance? Well, yes and no:

- Yes, because the processor can now divide tasks *between applications* among the cores (a process Intel calls HyperThreading). So if you're, say, compressing a large file, the processor can hand off that task to one core, and the other core is free to handle tasks from other programs.

- No, because the processor usually can't divide tasks *within an application* among the cores. For example, if you're compressing a large file, you won't be able to do anything else with that program until that task is complete. Note that it *is* possible to program individual applications to take advantage of two cores, and we're starting to see more of this as dual-core processors become mainstream.

However, there are times when you definitely do *not* want a program to utilize both cores. For example, if a program requires a lot of CPU resources, it might end up monopolizing both cores, which can slow the rest of your PC chores to a frustrating crawl. Similarly, many older programs don't play well with dual-core CPUs, and they may lock up (or *appear* to lock up by using 100 percent of the CPU resources).

To work around these sorts of problems, you can tell Windows to give the program access to just a single core. The program's performance might drop (but only slightly because it still has full access to a single core), but your overall PC performance should be noticeably faster.

Controlling which cores a program can access is called setting the *processor affinity*, and you do it by following these steps:

1. Launch the program you want to work with.

2. Press Ctrl+Alt+Delete to open the Windows Security screen and then click the Start Task Manager link.

3. Display the Processes tab.

4. Right-click your application's process to display its shortcut menu.

5. Click Set Affinity. (No Set Affinity command? Then your PC comes with only a single core. Too bad.) Task Manager displays the Processor Affinity dialog box.

6. Deactivate one of the check boxes, as shown in Figure 33.1.

> **TIP** To bypass the Windows Security screen, either press Ctrl+Shift+Esc or right-click an empty section of the taskbar and click Task Manager.

> **NOTE** If your PC is running a quad-core CPU, you see four check boxes (CPU 0 through CPU 3). In this case, you need to deactivate at least one check box.

FIGURE 33.1

Deactivate a CPU check box to restrict a program to a single core.

    7. Click OK.

Remove Hidden Windows Components

Medium

If you're trying to clean house on your Windows XP PC, you might decide to uninstall some accessories that you never use. So you select Start, Control Panel, Add or Remove Programs, and click Add/Remove Windows Components to run the Windows Components Wizard. To get to the accessories, you double-click Accessories and Utilities, then double-click Accessories. Figure 33.2 shows the Accessories dialog box that appears.

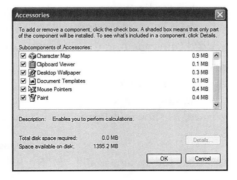

FIGURE 33.2

The Accessories dialog box lets you choose which XP accessories you want to remove.

This dialog box enables you to delete Calculator (not shown), Character Map, Clipboard Viewer, Desktop Wallpaper, Document Templates, Mouse Pointers, and Paint. However, where's WordPad? And how do you blow away useless accessories such as HyperTerminal and Phone Dialer?

These and a few other XP accessories are configured as hidden, so you don't see them in the Windows Components Wizard. However, it's possible to tweak XP to show these hidden accessories so you can uninstall them. Here's how:

1. Run Windows Explorer and navigate to `%SystemRoot%\inf` (where `%SystemRoot%` is usually `C:\Windows`).

2. Right-click the `sysoc.inf` file, click Open With, click Notepad, and then click OK.

3. Locate the accessory you want to uninstall. If it's hidden, it appears with the `HIDE` parameter, as in this example for WordPad:

   `MSWordPad=ocgen.dll,OcEntry,wordpad.ing,HIDE,7`

4. Delete just the `HIDE` text (leave the existing commas in place).

5. Repeat steps 3 and 4 for any other hidden accessories you want to uninstall:

   - **CommApps**—Remove `HIDE` for this item to add the Communications component to the Windows Components Wizard. This enables you to uninstall Chat, HyperTerminal, and Phone Dialer.

   - **MultiM**—Remove `HIDE` for this item to add the Multimedia component to the Windows Components Wizard. This enables you to uninstall Media Player, Sound Recorder, and Volume Control.

   - **AccessOpt**—Remove `HIDE` for this item to add the Accessibility Wizard component to the Windows Components Wizard.

   - **MSWordPad**—Remove `HIDE` for this item to add WordPad to the Windows Components Wizard, as shown in Figure 33.3.

6. Save and close the `sysoc.inf` file.

7. Run the Windows Components Wizard to uninstall the components.

> **NOTE** You'll see quite a few items in `sysoc.inf` that have the `HIDE` (or `hide`) parameter, but that doesn't mean all those components will appear in the Windows Components Wizard if you unhide them. Those components that are essential to the operation of Windows XP will never appear.

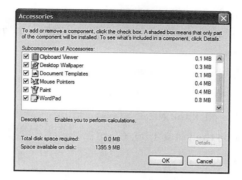

FIGURE 33.3

The Accessories dialog box with WordPad no longer hidden.

Shut Down Hung Programs Automatically

Medium

When you log off, restart, or shut down, Windows sends a message to each running program to shut itself down. Windows then waits politely for the program to close. If it doesn't, you see the End Task dialog box, which displays a message similar to the following:

```
This Windows application cannot respond to the End Task
request. It may be busy, waiting for a response from you, or it
may have stopped executing.
```

In some cases, you get three buttons:

- **Wait**—Click this button to have Windows give the program another five seconds to shut down.

- **End Task**—Click this button to shut down the program right away.

- **Cancel**—Click this button to bail out of the restart. This is the way to go if you know that the program is waiting for input from you (for example, to save changes to a file).

The problem is, Windows often waits quite a long time before displaying this message, which is annoying when a process hangs. It would be better if Windows XP simply killed hung programs automatically without wasting all that time.

Here's how to tweak XP to do this:

1. Select Start, Run, type **regedit**, and click OK. The Registry Editor appears.

2. Navigate to the following key:

   HKCU\Control Panel\Desktop

3. Double-click the AutoEndTasks setting.

4. Change the value from 0 to 1.

5. Click OK.

6. Double-click the HungAppTimeout setting.

7. Reduce the value from 20000 to 5000.

8. Click OK.

Write a Complete List of Installed Programs to a Text File

Medium

When you migrate to a new PC, most often you want to re-create the same setup as your old PC, and that means (in part) installing some or all of the same programs. Now I don't know about you, but I routinely install dozens of programs on my main Windows PC, so there's just no way that I can remember all of them (even back when I had a full complement of brain cells). Fortunately, I can get Windows to do the remembering for me by using a script that writes the name and version number of all my installed programs to a text file. Listing 33.1 shows the script.

> **NOTE** The file containing the script in Listing 33.1—WriteInstalledPrograms.vbs—is available from my website at http://mcfedries.com/cs/content/TweakItFreakIt.aspx. See Chapter 37, "Running Scripts," to learn how to run the script on your PC.

Listing 33.1 A Script That Writes a Complete List of a PC's Installed Programs to a Text File

```
Option Explicit
Dim strComputer, objWMI, collPrograms, objProgram, intPrograms
Dim objFSO, strFolder, objFile
'
' Get the WMI object
'
strComputer = "."
```

```
Set objWMI = GetObject("winmgmts:{impersonationLevel=impersonate}!\\" & _
            strComputer & "\root\cimv2")
'
' Change the following value to the path of the folder
' where you want to store the text file
'
strFolder = "d:\backups\"
'
' Initialize the file system object
'
Set objFSO = CreateObject("Scripting.FileSystemObject")
'
' Create the text file
'
Set objFile = objFSO.CreateTextFile(strFolder & "programs.txt", True)
'
' Return the collection of programs installed on the computer
'
Set collPrograms = objWMI.ExecQuery _
    ("Select * from Win32_Product")
'
' Run through each item in the collection
'
intPrograms = 0
For Each objProgram in collPrograms
    '
    ' Write the program's name and version number to the text file
    '
    objFile.WriteLine("Name: " & objProgram.Name)
    objFile.WriteLine("Version: " & objProgram.Version)
    objFile.WriteLine("")
    intPrograms = intPrograms + 1
Next
'
' Close the text file
'
objFile.Close
WScript.Echo "Wrote " & intPrograms & " program(s) to the text file."
```

The script sets up the usual Windows Management Instrumentation (WMI) object and then uses VBScript's `FileSystemObject` to get a hook into the PC's file system. In this case, the script uses `FileSystemObject` to create a new text file in the folder specified by `strFolder`. The script uses WMI to return the collection of installed programs, and then a `For Each...Next` loop writes the name and version number of each installed program to the text file.

Reset a Broken Service

Medium

If Windows is acting erratically (or, I should say, if it's acting more erratically than usual), the problem could be a service that's somehow gotten corrupted. How can you tell? The most obvious clue is an error message that tells you a particular service isn't running or couldn't start. You can also check the Event Viewer for service errors. Finally, if a particular feature of Windows is acting funny and you know that a service is associated with that feature, then you might suspect that service is causing the trouble.

To fix the problem (hopefully!), you can reset the broken service, a procedure that involves the following four general steps:

1. Find out the name of the service that is (or that you suspect is) broken.
2. Delete the service.
3. Load a backup copy of the system hive into the Registry.
4. Copy the service from the backup hive copy to service's actual Registry location.

To begin, follow these steps to determine the name of the service:

1. In Vista, select Start, type **services**, press Enter, and then enter your User Account Control credentials. (In XP, select Start, Run to open the Run dialog box, type **services.msc**, and click OK.) Windows opens the Services window.
2. Double-click the service you want to reset.
3. In the General tab, locate the Service Name value (see Figure 33.4) and make a note of it.
4. Click OK.

FIGURE 33.4

Open the service you want to reset and make note of the Service Name value.

Next, follow these steps to delete the service:

1. In Vista, select Start, type **command**, right-click Command Prompt in the result, click Run as Administrator, and then enter your User Account Control credentials. (In XP, select Start, Run to open the Run dialog box, type **cmd**, and click OK.) Windows opens a Command Prompt session.

2. Type the following (where *service* is the service name that you noted in the previous set of steps):

   ```
   sc delete service
   ```

3. Press Enter. Windows attempts to delete the service.

If the deletion works properly, you see the following message:

```
[SC] DeleteService SUCCESS
```

Note that you'll need the Command Prompt again a bit later, so leave the session open for now.

Now follow these steps to load a fresh copy of the system hive:

1. In Vista, select Start, type **regedit**, press Enter, and then enter your

> **NOTE** If the deletion isn't successful, double-check the service name. If you're sure you have the name right, try deleting the service using the Registry Editor, instead. Open the Registry Editor, navigate to the `HKLM\System\CurrentControl Set\Services` key, and then locate the service. Right-click the service and then click Delete.

User Account Control credentials. (In XP, select Start, Run to open the Run dialog box, type **regedit**, and click OK.)

2. Select the HKEY_LOCAL_MACHINE key.

3. Select File, Load Hive to open the Load Hive dialog box.

4. Open the system backup file:

   - **Vista**—%SystemRoot%\system32\config\RegBack\SYSTEM.OLD
   - **XP**—%SystemRoot%\repair\system.bak

5. Click Open. The Registry Editor prompts you for a key name.

6. Type **reset** and click OK.

You now have the backup copy of the system hive loaded into HKLM\reset key. Now you complete the operation by copying the service from this backup:

1. Return to the command prompt.

2. Type the following (where *service* is the service name that you noted in the first set of steps):

   ```
   reg copy hklm\reset\controlset001\services\service
   ➥hklm\system\currentcontrolset\services\service /s /f
   ```

3. Press Enter. Windows copies the backup version of the service to the original Registry location.

4. Reboot your PC to put the change into effect.

CHAPTER 34

Tweaking Windows with the Registry Editor

Both Windows Vista and Windows XP offer lots of tools for tweaking and customizing. All these tools are hidden so that novice users can't get their mitts on them and do untold damage to their PCs. Fortunately for the likes of you and me, most of these tweaking tools are hidden in plain sight, meaning that you can get to them with just a mouse click or three. For example, most Windows objects (such as the desktop and Start menu) have an associated property sheet with various customization options, and you display the property sheet by right-clicking the object and then clicking Properties. Similarly, the various icons in the Control Panel (click Start, Control Panel) are a customizer's delight.

You learned about these relatively easy-to-find tools throughout this book, but you also saw lots of tweaks that used a more deeply hidden tool called the Registry Editor. As its name implies, you use this program to edit the Registry, which is a massive storehouse of Windows settings, stored values, and saved data. If you can tweak an object, Windows almost certainly stores that object's settings somewhere in the Registry.

Most of the time, you change an object's Registry values using its property sheet or tools such as Control Panel and the Group Policy Editor (which you learn about in Chapter 35, "Controlling Windows with the Group Policy Editor"). However, tons of Windows tweaks happen *only* by adjusting some Registry setting directly, so it's crucial that you know how to operate the Registry Editor. This chapter tells you everything you need to know to find settings, modify them, and, most importantly, to keep the Registry safe.

Firing Up the Registry Editor

All the direct work you do with the Registry will happen inside the reasonably friendly confines of a program called the Registry Editor, which enables you to view, modify, add, and delete Registry settings. It also has a search feature to help you find settings and export and import features that enable you to save settings to and from a text file.

To launch the Registry Editor, use one of the following techniques:

- **Windows Vista**—Click Start, type `regedit` into the Search box, and then click `regedit.exe` in the results. (You can also press Windows Logo+R or select Start, All Programs, Accessories, Run to open the Run dialog box, type `regedit`, and click OK.) Enter your User Account Control credentials to continue.

- **Windows XP**—Press Windows Logo+R or select Start, Run to open the Run dialog box, type `regedit`, and click OK.

Figure 34.1 shows the Registry Editor window that appears. (Note that your Registry Editor window might look different if someone else has used the program previously. Close all the open branches in the left pane to get the view shown in Figure 34.1.)

CAUTION The Registry Editor is arguably the most dangerous tool in the Windows Vista arsenal. The Registry is so crucial to the smooth functioning of Vista that a single imprudent change to a Registry entry can bring your system to its knees. Therefore, now that you have the Registry Editor open, don't start tweaking settings willy-nilly. Instead, read the section titled "Keeping the Registry Safe," later in this chapter, for some advice on protecting this precious and sensitive resource.

FIGURE 34.1

Run the regedit *command to launch the Registry Editor, the program that enables you to work with the Registry's data.*

Taking a Tour of the Registry

The Registry Editor is divided into two sections:

- **Keys pane**—This is the left side of the Registry Editor window, and it contains the hierarchy of keys that Windows uses to organize the data in the Registry.

- **Settings pane**—This is the right side of the Registry Editor window, and it shows the settings associated with the currently selected key.

Getting Around in the Keys Pane

The keys pane is organized in a treelike hierarchy. The five keys that are visible when you first open the Registry Editor are special keys called *handles* (which is why their names all begin with HKEY). These keys are collectively referred to as the Registry's *root keys*. The root keys are your Registry starting points, so you need to become familiar with what kinds of data each key holds. Here's a quick summary:

- **HKEY_CLASSES_ROOT**—This root key—usually abbreviated as HKCR—contains data related to file extensions and their associated programs, the objects that exist in the Windows Vista system, as well as applications and their Automation information. There are also keys related to shortcuts and other interface features.

- **HKEY_CURRENT_USER**—This root key—usually abbreviated as HKCU—contains data that applies to the currently logged on user. It contains user-specific settings for Control Panel options, network connections, applications, and more.

- **HKEY_LOCAL_MACHINE**—This root key—usually abbreviated as HKLM—contains non-user-specific configuration data for your system's hardware and applications.

- **HKEY_USERS**—This root key—usually abbreviated as HKU—contains settings that are similar to those in HKEY_CURRENT_USER. HKEY_USERS is used to store the settings for users with group policies defined, as well as the default settings (in the .DEFAULT subkey), which get mapped to a new user's profile.

- **HKEY_CURRENT_CONFIG**—This root key—usually abbreviated as HKCC—contains settings for the current hardware profile.

These keys all contain subkeys, which you can display by clicking the plus sign (+) to the left of each key, or by selecting a key and pressing the plus-sign key on your keyboard's numeric keypad. When you open a key, the plus sign changes to a minus sign (-). To close a key, click the minus sign or highlight the key and press the minus-sign key on the numeric keypad.

Understanding Registry Settings

The settings pane on the right side of the Registry Editor window displays the settings contained in each key. The settings pane is divided into three columns:

- **Name**—This column tells you the name of each setting in the currently selected key.

- **Type**—This column tells you the data type of the setting. There are six possible data types (in Vista; XP has only five):

  REG_SZ—This is a string value.

  REG_MULTI_SZ—This is a series of strings.

  REG_EXPAND_SZ—This is a string value that contains an environment variable name that gets "expanded" into the value of that variable. For example, the %SystemRoot% environment variable holds the folder in which Windows Vista was installed. So, if you see a Registry setting with the value %SystemRoot%\System32\, and Windows Vista is installed in C:\Windows, the setting's expanded value is C:\Windows\System32\.

REG_DWORD—This is a double word value: a 32-bit hexadecimal value arranged as eight digits. For example, 11 hex is 17 decimal, so this number would be represented in DWORD form as 0x00000011 (17). (Why "double word"? A 32-bit value represents four bytes of data, and because a *word* in programming circles is defined as two bytes, a four-byte value is a *double word*.)

REG_QWORD (Vista only)—This is a quadruple word value: a 64-bit hexadecimal value arranged as 16 digits. Note that leading zeros are suppressed for the high 8 digits. Therefore, 11 hex appears as 0x00000011 (17) and 100000000 hex appears as 0x1000000000 (4294967296).

REG_BINARY—This value is a series of hexadecimal digits.

- **Data**—This column displays the value of each setting.

Keeping the Registry Safe

Windows is utterly dependent on the Registry, so it's not even remotely a stretch to say that if something bad happens to the Registry, chances are that Windows itself will go belly up. That sounds ominous and more than a little intimidating, no doubt, but I have two pieces of good news that I trust will mitigate these feelings. First, it's actually fairly hard to really mess up the Registry. I've been tweaking the Registry regularly on dozens of different Windows boxes over the past decade and half or so, and not once have I ever had a machine crash because of an improper Registry edit. Second, even if you do cause Windows to go haywire with an injudicious Registry edit, all is not lost because you can usually use System Restore or a backup copy of all or part of the Registry to recover with no permanent harm done.

So how can you avoid problems when mucking around in the Registry's innards? Here are the three most important pieces of advice you'll ever learn about working with the Registry:

- If you're not completely sure what a Registry setting does, don't mess with it. Ever. Seriously.

- If you're following someone else's directions for making a Registry edit (such as the directions you see throughout this book), make only the change (or changes) outlined in the steps. Don't suddenly go random and start modifying nearby settings "just to see what happens." Also, double-check your edits to make sure you've done them exactly as described in the steps.

■ Never delete anything from the Registry. If you want Windows to stop using a particular setting, rename it (as described a bit later) instead of deleting it. This way, if the results aren't what you want, you can usually recover just by restoring the setting's original name.

Preventing Other Folks from Messing with the Registry

Do you share your computer with other people? How brave! In that case, there's a pretty good chance that you don't want them to have access to the Registry Editor. In Windows Vista, User Account Control automatically blocks Standard users unless they know an administrator's password. For other administrators, or if you're using Windows XP, you can prevent any user from using the Registry Editor by setting a group policy (again, see Chapter 35):

1. Press Windows Logo+R to open the Run dialog box, type `gpedit.msc`, and then click OK.

2. In Windows Vista, enter your UAC credentials to continue.

3. Open the User Configuration, Administrative Templates, System branch.

4. Double-click the Prevent Access to Registry Editing Tools policy.

5. Click Enabled.

6. In the Disable Regedit from Running Silently? list, click Yes.

7. Click OK.

Note that *you* won't be able to use the Registry Editor, either. However, you can overcome that by temporarily disabling this policy prior to running the Registry Editor. Even better, you can run the following script, which toggles the Registry Editor between enabled and disabled:

> **NOTE** The code for this script is available on my website at http://www.mcfedries.com/cs/content/TweakItFreakIt.

```
Set objWshShell =
➥WScript.CreateObject("WScript.Shell")
'
' Get the current setting
'
intDisableRegistryTools =
```

```
Int(objWshShell.RegRead("HKCU\Software\Microsoft\
➥Windows\CurrentVersion\Policies\System\DisableRegistryTools"))
'
' Toggle the current setting
'
If intDisableRegistryTools = 0 Then
    objWshShell.RegWrite "HKCU\Software\Microsoft\Windows\CurrentVersion\
➥Policies\System\DisableRegistryTools", 2, "REG_DWORD"
    WScript.Echo "The Registry Editor is disabled."
Else
    objWshShell.RegWrite "HKCU\Software\Microsoft\Windows\CurrentVersion\
➥Policies\System\DisableRegistryTools", 0, "REG_DWORD"
    WScript.Echo "The Registry Editor is enabled."
End If
```

Note that in Vista you need to run this script as the Administrator. I show you a tweak for doing this in Chapter 12, "Taking Advantage of the Administrator Account."

➤   **See** "Run a Script as the Administrator," **p. 141**.

Backing Up the Registry in Vista

Windows Vista maintains what is known as the *system state*: the crucial system files that Windows Vista requires to operate properly. Included in the system state are the files used during startup, the system files, and, naturally, the Registry files. Windows Vista's Backup utility has a feature called Complete PC Backup that enables you to easily back up the current system state, so it's probably the most straightforward way to create a backup copy of the Registry should anything go wrong. See the "Backing Up Your Files" section in Chapter 26, "Building Better Backups," for the details.

➤   **See** "Create a Backup of Your Entire Computer," **p. 302**.

Backing Up the Registry in XP

Windows XP also maintains a system state, which includes the startup files, system files, and the Registry files. The Backup utility has a feature that enables you to easily back up the current system state, so

> **NOTE** In Windows XP, you must be logged on as a member of the Administrators group or the Backup Operators groups to back up the system state.

it's probably the most straightforward way to create a backup copy of the Registry should anything go wrong.

Here are the steps to follow to back up the system state in Windows XP:

1. Select Start, All Programs, Accessories, System Tools, Backup. (Note that if you're using Windows XP Home, you might need to install Backup from the Windows XP CD.)

2. If the Backup or Restore Wizard appears, click the Advanced Mode link.

3. Display the Backup tab.

4. In the folder tree, open the Desktop branch and then the My Computer branch, if they're not open already.

5. Activate the System State check box.

6. Choose your other backup options, click Start Backup, and then follow the usual backup procedure.

> **CAUTION** Depending on the configuration of your computer, the system state can be quite large—hundreds of megabytes. Therefore, make sure that the destination you choose for the backup has enough free space to handle such a large file.

Saving the Current Registry State with System Restore

Another easy way to save the current Registry configuration is to use the System Restore utility. This program takes a snapshot of your system's current state, including the Registry. If anything should go wrong with your system, the program enables you to restore a previous configuration. It's a good idea to set a system restore point before doing any major work on the Registry. Later in this book I show you a script that enables you to create an on-the-fly restore point; see Chapter 24, "Dealing with Disk Drives."

→ See "Create an Instant Restore Point," **p. 280**.

> **TIP** Another way to protect the Registry is to ensure that its keys have the appropriate permissions. By default, Windows Vista gives members of the Administrators group full control over the Registry. A Standard user gets Full Control permission only over the HKCU key when that user is logged on and Read permissions over the rest of the Registry. To adjust the permissions, right-click the key in the Registry Editor, and then click Permissions. Make sure that only administrators have the Full Control check box activated.

Protecting Keys by Exporting Them to Disk

If you're just making a small change to the Registry, backing up all its files might seem like overkill. Another approach is to back up only the part of the Registry that you're working on. For example, if you're about to make changes within the HKEY_CURRENT_USER key, you could back up just that key, or even a subkey within HKCU. You do that by exporting the key's data to a registration file, which is a text file that uses the .reg extension. That way, if the change causes a problem, you can import the .reg file back into the Registry to restore things the way they were.

Exporting the Entire Registry to a .reg File

The easiest way to protect the entire Registry is to export the whole thing to a .reg file on a separate hard drive or network share. Note that the resulting file will be 90 to 100MB, and possibly larger, so make sure the target destination has enough free space. Here are the steps to follow:

1. Open the Registry Editor.
2. Select File, Export to display the Export Registry File dialog box.
3. Select a location for the file.
4. Use the File Name text box to type a name for the file.
5. Activate the All option.
6. If you'll be importing this file into a system running Windows 9x, Windows Me, or Windows NT, use the Save As Type list to choose the Win9x/NT 4 Registration Files (*.reg) item.
7. Click Save.

Exporting a Key to a Registration File

Here are the steps to follow to export a key to a registration file:

1. Open the Registry Editor and select the key you want to export.
2. Select File, Export to display the Export Registry File dialog box.
3. Select a location for the file.
4. Use the File Name text box to type a name for the file.
5. Activate the Selected Branch option.

6. If you'll be importing this file into a system running Windows 9x, Windows Me, or Windows NT, use the Save As Type list to choose the Win9x/NT 4 Registration Files (*.reg) item.

7. Click Save.

> **NOTE** You also can import a .reg file by locating it in Windows Explorer and then double-clicking the file.

Importing a Registration File

If you need to restore the key that you backed up to a registration file, follow these steps:

1. Open the Registry Editor.

2. Select File, Import to display the Import Registry File dialog box.

3. Find and select the file you want to import.

4. Click Open.

5. When Windows Vista tells you the information has been entered into the Registry, click OK.

> **CAUTION** Many applications ship with their own .reg files for updating the Registry. Unless you're sure that you want to import these files, avoid double-clicking them. They might end up overwriting existing settings and causing problems with your system.

Working with Registry Entries

Now that you've had a look around, you're ready to start working with the Registry's keys and settings. In this section, I'll give you the general procedures for basic tasks, such as modifying, adding, renaming, deleting, and searching for entries, and more. These techniques will serve you well throughout the rest of the book when I take you through some specific Registry modifications.

Changing the Value of a Registry Entry

Changing the value of a Registry entry is a matter of finding the appropriate key, displaying the setting you want to change, and editing the setting's value. Unfortunately, finding the key you need isn't always a simple matter. Knowing the root keys, as described earlier, will certainly help, and the Registry Editor has a Find feature that's invaluable (I'll show you how to use it later).

To illustrate how this process works, let's work through an example: changing your registered owner name and company name. In versions of Windows prior to Vista, the installation process probably asked you to enter your name and, optionally, your company name. These registered names appear in several places as you work with Windows:

> **TIP** If you have keys that you visit often, you can save them as favorites to avoid trudging through endless branches in the keys pane. To do this, navigate to the key and then select Favorites, Add to Favorites. In the Add to Favorites dialog box, edit the Favorite Name text box, if desired, and then click OK. To navigate to a favorite key, pull down the Favorites menu and select the key name from the list that appears at the bottom of the menu.

- If you select Help, About in most Windows programs, your registered names appear in the About dialog box.

- If you install a 32-bit application, the installation program uses your registered names for its own records (although you usually get a chance to make changes).

Unfortunately, if you install a clean version of Windows Vista, Setup doesn't ask you for this data, and it takes your username as your registered owner name. (If you upgraded to Windows Vista, the owner name and company name were brought over from your previous version of Windows.) With these names appearing in so many places, it's good to know that you can change either or both names (for example, to put in your proper names if Vista doesn't have them or if you give the computer to another person). The secret lies in the following key:

`HKLM\SOFTWARE\Microsoft\WindowsNT\CurrentVersion`

To get to this key, you open the following branches in the Registry Editor's tree pane: `HKEY_LOCAL_MACHINE`, then `SOFTWARE`, then `Microsoft`, and then `Windows NT`. Finally, click the `CurrentVersion` subkey to select it. Here you see a number of settings, but two are of interest to us (see Figure 34.2):

`RegisteredOrganization`	This setting contains your registered company name.
`RegisteredOwner`	This setting contains your registered name.

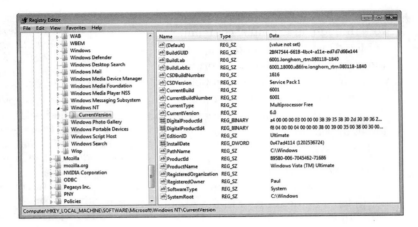

FIGURE 34.2

Navigate to `HKLM\SOFTWARE\Microsoft\Windows NT\CurrentVersion` *to see your registered names.*

To open the setting for editing, double-click it (or select the setting name and either select Edit, Modify or press Enter). The dialog box that appears depends on the value type you're dealing with, as discussed in the next few sections. Note that edited settings are written to the Registry right away, but the changes might not go into effect immediately. In many cases, you need to exit the Registry Editor and then either log off or restart Windows.

Editing a String Value

If the setting is a `REG_SZ` value (as it is in our example), a `REG_MULTI_SZ` value, or a `REG_EXPAND_SZ` value, you see the Edit String dialog box, shown in Figure 34.3. Use the Value Data text box to enter a new string or modify the existing string, and then click OK. (For a `REG_MULTI_SZ` multistring value, Value Data is a multiline text box. Type each string value on its own line. That is, after each string, press Enter to start a new line.)

FIGURE 34.3

You see the Edit String dialog box if you're modifying a string value.

Editing a DWORD or QWORD Value

If the setting is a REG_DWORD, you see the Edit DWORD (32-Bit) Value dialog box shown in Figure 34.4. In the Base group, select either Hexadecimal or Decimal, and then use the Value Data text box to enter the new value of the setting. (If you chose the Hexadecimal option, enter a hexadecimal value; if you chose Decimal, enter a decimal value.) Note that editing a QWORD value is identical, except that the dialog box is named Edit QWORD (64-Bit) Value, instead.

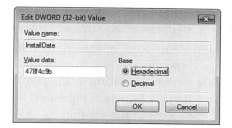

FIGURE 34.4

You see the Edit DWORD Value dialog box if you're modifying a double word value.

Editing a Binary Value

If the setting is a REG_BINARY value, you see an Edit Binary Value dialog box like the one shown in Figure 34.5.

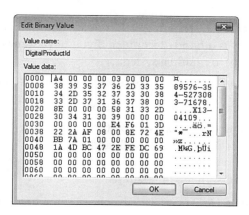

FIGURE 34.5

You see the Edit Binary Value dialog box if you're modifying a binary value.

For binary values, the Value Data box is divided into three vertical sections:

- **Starting Byte Number**—The four-digit values on the left of the Value Data box tell you the sequence number of the first byte in each row of hexadecimal numbers. This sequence always begins at 0, so the sequence number of the first byte in the first row is 0000. There are eight bytes in each row, so the sequence number of the first byte in the second row is 0008, and so on. You can't edit these values.

- **Hexadecimal Numbers (Bytes)**—The eight columns of two-digit numbers in the middle section display the setting's value, expressed in hexadecimal numbers, where each two-digit number represents a single byte of information. You can edit these values.

- **ANSI Equivalents**—The third section on the right side of the Value Data box shows the ANSI equivalents of the hexadecimal numbers in the middle section. For example, the first byte of the first row is the hexadecimal value 54, which represents the uppercase letter T. You can also edit the values in this column.

Editing a Registration File

If you exported a key to a registration file, you can edit that file and then import it back into the Registry. To make changes to a registration file, find the file in Windows Explorer, right-click the file, and then click Edit. Windows opens the file in Notepad.

Creating a Registration File

You can create registration files from scratch and then import them into the Registry. This is a handy technique if you have some customizations that you want to apply to multiple systems.

Windows Vista registration files always start with the following header:

```
Windows Registry Editor Version 5.00
```

Next is an empty line followed by the full path of the Registry key that will hold the settings you're adding, surrounded by square brackets. Here's an example:

```
[HKEY_CURRENT_USER\Test]
```

Below the key, you add the setting names and values, which use the following general form:

```
"SettingName"=identifier:SettingValue
```

> **TIP** If you're building a registration file for a Windows 9x, Me, or NT 4 system, change the header to the following:
>
> REGEDIT4
>
> If you want to add a comment to a .reg file, start a new line and begin the line with a semicolon (;).

SettingName   The name of the setting. Note that you use the @ symbol to represent the key's Default value.

identifier   A code that identifies the type of data. REG_SZ values don't use an identifier, but the other four types do:

dword   Use this identifier for a DWORD value.

hex(b)   Use this identifier for a QWORD value.

hex   Use this identifier for a binary value.

hex(2)   Use this identifier for an expandable string value.

hex(7)   Use this identifier for a multistring value.

SettingValue   This is the value of the setting, which you enter as follows:

String   Surround the value with quotation marks.

DWORD   Enter an eight-digit DWORD value.

QWORD   Enter eight two-digit hexadecimal pairs, separated by commas, with the pairs running from highest order to lowest. For example, to enter the QWORD value 123456789abcd, you would use the following value:

cd,ab,89,67,45,23,01,00

Binary   Enter the binary value as a series of two-digit hexadecimal numbers, separating each number with a comma.

Expandable   Convert each character to its hexadecimal equivalent string and then enter the value as a series of two-digit hexadecimal numbers, separating each number with a comma, and separating each character with 00.

TIP

To delete a setting using a .reg file, set its value to a hyphen (-), as in this example:

```
Windows Registry Editor
Version 5.00

[HKEY_CURRENT_USER\Test]

"BinarySetting"=-
```

To delete a key, add a hyphen to the start of the key name, as in this example:

```
Windows Registry Editor
Version 5.00


[-HKEY_CURRENT_USER\Test]
```

Multistring	Convert each character to its hexadecimal equivalent and then enter the value as a series of two-digit hexadecimal numbers, separating each number with a comma, separat-

ing each character with 00, and separating each string with space (00 hex).

> **CAUTION** Rename only those keys or settings that you're certain you need to change or that you created yourself. If you rename the wrong key or setting, Windows Vista might not work properly.

Renaming a Key or Setting

I mentioned earlier that instead of deleting an existing key or setting, it's much safer to rename the key or setting. This enables you to recover the data just by changing the name back to the original. Here are the steps to follow to rename a key or setting:

1. In the Registry Editor, find the key or setting you want to work with, and then highlight it.
2. Select Edit, Rename, or press F2.
3. Edit the name and then press Enter.

Creating a New Key or Setting

Many Registry-based customizations don't involve editing an existing setting or key. Instead, you have to create a new setting or key. Here's how you do it:

1. In the Registry Editor, select the key in which you want to create the new subkey or setting.
2. Select Edit, New. (Alternatively, right-click an empty section of the settings pane and then click New.) A submenu appears.
3. If you're creating a new key, select the Key command. Otherwise, select the command that corresponds to the type of setting you want: String Value, Binary Value, DWORD Value, Multi-String Value, or Expandable String Value.
4. Type a name for the new key or setting.
5. Press Enter.

Deleting a Key or Setting

Again, I strongly advise against deleting any of the Windows predefined keys or settings. However, if you've added your own data to the Registry, you can safely delete any of those keys or settings. Here are the steps to follow:

1. In the Registry Editor, select the key or setting that you want to delete.

2. Select Edit, Delete, or press Delete. The Registry Editor asks whether you're sure.

3. Click Yes.

Finding Registry Entries

The Registry contains only five root keys, but they contain hundreds of subkeys. The fact that some root keys are aliases for subkeys in a different branch only adds to the confusion. If you know exactly where you're going, the Registry Editor's treelike hierarchy is a reasonable way to get there. If you're not sure where a particular subkey or setting resides, however, you could spend all day poking around in the Registry's labyrinthine nooks and crannies.

To help you get where you want to go, the Registry Editor has a Find feature that enables you to search for keys, settings, or values. Here's how it works:

1. In the keys pane, select Computer at the top of the pane (unless you're certain of which root key contains the value you want to find; in this case, you can highlight the appropriate root key instead).

2. Select Edit, Find or press Ctrl+F. The Registry Editor displays the Find dialog box.

3. Use the Find What text box to enter your search string. You can enter partial words or phrases to increase your chances of finding a match.

4. In the Look At group, activate the check boxes for the elements you want to search. For most searches, you want to leave all three check boxes activated.

5. If you want to find only those entries that exactly match your search text, activate the Match Whole String Only check box.

6. Click the Find Next button. The Registry Editor highlights the first match.

7. If this isn't the item you want, select Edit, Find Next (or press F3) until you find the setting or key you want.

When the Registry Editor finds a match, it displays the appropriate key or setting. Note that if the matched value is a setting name or data value, Find doesn't highlight the current key. This is a bit confusing, but remember that the current key always appears at the bottom of the keys pane.

CHAPTER 35

Controlling Windows with the Group Policy Editor

You've seen in many places throughout this book that you can perform some pretty amazing tweaks by using a tool that's about as hidden as any Windows power tool can be: the Group Policy Editor. That Microsoft has buried this program in a mostly untraveled section of the Windows landscape isn't the least bit surprising because in the wrong hands the Group Policy Editor can wreak all kinds of havoc on a system. It's a kind of electronic Pandora's Box that, if opened by careless or inexperienced hands, can loose all kinds of evil upon the Windows world.

Of course, none of this doom-and-gloom applies to you, dear reader, because you're a cautious and prudent wielder of all the Windows power tools. This means that you'll use the Group Policy Editor in a safe, prudent manner and that you'll create a system restore point if you plan to make any major changes. I knew I could count on you.

As you see in this chapter, the Group Policy Editor isn't even remotely hard to use. However, it's such a powerful tool that it's important for you to know exactly how it works, which will help ensure that nothing goes awry when you're making your tweaks.

Understanding Group Policies

Put simply, group policies are settings that control how Windows works. You can use them to customize the Windows Vista interface, restrict access to certain areas, specify security settings, and much more.

Group policies are mostly used by system administrators who want to make sure that novice users don't have access to dangerous tools (such as the Registry Editor), or who want to ensure a consistent computing experience across multiple machines. Group policies are also ideally suited to situations in which multiple users share a single computer. However, group policies are also useful on single-user standalone machines, as you've seen throughout this book.

Group Policy Editor and Windows Versions

The power of the Group Policy Editor is aptly illustrated not only by the fact that Microsoft hides the program deep in the bowels of the system, but most tellingly by the fact that Microsoft doesn't even offer Group Policy Editor in the following Windows versions:

- Windows XP Home
- Windows Vista Home Basic
- Windows Vista Home Premium

In other words, those Windows versions that Microsoft expects novices to be using are the same Windows versions where Microsoft doesn't even include the Group Policy Editor, just to be safe.

Of course, plenty of experienced users use these Windows versions, mostly because they're cheaper than high-end versions such as XP Pro and Vista Ultimate. So what's a would-be tweaker to do when faced with having no Group Policy Editor?

The short answer is: Don't sweat it. That is, although the Group Policy Editor does provide an easy-to-use interface for many

> **TIP** Understanding that most group policies have parallel settings in the Registry is all fine and dandy, but how on earth are you supposed to know which of the Registry's thousands upon thousands of settings is the one you want? The old method was to export the Registry to a REG file, make the change in the Group Policy Editor, export the Registry again, and then compare the two files. *Way* too much work! (And impossible if all you have to work with is a Windows Home version.) Fortunately, Microsoft has an Excel workbook that lists every single Group Policy value and gives the corresponding Registry setting. You can download the Group Policy Settings Reference, which covers both Vista and XP, here:
>
> `http://www.microsoft.com/downloads/details.aspx?FamilyID=41DC179B-3328-4350-ADE1-C0D9289F09EF`

powerful settings, it's not the only way to put those settings into effect. Most group policies correspond to settings in the Windows Registry, so you can get the identical tweak on any Windows Home system by modifying the appropriate Registry setting, instead. Throughout this book, I've tried to augment group policy tweaks with the corresponding Registry tweak, just in case you don't have access to the Group Policy Editor.

NOTE Given a setting that you can tweak using either the Group Policy Editor or the Registry Editor (and assuming you're running a version of Windows that comes with the Group Policy Editor), which tool should you choose? I highly recommend using the Group Policy Editor, because (as you'll see below) it offers a simpler and more straightforward user interface, which means it saves time and you'll be much less likely to make an error.

Launching the Group Policy Editor

As I've said, you make changes to group policies using the Group Policy Editor, a Microsoft Management Console snap-in. To start the Group Policy Editor, follow these steps:

1. Press Windows Logo+R to open the Run dialog box. (In XP, you can also select Start, Run; in Vista, you can also select Start, All Programs, Accessories, Run.)

2. Type `gpedit.msc`.

3. Click OK.

4. In Vista, enter your administrator's credentials to continue.

Figure 35.1 shows the Local Group Policy Editor window that appears. (The word "Local" refers to the fact that you're editing group policies on your own computer, not on some remote computer.)

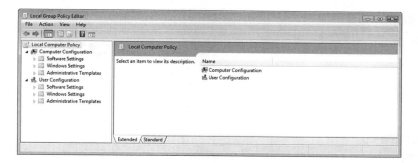

FIGURE 35.1

You use the Group Policy Editor to tweak group policies on your PC.

Working with Group Policies

The Group Policy window that appears is divided into two sections:

> **TIP** Windows comes with another tool called the Local Security Policy Editor, which displays only the policies found in the Group Policy Editor's Computer Configuration, Windows Settings, Security Settings branch. To launch the Local Security Policy Editor, open the Run dialog box, type **secpol.msc**, and click OK. As you might expect, this snap-in isn't available in the XP and Vista Home editions.

- **Left pane**—This pane contains a treelike hierarchy of policy categories, which is divided into two main categories: Computer Configuration and User Configuration. The Computer Configuration policies apply to all users and are implemented before the logon. The User Configuration policies apply only to the current user and, therefore, are not applied until that user logs on.

- **Right pane**—This pane contains the policies for whichever category is selected in the left pane.

The idea, then, is to open the tree's branches to find the category you want. When you click the category, its policies appear in the right pane. For example, Figure 35.2 shows the Group Policy window with the User Configuration, Administrative Templates, Start Menu and Taskbar category highlighted.

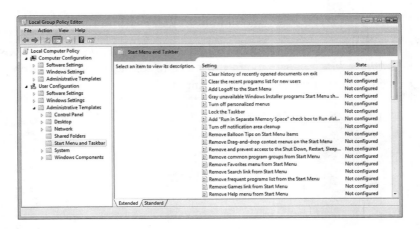

FIGURE 35.2

When you select a category in the left pane, the category's policies appear in the right pane.

In the right pane, the Setting column tells you the name of the policy, and the State column tells you the current state of the policy. Click a policy to see its description on the left side of the pane, as shown in Figure 35.3. If you don't see the description, click the Extended tab.

> **NOTE** Take note of the Supported On value in the dialog box. This value tells you which versions of Windows support the policy.

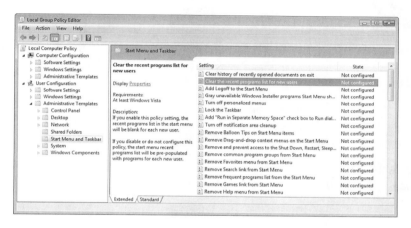

FIGURE 35.3

Click a policy to see its description.

To configure a policy, double-click it. The type of window you see depends on the policy:

- For simple policies, you see a window similar to the one shown in Figure 35.4. These kinds of policies take one of three states: Not Configured (the policy is not in effect), Enabled (the policy is in effect and its setting is enabled), and Disabled (the policy is in effect but its setting is disabled).

- Other kinds of policies require extra information when the policy is enabled. For example, Figure 35.5 shows the window for the Items Displayed in the Places Bar policy (described in detail in Chapter 19, "Useful and Fun Interface Mods"). When the Enabled option is activated, the various text boxes become enabled, and you use them to type paths for folders you want to display in the Places bar.

➡ **See** "Customize the Places Bar for Easier Navigation," **p. 222**.

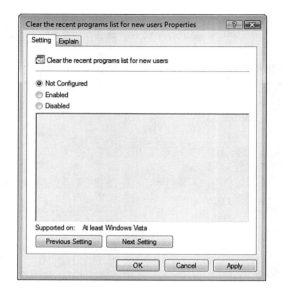

FIGURE 35.4

Simple policies are Not Configured, Enabled, or Disabled.

FIGURE 35.5

More complex policies also require extra information, such as a list of folders to display in the Places bar.

CHAPTER 36

Running the Command Prompt

A s you've seen in this book, tweaking Windows once in a while requires that you fire up a Command Prompt session and then enter one or more commands. And while it's true that getting the most out of Windows doesn't require you to become a Command Prompt guru (insert sigh of relief here), it will help a lot if you're at least comfortable in the not-so-friendly confines of the Command Prompt window.

To that end, this chapter provides you with just enough information to get you comfortable with the command prompt. You learn how to start a session, how to run DOS command, and I show you several useful techniques for working at the command prompt.

Starting a Command Prompt Session

NOTE For an in-depth look at Vista's command line, see *Windows Vista Guide to Scripting, Automation, and Command Line Tools* (Que 2009) by Brian Knittel. The XP version is called *Windows XP Under the Hood: Hardcore Windows Scripting and Command Line Power* (Que 2002).

To take advantage of Command Prompt and all its many useful commands, you need to start a Command Prompt session. Windows (as usual) offers a number of ways to get to the command prompt:

- Select Start, All Programs, Accessories, Command Prompt.
- In Vista, open the Start menu, type **comm** (or **cmd**) into the Search box, and then press Enter.
- Press Windows Logo+R (or select Start, All Programs, Accessories, Run in Vista, or Start, Run in XP), type **cmd** into the Run dialog box, and click OK.
- Create a shortcut for `%SystemRoot%\system32\cmd.exe` on your desktop (or some other convenient location, such as the taskbar's Quick Launch toolbar) and then launch the shortcut.
- Reboot your computer, press F8 to display the Windows Vista Advanced Options Menu, and select the Safe Mode with Command Prompt item.

If you start the session by running the Command Prompt command, the session begins in your main user profile folder, as shown in Figure 36.1 (`C:\Users\Paul`, in this case). If you start the session by running `cmd.exe` or by selecting the Safe Mode with Command Prompt startup item instead, the session begins in `%SystemRoot%\system32` (usually `C:\Windows\system32`).

FIGURE 36.1

When you launch a session with the Command Prompt command, the session begins in your main user profile folder.

➜ You can also configure the Windows Folder file type to open Command Prompt in Windows Explorer's current folder. To learn how, **see** "Open a Folder at the Command Prompt" **p. 262**.

PREVENTING COMMAND PROMPT ACCESS

If you share your computer with others, or if you're setting up a computer for kids or novice users, you might not want them stumbling upon Command Prompt and wreaking who knows what sort of havoc on the machine.

To prevent a user from accessing Command Prompt, log on as that user, press Windows Logo+R to open the Run dialog box (or select Start, All Programs, Accessories, Run in Vista; Start, Run in XP), type **gpedit.msc**, click OK, and then enter your UAC credentials to launch the Group Policy Editor. Open the User Configuration, Administrative Templates, System branch and then enable the Prevent Access to the Command Prompt policy.

Running Command Prompt as the Administrator

If you're running Windows Vista, once in a great while you not only need to start a Command Prompt session, but you need to start an *elevated* session. That's because certain Windows commands and utilities require Administrator-level permission. This is normally handled by User Account Control, which prompts you for administrator credentials before letting you continue with the operation. However, this is usually not the case with operations launched from the command prompt.

For example, in Chapter W3, "Creating Your Own Custom Startup," you learn how to use the BCDEDIT tool to edit the Vista's Boot Manager. This tool requires Administrator permissions, but you run it from the command prompt, so UAC doesn't come into play. To use BCDEDIT (or any Command Prompt utility or command that requires elevation) successfully, you need to run it within a Command Prompt session that has been elevated to Administrator status. Here's how it's done:

1. Select Start, All Programs, Accessories. (Alternatively, open the Start menu and type **comm** into the Search box.)

2. Right-click Command Prompt and then click Run as Administrator. UAC prompts you for your credentials.

3. Enter your administrator credentials to continue.

> **NOTE** When you start your computer using the Safe Mode with Command Prompt startup option, the Command Prompt session you get is an Administrator session.

In this case, the Command Prompt window still appears, but the title bar reads Administrator: Command Prompt to remind you that you're in an elevated session (see Figure 36.2).

FIGURE 36.2

When you launch an elevated Command Prompt session, Windows includes Administrator: in the window title bar.

Using CMD.EXE Switches

For the methods that use the CMD executable, you can specify extra switches after the cmd.exe filename. Most of these switches aren't particularly useful, so I'll just show you the simplest syntax that you'll use most often:

```
cmd [[/s] [/c ¦ /k] command]
```

/s	Strips out the first and last quotation marks from the *command*, provided that the first quotation mark is the first character in *command*
/c	Executes the *command* and then terminates
/k	Executes the *command* and remains running
command	The command to run

For example, if your ISP provides you with a dynamic IP address, you can often solve some connection problems by asking the ISP for a fresh address. You do that by running the command ipconfig /renew at the command prompt. In this case, you don't need the Command Prompt window to remain open, so you can specify the /c switch to shut down the Command Prompt session automatically after the IPCONFIG utility finishes:

```
cmd /c ipconfig /renew
```

On the other hand, you often either want to see the results of the command, or you want to leave the Command Prompt window open so that you can run other commands. In those cases, you use the /k switch. For example, the following command runs the SET utility (which displays the current values of the Windows environment variables) and then leaves the Command Prompt session running:

```
cmd /k set
```

Running Commands

Although many of the Windows accessories provide more powerful and easier-to-use replacements for nearly all commands, a few commands still have no Windows peer. These include the REN command, as well as the many Command Prompt–specific commands, such as CLS, DOSKEY, and PROMPT.

Running Internal and External Commands

How you run a command depends on whether it's an internal or external command, and on what you want Windows to do after the command is finished. For an internal command, you have two choices: You can either enter the command in Command Prompt or include it as a parameter with cmd.exe. As you saw earlier, you can run internal commands with cmd.exe by specifying either the /c switch or the /k switch. If you use the /c switch, the command executes and then the Command Prompt session shuts down. This is fine if you're running a command for which you don't need to see the results. For example, if you want to redirect the contents of drive C's root folder in the text file root.txt, entering the following command in the Run dialog box (for example) will do the job:

cmd.exe /c dir c:\ > root.txt

On the other hand, you might want to examine the output of a command before the Command Prompt window closes. In that case, you need to use the /k switch. The following command runs DIR on drive C's root folder and then drops you off in Command Prompt:

cmd.exe /k dir c:

> **NOTE** Command-line commands that exist as separate executable files—such as CHKDSK, DEFRAG, and XCOPY—are called *external commands*; all other command-line commands—such as DIR, CD, and CLS—are part of the CMD shell and are known as *internal commands*.

For an external command, you have three choices: enter the command at the command prompt, enter the command by itself from within Windows, or include it as a parameter with `cmd.exe`.

To enter a command by itself from within Windows means launching the command's file in Explorer, entering the command in the Run dialog box, or creating a shortcut for the command. For the latter two methods, you can embellish the command by adding parameters and switches. The problem with this method is that Windows automatically closes the Command Prompt window when the command completes. To change this behavior, follow these steps:

> **NOTE** When you use the command line or the Run dialog box to start an external Command Prompt command, you don't need to use the command's full pathname. For example, the full pathname for `mem.exe` is `%SystemRoot%\System32\mem.exe`, but to run this command, you need to enter only `mem`. The reason is that the `%SystemRoot%\System32` subfolder is part of the PATH statement for each Command Prompt session.

1. Find the command's executable file in the `%SystemRoot%\System32` folder.

2. Right-click the executable file and then click Properties to display the command's properties sheet.

3. Display the Program tab. (Note that this tab doesn't appear for all commands.)

4. Deactivate the Close on Exit check box.

5. Click OK.

Adding Parameters and Switches to a Command Prompt Command

If you use the command line or the Run dialog box to enter your Command Prompt commands, you can easily tack on any extra parameters or switches you want to use to modify the command. If, however, you start an external command from Explorer, the command runs without any options. To modify how an external command operates, you can add parameters and switches by following these steps:

1. Use Windows Explorer to find the command's executable file.

> **CAUTION** Vista sets up the `%SystemRoot%\System32` folder as read-only for security purposes. This means that you cannot change the properties of any file in the folder, including Command Prompt stalwarts such as MEM and EDIT. To modify the properties of these programs, you must copy them (or a shortcut to them) to a folder within your user profile, and you run the program from there.

2. Right-click the executable file and then click Properties to display the command's properties sheet.

3. Display the Program tab.

4. In the Cmd Line text box, add a space after the command and then add your parameters and switches. Figure 36.3 shows an example.

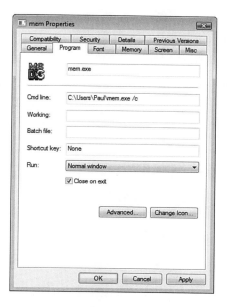

FIGURE 36.3

Use the Cmd Line text box to append extra parameters to an external command.

5. Click OK.

PROGRAM INFORMATION FILES

After you've modified a command's properties sheet, Windows creates a *program information file* (PIF) for the command. This is a separate file that has the same name as the command, but with a `.pif` extension. Unfortunately, Windows Explorer always hides the `.pif` extension. You can recognize the PIF, however, if you display Explorer in Details view: The PIF says `Shortcut to MS-DOS Program` in the Type column. If you

continues

prefer to display the `.pif` extension, head for the following Registry key:

    HKCR\piffile

Rename the `NeverShowExt` setting to `AlwaysShowExt` (or something similar). When you next restart your computer, Windows will show the `.pif` extensions.

If you want to vary the parameters each time you run the command, add a space and a question mark (?) to the end of the command, like so:

    %UserProfile%\mem.exe ?

Each time you run the command (whether from Explorer or from the Run dialog box), Windows displays a dialog box similar to the one shown in Figure 36.4. Use the text box to type your switches and options, and then click OK.

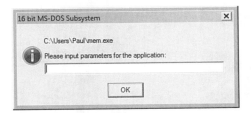

FIGURE 36.4

If you add a question mark (?) to the end of the command, Windows displays a dialog box similar to this one each time you run the command.

Working with Long Filenames

Unlike the old DOS, you can work with long filenames within a Windows Command Prompt session. If you want to use long filenames in a command, however, you need to be careful. If the long filename contains a space or any other character that's illegal in an 8.3 filename, you need to surround the long name with quotation marks. For example, if you run the following command, Windows will tell you that `The syntax of the command is incorrect`:

    copy Fiscal Year 2008.doc Fiscal Year 2009.doc

Instead, you need to enter this command as follows:

    copy "Fiscal Year 2008.doc" "Fiscal Year 2009.doc"

Long filenames are, of course, long, so they tend to be a pain to type in Command Prompt. Fortunately, Windows offers a few methods for knocking long names down to size:

- In Explorer, drag a folder or file and drop it inside the Command Prompt window. Windows pastes the full pathname of the folder or file to the end of the prompt.

- In Explorer, hold down Shift, right-click the folder or file, and then click Copy as Path to copy the object's full pathname to the Clipboard. Use the technique shown later in the "Pasting Text to the Command Prompt" section to paste the pathname into your Command Prompt session.

- If you're trying to run a program that resides in a folder with a long name, add the folder to the PATH. This technique enables you to run programs from the folder without having to specify the full pathname. (I talk about this in more detail in the next section.)

- Use the SUBST command to substitute a virtual drive letter for a long pathname. For example, the following command substitutes drive Z for the current user's Accessories folder:

```
subst z: "%UserProfile%\AppData\Roaming\Microsoft\Windows\Start Menu\
➥Programs\Accessories"
```

Starting Applications from Command Prompt

You can also use the command prompt to start Windows applications, launch documents, and even open folder windows. As with DOS programs, you start a Windows application by entering the name of its executable file.

This works fine if the executable file resides in the main Windows folder, because that folder is part of the PATH. But most Windows applications (and even some Windows accessories) store their files in a separate folder and don't modify the PATH to point to these folders. Instead, the Registry has an AppPaths key that tells Windows where to find an application's files. Command Prompt can't use the Registry-based application paths directly, but there's a Windows command that can. This command is START, and it uses the following syntax:

```
START ["title"] [/Dpath] [/I] [/MIN] [/MAX] [/SEPARATE ¦ /SHARED]
[/LOW ¦ /NORMAL ¦ /HIGH ¦ /REALTIME ¦ /ABOVENORMAL ¦ /BELOWNORMAL]
[/AFFINITY hex value] [/WAIT] [/B] [filename] [parameters]
```

"title"	Specifies the title to display in Command Prompt's window title bar.
/Dpath	Specifies the program's startup folder.

/B	Starts the program without creating a new window.
/I	Tells Windows that the new Command Prompt environment will be the original environment passed to cmd.exe and not the current environment.
/MIN	Starts the program minimized.
/MAX	Starts the program maximized.
/SEPARATE	Starts a 16-bit Windows program in a separate memory space.
/SHARED	Starts a 16-bit Windows program in a shared memory space.
/LOW	Starts the program using the IDLE priority class.
/NORMAL	Starts the program using the NORMAL priority class.
/HIGH	Starts the program using the HIGH priority class.
/REALTIME	Starts the program using the REALTIME priority class.
/ABOVENORMAL	Starts the program using the ABOVENORMAL priority class.
/BELOWNORMAL	Starts the program using the BELOWNORMAL priority class.
/AFFINITY	Starts the program with the specified processor affinity mask, expressed as a hexadecimal number. (On a multiprocessor system, the affinity mask indicates which processor you want the program to use. This prevents Windows from moving the program's execution threads from one processor to another, which can degrade performance.)
/WAIT	Waits until the program has finished before returning to Command Prompt.
filename	Specifies the name of the executable file or document. If you enter a document name, be sure to include the extension so that Windows can figure out the file type.
parameters	Specifies options or switches that modify the operation of the program.

When you use START to launch a program, Windows checks not only the current folder and the PATH, but also the Registry. For the Registry, Windows looks for an `AppPaths` setting or a file type (if you entered the name of a document). For example, if you type **wordpad** and press Enter at the command prompt, you get a `Bad command or file name` error (unless you happen to be in the `%Program Files%\Windows NT\Accessories` folder). If, however, you enter **start wordpad**, WordPad launches successfully.

> **NOTE** The START command's /WAIT switch is useful in batch files. If you launch a program from within a batch file by using START /WAIT, the batch file pauses while the program runs. This enables you, for example, to test for some condition (such as an ERRORLEVEL code) after the program has completed its work.

Recalling and Editing Commands

Windows loads the DOSKEY utility by default when you start any Command Prompt session. This useful little program brings a number of advantages to your command-line work:

- You can recall previously entered commands with just a keystroke or two.
- You can enter multiple commands on a single line.
- You can edit commands instead of retyping them.

The next three sections provide the details.

Recalling Command Lines

The simplest DOSKEY feature is command recall. DOSKEY maintains a *command history buffer* that keeps a list of the commands you enter. To scroll through your previously entered commands in reverse order, press the Up Arrow key; when you've done that at least once, you can change direction and run through the commands in the order you entered them by pressing the Down Arrow key. To rerun a command, use the arrow keys to find it and then press Enter.

Table 36.1 lists all the command-recall keys you can use.

> **TIP** If you don't want to enter any commands from the history buffer, press Esc to get a clean command line.

Table 36.1 DOSKEY Command-Recall Keys

Press	To
Up Arrow	Recall the previous command in the buffer.
Down Arrow	Recall the next command in the buffer.
Page Up	Recall the oldest command in the buffer.
Page Down	Recall the newest command in the buffer.
F7	Display the entire command buffer.
Alt+F7	Delete all commands from the buffer.
F8	Have DOSKEY recall a command that begins with the letter or letters you've typed on the command line.
F9	Have DOSKEY prompt you for a command list number (you can see the numbers with the F7 key). Type the number and press Enter to recall the command.

Entering Multiple Commands on a Single Line

DOSKEY enables you to run multiple commands on a single line. To do this, insert the characters && between commands. For example, a common task is to change to a different drive and then run a directory listing. Normally, you'd do this with two separate commands:

```
e:
```

```
dir
```

With DOSKEY, however, you can do it on one line, like so:

```
e:&&dir
```

Editing Command Lines

Rather than simply rerunning a previously typed command, you might need to run the command again with slightly different switches or parameters. Rather than retyping the whole thing, DOSKEY enables you to

> **TIP** The command history buffer holds 50 commands, by default. If you need a larger buffer, run DOSKEY with the /LISTSIZE=*buffers* switch, where *buffers* is the number of commands you want to store. For example, to change the buffer size to 100, enter the following command:
>
> **doskey /listize=100 / reinstall**

> **TIP** You can enter as many commands as you like on a single line, but just remember that the total length of the line can't be more than 8,191 characters (which should be plenty!).

edit any recalled command line. You use various keys to move the cursor to the offending letters and replace them. Table 36.2 summarizes DOSKEY's command-line editing keys.

Table 36.2   DOSKEY **Command-Line Editing Keys**

Press	To
Left Arrow	Move the cursor one character to the left.
Right Arrow	Move the cursor one character to the right.
Ctrl+Left Arrow	Move the cursor one word to the left.
Ctrl+Right Arrow	Move the cursor one word to the right.
Home	Move the cursor to the beginning of the line.
End	Move the cursor to the end of the line.
Delete	Delete the character over the cursor.
Backspace	Delete the character to the left of the cursor.
Ctrl+Home	Delete from the cursor to the beginning of the line.
Ctrl+End	Delete from the cursor to the end of the line.
Insert	Toggle DOSKEY between Insert mode (your typing is inserted between existing letters on the command line) and Overstrike mode (your typing replaces existing letters on the command line).

Sharing Data Between the Command Prompt and Windows Applications

Command Prompt sessions don't know about the Clipboard, so they don't support the standard cut, copy, and paste techniques. However, there are methods you can use to share data between the command prompt and Windows applications. I spell them out in the next two sections.

Copying Text from the Command Prompt

The best way to copy text from the command prompt is to highlight the text you want and then copy it. The following procedure takes you through the required steps:

1. Make sure that the text you want to copy is visible in the Command Prompt window.

2. Pull down the window's control menu and select Edit, Mark to put the window into Select mode. (You can also right-click the title bar and then select Edit, Mark.)

3. Use the mouse or keyboard to select the data you want to copy.

4. Pull down the window's control menu and select Edit, Copy to copy the selected data to the Clipboard. (You can also either press Enter or right-click the title bar and then select Edit, Copy.)

5. Switch to the Windows application you want to use as the destination and position the insertion point where you want the copied data to appear.

6. Select Edit, Paste (or press Ctrl+V).

> **TIP** If you have a lot of text to copy, you might find it easier to activate the Windows QuickEdit option. QuickEdit mode leaves the Command Prompt window in Select mode permanently so that you can select text anytime you like. (The downside, however, is that you can no longer use the mouse to manipulate the Command Prompt program itself.) To enable QuickEdit, pull down the window's control menu and select Properties to open the properties sheet for the program. In the Options tab, activate the Quick-Edit Mode check box.

Pasting Text to the Command Prompt

If you've sent some text to the Clipboard from a Windows application, it's possible to copy the text into a Command Prompt session.

First, position the command prompt cursor at the spot where you want the pasted text to appear. Then pull down the window's control menu and select Edit, Paste (or right-click the title bar and then select Edit, Paste).

CHAPTER 37

Running Scripts

You've seen throughout this book that tweaking Windows involves making changes to object properties, program options, Registry settings, group policies, and other under-the-hood adjustments. It's surprising how often a simple change—such as checking or unchecking a check box or activating an option button—can make a major difference (hopefully for the better!) in how Windows works.

However, there are lots of Windows tweaks where these more straightforward adjustments aren't enough. Instead, you have to bring out the heavy-duty tools: scripts. Throughout this book, I've helped you unlock the potential of Windows by providing you with sample scripts that automate routine or cumbersome tasks and take advantage of the power that only scripting and programming can provide. This isn't a programming book, so I've tried not to overwhelm you with too many scripts. However, there are quite a few, and it's important that you know how to get those scripts onto your system and run them.

That's the goal of this chapter. You won't learn how to program scripts, but you will learn how to unlock their power by running them on your system.

Understanding Windows Script Host

As you might know, Internet Explorer is really just an empty container application that's designed to host different data formats, including ActiveX controls, various file formats (such as Microsoft Word documents and Microsoft Excel worksheets), and several ActiveX scripting engines. A *scripting engine* is a dynamic link library (DLL) that provides programmatic support for a particular scripting language. Internet Explorer supports two such scripting engines: VBScript (`VBScript.dll`) and JavaScript (`JSscript.dll`). This enables web programmers to write small programs—*scripts*—that interact with the user, control the browser, set cookies, open and close windows, and more. Although these scripting engines don't offer full-blown programmability (you can't compile scripts, for example), they do offer modern programming structures such as loops, conditionals, variables, and objects. In other words, they're a huge leap beyond what a mere batch file can do.

> **NOTE** This chapter does not teach you how to program in either VBScript or JavaScript. If you're looking for a programming tutorial, my *VBA for the Office 2007 System* (Que, 2007) is a good place to start. (VBScript is a subset of VBA—Visual Basic for Applications.) For JavaScript, try my *Special Edition Using JavaScript* (Que, 2001).

The Windows Script Host is also a container application, albeit a scaled-down application in that its only purpose in life is to host scripting engines. Right out of the box, the Windows Script Host supports both the VBScript and JavaScript engines. However, Microsoft designed the Windows Script Host to be a universal host that can support any ActiveX-based scripting engine. Therefore, third-party vendors also offer scripting engines for languages such as Perl, Tcl, and Rexx.

The key difference between Internet Explorer's script hosting and the Windows Script Host is the environment in which the scripts run. Internet Explorer scripts are web page–based, so they control and interact with either the web page or the web browser. The Windows Script Host runs scripts within the Windows shell or from the command prompt, so you use these scripts to control various aspects of Windows. Here's a sampling of the things you can do:

- Execute Windows programs.
- Create and modify shortcuts.
- Use Automation to connect and interact with Automation-enabled applications such as Microsoft Word, Outlook, and Internet Explorer.

- Read, add, and delete Registry keys and items.

- Access the VBScript and JavaScript object models, which give access to the file system, runtime error messages, and more.

- Use pop-up dialog boxes to display information to the user and determine which button the user clicked to dismiss the dialog box.

CAUTION Scripts are obviously very powerful and can access and modify the sensitive innards of your system. Therefore, take extra care if you decide to download scripts from the Internet. In fact, I highly recommend that you only grab scripts from sources that you trust completely.

- Read environment variables, which are system values that Windows Home Server keeps in memory, such as the folder into which Windows Home Server is installed—the %SystemRoot% environment variable—and the name of the computer—the %ComputerName% environment variable.

- Deal with network resources, including mapping and unmapping network drives, accessing user data (such as the username and user domain), and connecting and disconnecting network printers.

- Script the Windows Management Instrumentation (WMI) interface.

What about speed? After all, you wouldn't want to load something that's the size of Internet Explorer each time you need to run a simple script. That's not a problem because, as I've said, the Windows Script Host does nothing but host scripting engines, so it has much less memory overhead than Internet Explorer. That means that your scripts run quickly. For power users looking for a Windows-based batch language, the Windows Script Host is a welcome tool.

Introducing Script Files

Scripts look complex, but they're actually nothing but simple text files. This means that you can create and edit script files using Notepad or some other text editor. You can use a word processor such as WordPad to create and edit scripts, but you must make sure that you save these files using the program's Text Only document type. For VBScript, a good alternative to Notepad is the editor that comes with either Visual Basic or any program that supports VBA (such as the Office suite). Just remember that VBScript is a subset of VBA (which is, in turn, a subset of Visual Basic), so it does not support all objects and features.

In a web page, you use the `<script>` tag to specify the scripting language you're using, as in this example:

`<SCRIPT LANGUAGE="VBScript">`

With the Windows Script Host, the script file's extension specifies the scripting language:

- For VBScript, save your text files using the `.vbs` extension (which is registered as the following file type: VBScript Script File).
- For JavaScript, use the `.js` extension (which is registered as the following file type: JScript Script File).

As described in the next three sections, you have three ways to run your scripts: by launching the script files directly, by using `WScript.exe`, or by using `CScript.exe`.

Running Script Files Directly

The easiest way to run a script from within Windows is to launch the `.vbs` or `.js` file directly:

- Locate the script file in Windows Explorer and then double-click the file.
- Open the Run dialog box, type the file's path and name, and then click OK.
- In Vista, if you stored the script file within your user profile folders, open the Start menu, type the name of the script file into the Search box, and then click the script file in the results.

Note, however, that these techniques don't work at the command prompt. For that, you need to use the CScript program described a bit later.

Using WScript for Windows-Based Scripts

The `.vbs` and `.js` file types have an `open` method that's associated with WScript (`WScript.exe`), which is the Windows-based front-end for the Windows Script Host. In other words, launching a script file named, for example, `MyScript.vbs` is equivalent to entering the following command in the Run dialog box:

`wscript myscript.vbs`

The WScript host also defines several parameters that you can use to control the way the script executes. Here's the full syntax:

```
WSCRIPT [filename] [arguments] [//B] [//D] [//E:engine] [//H:host] [//I]
➥[//Job:xxxx] [//S] [//T:ss] [//X]
```

`filename`	Specifies the filename, including the path of the script file, if necessary.
`arguments`	Specifies optional arguments required by the script. An *argument* is a data value that the script uses as part of its procedures or calculations.
`//B`	Runs the script in batch mode, which means script errors and `Echo` method output lines are suppressed.
`//D`	Enables Active Debugging. If an error occurs, the script is loaded into the Microsoft Script Debugger (if it's installed), and the offending statement is highlighted.
`//E:engine`	Executes the script using the specified scripting *engine*, which is the scripting language to use when running the script.
`//H:host`	Specifies the default scripting host. For *host*, use either `CScript` or `WScript`.
`//I`	Runs the script in interactive mode, which displays script errors and `Echo` method output lines.
`//Job:id`	In a script file that contains multiple jobs, executes only the job with `id` attribute equal to `id`.
`//S`	Saves the specified WScript arguments as the default for the current user; uses the following Registry key to save the settings:
	`HKCU\Software\Microsoft\Windows Script Host\Settings`
`//TT:ss`	Specifies the maximum time in seconds (*ss*) that the script can run before it shuts down automatically.
`//X`	Executes the entire script in the Microsoft Script Debugger (if it's installed).

For example, the following command runs `MyScript.vbs` in batch mode with a 60-second maximum execution time:

```
wscript myscript.vbs //B //TT:60
```

CREATING SCRIPT JOBS

A script *job* is a section of code that performs a specific task or set of tasks. Most script files contain a single job. However, it's possible to create a script file with multiple jobs. To do this, first surround the code for each job with the `<script>` and `</script>` tags, and then surround those with the `<job>` and `</job>` tags. In the `<job>` tag, include the `id` attribute and set it to a unique value that identifies the job. Finally, surround all the jobs with the `<package>` and `</package>` tags. Here's an example:

```
<package>
<job id="A">
<script language="VBScript">
    WScript.Echo "This is Job A."
</script>
</job>

<job id="B">
<script language="VBScript">
    WScript.Echo "This is Job B."
</script>
</job>
</package>
```

Save the file using the Windows Script File (`.wsf`) extension.

Using CScript for Command-Line Scripts

The Windows Script Host has a second host front-end application called CScript (`CScript.exe`), which enables you to run scripts from the command line. In its simplest form, you launch CScript and use the name of the script file (and its path, if required) as a parameter, as in this example:

```
cscript myscript.vbs
```

NOTE If you write a lot of scripts, the Microsoft Script Debugger is an excellent programming tool. If there's a problem with a script, the debugger can help you pinpoint its location. For example, the debugger enables you to step through the script's execution one statement at a time. If you don't have the Microsoft Script Debugger, you can download a copy from msdn2.microsoft.com/ en-us/library/ms950396.aspx.

The Windows Script Host displays the following banner and then executes the script:

```
Microsoft (R) Windows Script Host Version 5.6 for Windows
Copyright (C) Microsoft Corporation. All rights reserved.
```

As with WScript, the CScript host has an extensive set of parameters you can specify:

```
CSCRIPT [filename] [arguments] [//B] [//D] [//E:engine] [//H:host] [//I]
➡[//Job:xxxx] [//S] [//T:ss] [//X] [//LOGO ¦ //NOLOGO] [//U]
```

This syntax is almost identical to that of WScript, but it adds the following three parameters:

//LOGO	Displays the Windows Script Host banner at startup
//NOLOGO	Hides the Windows Script Host banner at startup
//U	Uses Unicode for redirected input/output from the console

Script Properties and .wsh Files

In the previous two sections, you saw that the WScript and CScript hosts have a number of parameters you can specify when you execute a script. It's also possible to set some of these options by using the properties associated with each script file. To see these properties, right-click a script file and then click Properties. In the properties sheet that appears, display the Script tab, shown in Figure 37.1. You have two options:

Stop Script After Specified Number of Seconds—If you activate this check box, Windows shuts down the script after it has run for the number of seconds specified in the associated spin box. This is useful for scripts that might hang during execution. For example, a script that attempts to enumerate all the mapped network drives at startup might hang if the network is unavailable.

Display Logo When Script Executed in Command Console—As you saw in the previous section, the CScript host displays some banner text when you run a script at the command prompt. If you deactivate this check box, the Windows Script Host suppresses this banner (unless you use the //LOGO parameter).

FIGURE 37.1

In a script file's properties sheet, use the Script tab to set some default options for the script.

When you make changes to these properties, the Windows Script Host saves your settings in a new file that has the same name as the script file, except with the .wsh (Windows Script Host Settings) extension. For example, if the script file is MyScript.vbs, the settings are stored in MyScript.wsh. These .wsh files are text files organized into sections, much like .ini files. Here's an example:

```
[ScriptFile]
Path=C:\Users\Paul\Documents\Scripts\
CreateShortcut.vbs
[Options]
Timeout=10
DisplayLogo=0
```

To use these settings when running the script, use either WScript or CScript and specify the name of the .wsh file:

```
wscript myscript.wsh
```

NOTE Rather than setting properties for individual scripts, you might prefer to set global properties that apply to the WScript host itself. Those global settings then apply to every script that runs using the WScript host. To do this, run WScript.exe without parameters. This displays the properties sheet for WScript, which contains only the Script tab shown in Figure 37.1. The settings you choose in the properties sheet are stored in the following Registry key:

```
HKLM\Software\Microsoft\
Windows Script Host\Settings
```

INDEX

Numerics

802.11n standard, 6

A

abbreviating long filenames in Command Prompt, 432-433

Access Denied message, configuring for standard users, 127-128

accessing
Mac shares in Windows, 331, 334
router setup pages, 22
Run command, 30

activating Administrator account, 136-139

Activity Reporting (Parental Controls), 116

ad hoc wireless networks, creating, 374-376

adding
icons to Quick Launch toolbar, 380
parameters to Command Prompt commands, 430-432
programs with Open With dialog box, 319
switches to Command Prompt commands, 430-432
tabs to Windows Explorer, 320-321

Address bar (Internet Explorer)
editing, 41
list, clearing, 106-108
searching with, 184-186

adjusting
blink rate of cursor, 206
font size, 207-209

admin approval mode (Administrator account), activating, 139

administrative hidden shares, disabling, 342

Administrator account, 126, 135
activating, 136, 138
admin approval mode, activating, 139
Command Prompt, running automatically, 140-141
programs, running, 143-144
renaming, 71-72
scripts, running, 141-142

Administrators group, 126

ads, removing from recorded TV shows, 252-254

advanced filters, 287

Aero Glass, 202

Aero interface, turning off, 202

animated GIFs, disabling, 43

anonymous proxy servers, 112
configuring, 114
web proxies, 112